*f*P

INNOVATION NATION

How America Is Losing Its Innovation Edge,

Why It Matters,

and What We Can Do to Get It Back

JOHN KAO

FREE PRESS

NEW YORK   LONDON   TORONTO   SYDNEY

*f*P

Free Press
A Division of Simon & Schuster, Inc.
1230 Avenue of the Americas
New York, NY 10020

First Free Press hardcover edition October 2007

FREE PRESS and colophon are trademarks of Simon & Schuster, Inc.

For information about special discounts for bulk purchases, please contact
Simon & Schuster Special Sales at 1-800-456-6798
or business@simonandschuster.com

Designed by Joseph Rutt

Manufactured in the United States of America

10 9 8 7 6 5 4

Library of Congress Cataloging-in-Publication Data
Kao, John J.
    Innovation nation/John Kao.
        p. cm.
    Includes bibliographical references and index.
    1. Technological innovation—United States.   2. Technological innovations—
United States—Management.   I. Title.
HD45.K337 2007
338′.06—dc22   2007022484

ISBN-13: 978-1-4165-3268-2
ISBN-10: 1-4165-3268-4

For Jackson, Emeline, and Desmond,
new citizens of Innovation Nation
And for Laurel, who already lives there

The American people always do the right thing after they've tried every other alternative.

—Winston Churchill

CONTENTS

INNOVATION NATION

INTRODUCTION

The New Frontier is not a set of promises. It is a set of challenges.

　　　　　　　　　　　　　　　　—John F. Kennedy

Only yesterday, we Americans could afford to feel smug about our preeminence. Destiny, it seems, had appointed us the world's permanent pioneers, forever striding beyond the farthest cutting edge. From the Declaration of Independence to the Creative Commons, from the movies to Internet media, from air travel to integrated circuits, from the Mac to MySpace, we led the way to the new. We owned the future. Other countries would have to settle for being followers, mere customers, or imitators of our fabulous creations.

That was yesterday. Today, things are vastly different. Innovation has become the new currency of global competition as one country after another races toward a new high ground where the capacity for innovation is viewed as a hallmark of national success. These competitors are beginning to seriously challenge us as magnets for venture capital, R & D, and talent, and as the hot spots of innovation from which future streams of opportunity will emerge.

You know the world has changed when the Chinese politburo—historical bastion of Marxist-Leninist-Maoist thought—puts innovation squarely in the middle of its next five-year plan, as it did in

2006, by setting the goal of building an "innovative country," on a "rich talent base," to drive economic and social development.

Meanwhile, our own national capacity for innovation is eroding, with deeply troubling implications for our future. I know this because, as part of my work on innovation, I advise governments, established market-leading companies, and upstart ventures around the world. They come to me to develop not just new products or services but also new business models and visions of possibility. Constantly on the lookout for best practices and emerging trends, I have watched a drama unfold from my ringside seat.

We live in a country in which more money is now spent on astrology than astronomy, one in which our handling of such fundamental issues as education, science, and investment in basic research seems increasingly at odds with a new set of global best practices pioneered by others. In Chapter 2 of this book, I reveal a set of dismal and disconcerting facts in a "report card" on American innovation.

Though we still enjoy the lead position, other parts of the world are moving ahead at a rapid pace. Indeed, my work has shown me that innovation is fast becoming a guiding force for public policy in one country after another—but not our own. Other countries are ramping up innovation efforts and spending serious amounts of money to devise new kinds of incentives, nurture talent, and actively sponsor large-scale innovation initiatives. My desk is piled high with national innovation strategies and white papers from Sweden, China, Australia, Canada, and Singapore.

Most people are unaware of just how rapidly such strategies, driven by a new global economic calculus, are reshaping the competitive landscape. By 2010, for example, experts estimate that Beijing will have the world's largest nanotechnology research infrastructure, with ten times as many researchers in one location as any comparable U.S. facility. The second largest by then? Shanghai. And while America retains its lead in the life sciences, countries from

China to Hungary are striving to become world-class players and realize world-class economic payoffs. And they are succeeding. Countries we don't even acknowledge as serious competitors are beginning to outpace us in some vital areas as we squander our long-held advantage.

It is a crucial moment in time, a historic tipping point perhaps. Just as we are beginning to slack off, others are stepping on the gas. And, at some point—sooner than we might think—the curves of our decline and the rest of the world's ascent will cross. In tomorrow's world, even more than today's, innovation will be the engine of progress. So unless we move to rectify this dismal situation, the United States cannot hope to remain a leader. What's at stake is nothing less than the future prosperity and security of our nation.

The accumulating evidence has made me increasingly concerned about, and disturbed by, the health of our national innovation engine. I see a crisis brewing, and it makes me angry. We should be doing much better than we are. We have the talent, money, track record, and infrastructure necessary for continued success. But we are rapidly becoming the fat, complacent Detroit of nations. We are losing our collective sense of purpose along with our fire, ambition, and determination to achieve. To make matters worse, the opening years of the twenty-first century have witnessed what I call a crisis of national competence. Think Hurricane Katrina. Think national security.

I had an inkling of how cramped our vision had become shortly after 9/11, when I attended a conference sponsored by the intelligence community on methodologies for thinking about the future. I remarked on what I imagined had been a substantial uptick in new approaches to counterterrorism, use of new technologies, and new concepts of operations since that horrible event. "Oh, no," was the reply from the other side of the conversation. "Unfortunately, it's probably going to take another major episode before we wake up and take real positive action." I was stunned.

As a student of military history, I think back to 1941 and the dark days after Pearl Harbor. That attack left the U.S. Navy with only a handful of aircraft carriers—most of which the Japanese sank soon after the vast war in the Pacific began—to hold the line. Yet a mere three years later, America had a hundred aircraft carriers fully armed with new planes, pilots, tactics, and escort ships, backed by new approaches to logistics, training methods, aircraft plants, shipyards, and women workers. That's not counting the rapid mobilization of a huge force deployed in both Asia and Europe and such game-changing innovations as the B-29, landing craft, and nuclear fission. Have we worked at anything approaching that tempo in the present era?

Americans love the national narrative of a good come-from-behind story and are confident, perhaps overly so, in our ability to catch up quickly when we need to. And we certainly enjoy the idea of being number one. But, unfortunately, we're also very good at drifting along in our current direction—sideways. And at present, we lack a national consensus about what we stand for as a country and our role in the world, as well as a clear, vital sense of purpose.

Amplifying the dangers we face are the precipitous decline in our world standing and the concurrent loss of respect for our ability to lead. Do I exaggerate? Not according to the Pew Global Attitudes Project, the largest survey to date of world public opinion. It reveals, for example, that our image in Indonesia, the most populous Muslim nation on earth, has badly deteriorated. Whereas 61 percent of Indonesians viewed the United States favorably in 2002, the numbers plummeted to just 15 percent in 2003 on the heels of our march into Iraq. Then, after two former U.S. presidents and a carrier battle group headed to Indonesia to help provide tsunami relief in 2005, our favorability rating rallied somewhat, but it still stood at only 30 percent in 2006, just half of what it was before the Iraq invasion.

The story is much the same among more traditional allies like

Germany. In 2002, 61 percent of Germans viewed us favorably; by 2006, only 37 percent did. And in China, according to the Pew survey, the United States is viewed as a "great danger" to world peace by more people, more than Iran, North Korea, or the Israeli-Palestinian conflict.

Our political leaders are not blind to the threat posed by our loss of global prestige, although strong evidence of a new national narrative and fresh approach to our innovation challenges are not apparent at present. President Bush has put forward an American Competitiveness Initiative. It includes, among other elements, more basic research in such areas as supercomputing, alternative energy, and nanotechnology; a permanent business tax credit for R & D spending; and a push to train 70,000 additional high-school science and math teachers. Speaker of the House Nancy Pelosi has long championed a national innovation strategy that stresses a rejuvenated role for government in basic research. Her plan aims at improved math and science education, doubled funding for the National Science Foundation, a renewed emphasis on basic research at the Defense Advanced Research Projects Agency (DARPA), and a research-led drive for energy independence. And reports have been issued by numerous other stakeholder groups, including the National Academy of Sciences, The Council on Competitiveness, the National Governors Association, the Asia Society, and the TechNet Alliance. But what is currently on the table is a strategy largely of "more," not "different," when what we need is a fresh approach to innovation, one that aspires to change the nature of the conversation.

There is no single answer or remedy. What is required is nothing less than a major commitment of America's resources, human and financial, to rejuvenate our innovation engine. And the obvious first step is simply to acknowledge the challenges we face at a national level. After which, we must develop a compelling vision and a blueprint for action that will reinvent the way we educate our children, marshal our resources, pursue our research projects, communicate and share our discoveries, and conduct ourselves in the world community. Incrementalism will not take us where we need to go; we are at what biologists call a "punctuated equilibrium" moment, in which a rapidly altering context demands an equally rapid evolution of our ability to adapt.

Our challenge is to seize a day that is well past noon.

There will be those who label a national innovation strategy a quixotic or unrealistic goal, because most Americans are not fans of top-down policies. Instead, we prefer an economic model that defers to the so-called invisible hand of free-market incentives to guide the progress of business, science, and social development. But, in fact, we've marshaled our resources to address large-scale challenges before, and to great effect. Think of Sputnik. After the Soviet Union pricked our bubble of complacency and challenged America's sense of confidence in our global leadership by sending a manmade object orbiting around the planet, we responded with massive funding for education, revamped school curricula in science and math, and launched a flurry of federal initiatives that eventually put Neil Armstrong in position to make his "giant leap for mankind." No president has yet matched John F. Kennedy's thrilling call for targeted innovation when he vowed to send the first man to the moon nearly half a century ago.

Instructive as the Apollo example is, today's challenge is different. As I will explain, today's threat is a "silent" Sputnik, a threat that is neither obvious—looming in the night sky—nor capable of endangering our security and way of life, at least at the outset. Nevertheless, our response must be equally vigorous—to enlist our resource base and abundant talent in a drive to spur innovation nationally, in order to affirm and revitalize our position of leadership in the twenty-first century.

This book is intended to support that mission by diagnosing our current situation, describing innovation best practices from around the world, explaining how innovation works at a national level, and putting forth a proposal for a U.S. strategy that all stakeholders can get behind. In my view, a national strategy offers us the opportunity to become what I call an Innovation Nation, a country with a widely shared, well-understood objective of continuously improving our innovation capabilities in order to achieve world-changing goals.

I decided to write this book out of a feeling of alarm over the nation's ever-duller cutting edge. In some ways, our country is in the position of someone suffering from anosognosia, a brain malfunction I first encountered as a medical student at Yale. Imagine a stroke victim with a paralyzed left arm and leg who denies that he is paralyzed. Anosognosia often begins with a right-brain injury that typically blocks the patient from feeling or even comprehending the left side of his body. The only known relief from anosognosia is a squirt of ice water in the patient's left ear, the shock causing a temporary return of feeling.

This book is my attempt to squirt ice water in America's ear. It was conceived not as a policy tome or an academic treatise, but as a conversation with my fellow citizens, a way to share what I have learned from an unusual set of professional and life experiences. In what has been a consuming journey for me in searching for innovation around the world, I have been presented with four epiphanies, each one deepening my understanding of innovation and collectively leading me to see that our task at hand as a nation is to innovate the process of innovation itself. Without a new awareness of how to do so, I fear we will fall far short of the mark, despite our best intentions.

The first epiphany turned on a significant misunderstanding from my youth. At the age of ten, I happened on A. E. van Vogt's *Voyage of the Space Beagle*, one of the original science-fiction space operas. It was the gripping tale of an interstellar expedition gone wrong. The ship's crew encountered, among other horrors, a galaxy-spanning consciousness called Ixtl that lured them into a deep-space chase they could not escape for decades. A power struggle erupted among the specialists—chemists, soldiers, anthropologists, and the like—who comprised the crew but could not work together because they couldn't think outside their specialties. The hero was Dr. Elliott Grosvenor, the ship's sole "nexialist," a new discipline (its name derived from "nexus") that integrated many practical systems of knowledge. As total disaster loomed, Grosvenor was forced to take charge of the ship, using a potent mix of psychological techniques, management and military sciences, and communication skills that unified the crew, finally enabling them to escape.

"Wow!" I thought. "A nexialist is what I want to be." Only sometime later did I discover that nexialism wasn't a real discipline; it was the author's neologism. All the same, I have spent much of my life turning my polymath aspirations into a career that in some ways approaches nexialism. In my hunger to find the wellsprings of innovation, I have been an entrepreneur, a film and Broadway producer, psychiatrist, business school professor, consultant, and author.

In some respects, my real job description today is that of arbitrageur. I like to take on complex topics—call them emerging agendas or wicked problems—that are beyond the effective range of narrowly defined disciplines and then figure out who is making headway with them. In business, the arbitrageur exploits price differences in stocks or other financial instruments between markets worldwide, buying at a low price and selling at a higher one. My version of arbitrage involves creating value by finding the seams between disciplines and between traditional points of view, by bringing knowledge from where it is established to where it is needed. Specifically, I trade findings about innovation—new methods, big developments—in the global marketplace of ideas.

As an arbitrageur, I have had the opportunity to consider a bountiful array of interesting questions. For example, how can an understanding of story and narrative inform the discipline of strategy? Why is psychiatry useful in the study of military affairs? How can knowledge of Hollywood production values help create memorable educational experiences? Why are environments like recording studios and sound stages especially conducive to innovation?

What I have learned is that innovation—creating what is both new and valuable—is not a narrowly defined, technical area of competence. It cannot be reduced to a single frame of reference, way of thinking, or set of methods. Rather, innovation emerges when different bodies of knowledge, perspectives, and disciplines are brought together.

I experienced my second epiphany about innovation shortly after I arrived as a newly minted assistant professor at the Harvard Business School. I sought out faculty reaction to my plans for teaching and researching the topic. One of my colleagues, a distinguished-looking professor with a shock of white hair and a desk the size of a small battleship, looked me over and said, "Let me give you some advice. Innovation is not a good subject for you to teach here." "Why not?" I asked. His reply: "Because everything that is important about the subject has already been reflected in the literature." That's when I knew I was onto something big. And from then on, the common theme for all my nexialist efforts would be innovation.

During my time at Harvard, I looked into why some businesspeople seem to be born innovators, casually sharpening and strengthening whatever they touch, wherever they go. It's a set of talents expressed in observable skills—like the ability of a great jazz musician to achieve exquisite harmony without necessarily being able to read music. It's the knack of being able to sense emerging opportunities, to marshal resources "just in time" to realize something tangible from an idea. It's the blending of the intuitive and the practical, of the optimistic and the pragmatic. All these skills are routinely and often unconsciously practiced by innovators at the top of their game. To hone my own understanding, I sought out and studied an eclectic array of master practitioners—Richard Branson, Lou Gerstner, Leo Castelli, Stephen Schwartzman, and Frank Zappa, among others—absorbing bits and pieces of their lore as I learned more and more about the theory and practice of innovation.

I also set out on a worldwide quest—San Francisco to Singapore, Dubai to Denmark—to identify best practices for innovation. I also discovered that those practices could be usefully employed in ways not originally foreseen. The design principles that applied to generating the best environment for creative individuals and teams, for example, were also relevant to crafting the innovation strategies of large-scale enterprises. Culture, agility, vision, and ambience were revealed as scalable phenomena. There were ways to take the lessons from hot teams and apply them to companies, and to draw a conceptual bridge between hot companies and hot countries. I began to see innovation not only in terms of lightning-bolt bursts of creativity from a lone genius or the jam sessions of a design team, but also as the product of a complex organizational and social weave whose many attributes all demanded attention.

In nearly every organization, an understanding of systems is commonplace and necessary. If you ask where the money in an organization is located and how it is handled, for instance, hopefully someone can point to a system of trained accounting and finance professionals, computer-based records, bank accounts, and so on. But up to now, innovation has not typically been thought of as a system, even though every organization has some kind of ad hoc scheme through which people generate ideas that are supported or ignored until they either do or do not pan out. In most organizations, these innovation systems operate without conscious design or planning. How, I began to wonder, could a more conscious systems approach help foster innovation capability, not just for companies, but at a national level?

A few years later, near the end of the 1990s, I had my third epiphany while advising various U.S. national security agencies and departments. I was working with both military officers and civilians on the intricacies of anticipating future wars, giving thought to the accelerating rate of social and technological change, the nature of future threats and opportunities, and the need for new measures of success in a world where winning the peace was equally if not more important than winning a war.

While visiting the USS *Abraham Lincoln*, a Nimitz-class aircraft carrier cruising off San Diego, I realized that the design for the next version of this ship depended almost entirely on the navy's ability to envision an unknown and perhaps unfathomable future field of engagement. Who might our future adversaries be? What kind of planes, manned and unmanned, would be carried on board? What kind of ground campaigns would require support in what sort of geopolitical environment? And what would be the overall concept of operations?

My challenge was to identify the unknowns well before they emerged, to prod leadership into creative consideration of their options, and to help generate the innovations needed to deal with future realities. It was somewhat like training a dinosaur—or, more charitably, an elephant—to dodge a meteorite that might not crash into the earth for another fifty years.

The next generation of aircraft carriers, now on the drawing boards, will likely still be afloat in the twenty-second century. The captain of the last ship in the planned series probably hasn't been born yet. His (or her) grandfather may be the commander of one of the current carriers. How can today's skipper guess what crises his or her grandchild will face? For that matter, how was I supposed to know? Obviously, I didn't. But my job was to imagine the possibilities and outline ways of dealing with them.

Aircraft carriers are the largest single line item in our nation's budget, and they are controversial. Their defenders insist they're indispensable: size will always matter in naval combat, they say, and carriers project U.S. power wherever dispatched. Nothing pacifies a restless nation, or so the reasoning goes, quite like the specter of a giant floating air base and its shrieking fighter jets looming out of the fog offshore.

Carrier critics, however, say they cost too much; they muscle out of the budget many programs that would be more flexible and useful. Furthermore, carriers are always in danger of becoming obsolete in a fast-changing world. One noted military strategist told me that the very sight of an aircraft carrier made him "want to puke."

Juggling such opposing viewpoints greatly expanded my perspective on where and how innovation could be managed. It also convinced me of the relevance of private-sector knowledge in dealing with public-sector concerns. But the key piece of knowledge gleaned from this experience was that simply improving an existing product—in the language of Silicon Valley, going for "better, faster, cheaper"—would not necessarily justify the mammoth investment of designing a next-generation aircraft carrier. We had to move beyond old, established ways of thinking. We had to be able to entertain "impossible" possibilities, consult outsiders with widely divergent opinions and backgrounds, conduct meaningful experiments, and take daring intellectual risks in order to win the desired future.

My fourth, and so far final, epiphany about innovation was simply that too many of our leaders—both national and international—in government, business, and academe have a dangerously limited understanding of what it is. I remember asking a senior United Nations official, in one of many such conversations, which of his colleagues was in charge of innovation. After a long silence, he replied that it must be someone in intellectual property law, or perhaps someone who dealt with high tech. He just wasn't sure.

You would think that a great organization's stakeholders would be so intent on its (and their) future that innovation—the key to that future—would be their first priority, or at least among their top three. But, sad to say, that is far from true. Even among those who are thinking and writing about innovation, much of the discussion—fueled by stacks of white papers, statistics, and studies—is hamstrung by distressingly limited, conventional definitions of innovation and outmoded views of how to make it happen. It's as though the writers were recommending twentieth-century best practices derived from nineteenth-century manufacturing hierarchies as scripture for twenty-first-century networked innovators. (Chapter 1 will address this dilemma in greater detail.)

In contrast, my four epiphanies taught me that our national approach to innovation must itself be highly innovative. It must be interdisciplinary and cross boundaries. It must draw from insights about best practices on a worldwide basis. It must be more ambitious and inventive than simply doing what we've been doing, only better. And it must be supported by a higher level of awareness and urgency on the part of our political and business leaders.

If we are to maintain our ascendancy, we must open our minds to new ways of thinking about innovation. I'm reminded of the debate raging among mountain climbers, pitting those who subscribe to the traditional slow-and-steady expedition approach against those who practice the light-and-fast style. The newcomers bring different gear and climbing techniques to the mountain, along with a different mind-set. Free of legacy thinking and with little to lose, they approach the challenge not in terms of "conquering" a mountain but with a sense of respect and a desire to engage and merge with it.

Our nation needs to deal with innovation in just that way. Instead of treating innovation as a discrete, tactical agenda that can be improved by tossing in an occasional research grant or biotech lab, I say we need to immerse ourselves as a society in the challenge and look at innovation with fresh eyes. To receive the priority it deserves, it must become part of the very core of our national vision and strategy, beginning in our schools and homes, and continuing throughout our lives.

I have coined the phrase Innovation Nation to refer to a country that is mobilizing its resources in such a pervasive and innovative way. An Innovation Nation is, to my mind, a country that is committed to constantly reinventing the nature of its innovation capabilities to improve the lot of humanity. Right now, there are no Innovation Nations. But America has the potential to become the first, a blend of enlightened self-interest and outward-reaching altruism.

Will the United States rise to its innovation challenge, heeding the call for renewed national greatness? Or will we take the path of least resistance, basking in our fading glory and milking aging cows on the verge of going dry? The choice to overcome denial is ours to make, and we must do it now.

ONE

BRINGING INNOVATION TO INNOVATION

Do something. Do something to that, and then do something to that. Pretty soon you've got something.

—Jasper Johns, painter

Not long ago, while prepping to deliver a speech at Google headquarters in Mountain View, California, I decided to eat the company's cooking and Google the word "innovation." Though I expected to see a lot of hits, I had no idea just how popular the word would be in the Googly universe of "all the world's information at your fingertips." Wham, the search came back—330 million references to innovation.

Those of you who, like me, constantly scan the new arrivals in the business section at your local bookseller may be aware of a similar phenomenon. Innovation—or at least the notion of innovation—is hot. The titles tell the story: *Open Innovation, The Art of Innovation, Fast Innovation, Customer-Driven Innovation, The Innovator's Dilemma, The Innovator's Solution, Dynamics of Innovation, Seeds of Innovation,* and so on. New titles appear nearly every month in an endless proliferation of arguments, a debate about innovation that is itself symptomatic of our core problem with innovation.

I'm not exaggerating when I say that the biggest obstacle to developing a national innovation agenda is not how many Ph.Ds or how much venture capital or how much wireless capacity we have. Rather, it's our level of knowledge about innovation that counts. And the ways we currently define it do not, for the most part, fit new global realities. Neither comprehensive nor specific enough, the plethora of definitions actually masks an underlying lack of consensus. In short, we know everything and nothing about innovation.

I know firsthand that there is confusion about innovation because I constantly receive calls from people—some quite nervous at first—who identify themselves as some version of a new "innovation process owner," meaning they are in charge, somehow, of innovation in their organization. My first question is typically, "What do you mean by innovation?" The variety of responses I've received over the years would fill a very long list, but it would be as short in internal consistency as it is abundant in quantity.

Neither is experience a guarantee of expertise. When I teach senior executives about innovation, I sometimes use a slide showing a number of management terms scattered across a page. Innovation is among them, as are strategy, creativity, transformation, and leadership. I ask the executives to define innovation and describe how the various concepts relate to one another. Their responses are typically as scattered as the words projected on the screen. Is strategy part of innovation or innovation part of strategy? How far in the future should innovation initiatives be targeted? Is innovation about being creative or is creativity about being innovative?

I believe we are in what might be called a pre-Copernican period with regard to innovation. It's as if we don't yet know which heavenly bodies revolve around which others. We don't even know where all the planets are located, nor do we have a viable theory of planetary motion. We rely on metaphors and images to express an as yet imprecise and unsystematic understanding.

Little wonder that one of the first tasks I set in my teaching days was to ask my students to define innovation, prompting more than a few of them to mutter under their breaths about "semantic hell." No matter. The importance of being as clear as possible about the journey on which you are embarking, whether as an inventor in your garage or a scientist in a federally funded lab, can scarcely be overstated. Your understanding shapes, in turn, how you measure innovation and what you decide to do about it. If innovation is equated with intellectual capital, you'll count patents; if it's an educated workforce, you'll count Ph.D.s; if it's infrastructure, you'll count broadband networks and bits per second; if it's culture, you'll count pieces of public art and symphony orchestras.

Many of us assume that the tools and methods of innovation are mature, simply waiting to be deployed. The truth is otherwise; we have few if any mature standards for how to practice innovation and measure the effectiveness of our efforts, let alone for how to train people to become master practitioners.

In contrast, consider the mature discipline of accounting. The need for audits became necessary as organizations became more complex, and a management technology was developed in response. If you wanted to know where a company's money came from and where it was deployed, you could find the answers by going to the accounting department, talking with the chief financial officer, looking at online financial data, consulting Generally Accepted Accounting Principles (GAAP), and scanning annual reports and 10Ks. But when it comes to innovation, most organizations lack anything like a comparable level of tangibility or management method.

What is more, there is an aura around innovation that clouds our perspective and often introduces an emotional component to the rational. Hmm, over in this corner is the sexy, expeditionary, wealth-generating, cool stuff, while over here is the structured, bureaucratic, legacy stuff. Which of these is more *moi*? We can safely assume that nobody wants to be known as un-innovative. But if innovation is seen as just another management mantra, another synonym for "good," then the cause is lost. The truth of the matter is that innovation is hard work, and it has passed through many incarnations and many attempts to explain it over the years.

Probably, the most widely shared misconception about innovation is that it's all about science and high tech. The rise of microlending, one of the most powerful innovations in recent years, shatters that notion.

Economist Muhammad Yunus came up with the idea of microcredit in 1974, after giving a woman in the village of Jobra, Bangladesh, $27 from his own pocket to help her make bamboo furniture. Previously, women in a village like Jobra either had no access to capital or they had to pay usurious rates to local loan sharks. Realizing that poor women were actually excellent credit risks and that giving them small loans could transform an entire local economy, Yunus formed Grameen Bank in 1976 to institutionalize what he called microcredit. The bank has now loaned more than $6 billion to more than 7 million borrowers, and Yunus took home a Nobel Peace Prize in 2006 in recognition of his innovative efforts.

Microlending is not the only social innovation of recent years. We can also cite the advent of impartial consumer testing of products, carpool lanes on busy highways, carbon-offset schemes, and a thousand other examples.

Nontechnological innovations abound in business as well. The classic example is Herb Kelleher and what he's accomplished at Southwest Airlines. Built on the simple idea of short-hop flights, no-frills service, and a clear, low-cost fare structure, Southwest has achieved phenomenal success and changed U.S. air travel in the process. Or how about John Bogle, who invented the index fund for individual investors and built the Vanguard Group of investment companies? Dov Charney proved with American Apparel that clothing could be manufactured in the United States by workers enjoying good wages and benefits. And what about W Hotels? Who would have thought a hotel chain could be hip?

These examples are not intended to discount the vital role of science and technology. Indeed, breakthrough technologies regularly set the stage for staggering waves of innovation. We're in the early stages of one of these transformations now that has been enabled by Internet-related technology. It is also easy to agree with analysts who reckon this century will see explosions of innovation, thanks especially to the revolutions in life sciences, nanotechnology, and clean technology. And there is an increasing amount of discussion on the innovation potential of our fast-evolving understanding of the brain and consciousness.

The point is not that technology isn't crucial—it is—but that we must think more broadly. My own definition of innovation is both integrative and aspirational. I define it as the ability of individuals, companies, and entire nations to continuously create their desired future. Innovation depends on harvesting knowledge from a range of disciplines besides science and technology, among them design, social science, and the arts. And it is exemplified by more than just products; services, experiences, and processes can be innovative as well. The work of entrepreneurs, scientists, and software geeks alike contributes to innovation. It is also about the middlemen who know how to realize value from ideas. Innovation flows from shifts in mind-set that can generate new business models, recognize new opportunities, and weave innovations throughout the fabric of society. It is about new ways of doing and seeing things as much as it is about the breakthrough idea.

Seen in this way, innovation is always in a state of evolution, with the nature of its practice evolving along with our ideas about the desired future. That is why innovation has meant different things at different periods in our nation's history, a state of flux that has made it difficult to fashion a consensus around any one meaning of innovation itself.

Version 1.0 of our national innovation capability, for instance, featured individual visionary inventors. Central casting gave us Benjamin Franklin and his kite, what we might call the artisanal model of innovation.

Geniuses in their workshops and garages, men like Thomas Edison and Henry Ford, later came up with inventions that inspired large-scale enterprises, ushering in version 2.0—the industrial model of innovation. Business requirements gave rise to mammoth, centralized corporate research groups that reached their zenith in such venerable institutions as Bell Labs, HP Labs, and the Xerox Palo Alto Research Center (PARC).

In the days before CEOs obsessed about shareholder value and financial metrics, some of these centers were true hotbeds of innovative R & D. Engineers and scientists were encouraged to follow their instincts, budgets were loosely scrutinized, and indulgent managers protected talented visionaries from cost-cutting bean counters. A story told of Bill Hewlett—who, along with Dave Packard, founded Hewlett-Packard—describes the creative atmosphere that once prevailed. Upon finding a locked storeroom at HP Labs, Hewlett is said to have returned with bolt cutters to destroy the lock. He wanted his engineers to be able to wander at will and make serendipitous discoveries, no authorization and voluminous forms needed.

In the public sector, the move to large-scale, organized innovation was expressed by the creation of the National Science Foundation, the National Institutes of Health, and other centralized edifices of government that provided national funding and administrative functions.

Version 3.0 deinstitutionalized innovation and featured the innovator-entrepreneur, financed by venture capital and devoted to the "just-in-time" organization. In this world, while corporate giant Xerox PARC developed the graphical user interface, upstart Apple Computer commercialized it. Big pharmaceutical companies got out of basic research, preferring to innovate by buying upstart biotech companies with valuable technology. In other words, it was innovation by merger and acquisition, not by R & D. And in another twist, Procter & Gamble, historically a bastion of proprietary knowledge, announced a plan to find the majority of its innovations from outside its corporate walls. More recently, Version 3.0 has seen the rise of entrepreneurial communities and open networks enabled by the Internet and new kinds of digital collaboration tools, such as Groove, MySpace, and the explosive expanse of social networking in all its forms.

Version 4.0, where we are today, is fast evolving—in beta, as techies are fond of saying. Many of the most important contributors to the process, however, reside outside the United States. Indeed, 4.0 is fundamentally about adapting to new innovation business models that may originate anywhere. It is driven by a global diffusion of innovation capability that has ended America's monopoly. For China, the key innovation model today may be a kind of brute force that comes from increasingly sophisticated massed minds working together. For Singapore, it is competitive specialization—for now in biotech, digital media, and environmental technology—as its vehicle to ride the rising tides of globalization. For India, it is building on the booming outsourcing industry. And oil-rich nations have a time-limited opportunity to buy into the game.

Countries everywhere are seeking their own sources of comparative advantage in the innovation landscape. And the logic of self-interest is clear. Robert Solow won the Nobel Prize in economics for, among other things, demonstrating that as much as 80 percent of GDP growth comes through the introduction of new technologies. And the Boston Consulting Group, in a study conducted for *BusinessWeek*, concluded that innovative companies achieved median profit margin growth of 3.4 percent as compared with 0.4 percent for the median S & P Global 1200. Furthermore their annualized stock returns of 14.3 percent were a full 3 percent better than the S & P 1200 over the same decade.

So innovation pays. As we struggle to get a fix on the ways in which our innovation processes must evolve in this rapidly globalizing world, experts are eager to step forward with a plethora of new ideas about the latest and greatest keys to innovation: S-curves, chasm crossing, customer-driven innovation, anthropological and design-driven approaches, and taxonomies of roles in the innovation process. Each concept has its merits, but one of my favorites was put forth by Clayton M. Christensen, a Harvard Business School professor, in his 1997 book, *The Innovator's Dilemma*. Christensen made a vital distinction between innovation that simply improves what is and innovation that defines what could be.

When management theorists started looking at innovation in the 1960s and '70s, they concentrated on the kind of stepwise product development best suited to an era of centralized, industrial, hierarchical business models. (You may recall that, when I started at Harvard Business School, I was told there was "nothing more to say" about innovation.) But upstarts began to challenge the incumbents with startling success. Two kids started Apple Computer. A Harvard dropout became the world's richest man. The iconic Xerox was nearly destroyed by Canon. A merchant from Bentonville, Arkansas, capitalized on the world's low-price infatuation and became its biggest retailer. And on and on. Clearly, more was at work here than nice, steady progression.

Innovation for improvement is a carefully limited and controlled kind of risk taking. Oreo sandwich cookies, for example, begat Oreo minis, which begat mint-flavored Oreos, which begat limited-edition white fudge–covered Oreos, Easter Oreos, Halloween Oreos, and so on. There are currently forty Oreo brand extensions on the market, including Oreo piecrust and ice-cream cones. If the incremental approach doesn't work, no problem. We'll simply adjust it.

There's nothing wrong with incremental innovation. In fact, it's essential for ordinary progress: Semiconductors get faster every year; medications become more effective; cars become more stylish and, is hoped, more fuel efficient; government makes itself more efficient (or not).

Game-changing innovation, however, requires one to assume a far higher level of risk. You really don't know how things are going to turn out, so all those linear, predictive models just don't apply. Forget the Oreo, let's launch a personal music device called a Walkman, or let's transform the computer industry by making computers personal, or let's make it possible for people to sell their stuff online. This is the sort of change I will be focusing on, because the mastery of disruptive innovation on a national scale is required to revitalize America's innovation capability.

China, India, Singapore, and the European Union (EU) will all ramp up their own models to benefit from their particular comparative advantages. It is my proposal that the United States specialize in a more comprehensive, transformational style of innovation, one that allows for placing big bets on the future, deploying its enormous resources, carrying out ambitious and mold-breaking experiments, reinventing the way we educate our young, aligning our federal, state, and local agendas, and recharging the magnetism of openness and opportunity that has historically attracted the world's talent to our shores.

By adopting this innovative approach to innovation, I believe the United States can step up to a revitalized national idea. What would it be like as a nation to be able to continuously innovate in service of ambitious, compelling, world-changing goals? We are not speaking of the pedestrian innovation described in business textbooks—a way to maximize return on investment, prime the product pipeline, or squeeze a little more performance out of R & D. No, I envision a concentrated application of our vast resources to innovate on a huge scale for human benefit. In short, I want America to be in the wicked problems business.

Various pundits have proposed a global priority list of wicked problems, including climate change, environmental degradation, communicable diseases, education, water quality, poverty, population migration, and energy sufficiency. Such wicked problems also hold the keys to making the most consequential breakthroughs of the twenty-first century. They interest me because they become opportunities when flipped on their heads. Innovation applied to a wicked problem can realize an enormous amount of social and economic value by setting new commercial standards, creating new businesses, and generating new sources of value. For a country that aspires to become an Innovation Nation, the search for opportunities to do good and still do well will allow it to exercise its innovation muscle.

The term "wicked problem" isn't new—although I have a different take on it. In 1973, the journal *Policy Sciences* published an article entitled "Dilemmas in a General Theory of Planning." Its authors, Horst W. J. Rittel and Melvin M. Weber, two scholars from the University of California, Berkeley, sought to describe planning problems—building a highway through the middle of a city, for example—that involved social issues so complex as to be virtually unsolvable. "At best," they wrote, the problems "are only re-solved—over and over again."

The wicked problems of our time rarely have clear-cut solutions that can be unlocked by a single discipline. They are complex and ambiguous. Issues such as climate change, health care, and national security are, at once, political and psychological, financial and technological. They require breakthrough business models and new ways of thinking about how to change the status quo. Above all, they require integrative approaches that blend necessary perspectives into a new way of doing the actual work of innovation.

But this is hard work without a road map. Every effort to find a solution to a wicked problem can trigger obdurate opposition from vested interests with different perspectives. You say the sheer weight of development is destroying the world supply of clean water? It's appalling, yes, but are we really willing to pay the political and economic price of water conservation? How do we define, let alone agree on, the relevant issues and measures? Are builders willing to halt expansion, farmers to limit crops, industries to cut emissions, politicians to alienate campaign donors—all to cope with someone else's creeping desert or toxic swamp?

The common answer, or so the political record suggests, is neither a flat yes or no, but something on the order of a shrug of maybe. The problem is just too big, too amorphous—just too wicked.

In contrast, we are accustomed to dealing with tame problems, ones that are easily defined and have clear boundaries that lend themselves to orderly, linear thinking. Buying a car, for instance, is relatively straightforward. We know we need a new car because the old one is wearing out. So we comparison shop, analyze the variables involved, narrow our choices, and make a decision. In short, we begin by defining the dilemma and then proceed in a straight line through a statement of options, the winnowing of possibilities, and the selection of the optimum product. Voilà, closure!

There's nothing simple about a wicked problem. In fact, just working on it may change its nature or make other wicked problems even worse. Finding an economical way to extract oil from shale, for instance, might reduce America's energy dependency and power the world for another century—but at the cost of new eruptions of greenhouse gases and potentially faster climate change. It's not even possible to say for sure that a wicked problem has been solved. How can we know for certain that we've won the so-called global war on terrorism or achieved a satisfactory level of health in society?

Or take the development of new disease-busting drugs. A variety of stakeholders populate the field. Some are entrenched in established business models—call them big pharma or national laboratories. Others are the insurgents—call them venture-backed start-ups. Patient groups, academics, policy think tanks, advocacy groups, and an entire ecosystem of other industry stakeholders also must be considered, because all have a vested interest in the outcome—whether it be economic, political, or social—and anyone can throw a wrench into the works by raising objections in a public forum or by getting legislators involved. The latter is almost a given because, like myriad issues in our society these days, the question of drug discovery has, unfortunately, become highly politicized. It is hard to see how the system for drug discovery can ever be improved when the possibility of creating consensus seems elusive at best.

The energy agenda is emerging as a key wicked problem of this generation. We may not be able to say why certain forms of energy are "alternative" or certain technologies "clean." But that has not stopped the challenge from rising to the top of the pile, as seen in calls for an agency modeled along the lines of the Defense Advanced Research Projects Agency (DARPA) and the rise of venture capital investment in green technologies. The bellwether *New York Times* columnist Thomas Friedman has even gone so far as to call green the "new red, white, and blue," redefining environmentalism in terms of patriotic self-interest. If our national energies are redirected toward green and clean technology, the logic goes, our global image will be overhauled, our economy will get an enormous boost, and the planet will get a critically needed clean-up.

However, global civil society has difficulty getting traction on such wicked problems because it lacks the wherewithal to bring together the diverse group of stakeholders from various disciplines that is needed to forge even a partial solution. To have a chance of success, we will need new approaches that blend facilitation and collaboration processes, new kinds of places, technology, tools, knowledge management practices, and more into a different way of working. It is not an overstatement to say that much of what follows in this book is a national toolbox for tackling wicked problems.

In succeeding chapters, I'll take you on a tour of innovation hot spots around the world to find emerging best practices. It will be a look at what might be called the new geography of innovation and the requisite new tools for innovation on a national scale. First, though, let's examine the troubling erosion of our innovation capacity at home.

TWO

SILENT SPUTNIK

Once the invisible hand has taken all those historical inequities and smeared them out into a broad global layer of . . . prosperity—y'know what? There's only four things we do better than anyone else: music, movies, microcode software, high-speed pizza delivery.

—Neal Stephenson, *Snow Crash*

The eighteenth-century Scottish writer Alexander Tytler is said to have argued that all great nations reenact an inevitable cycle that takes them from bondage through liberty to abundance, and then from complacency through dependence back into bondage. If the United States is to be an exception to that theory, we must start by confronting the dismal facts of our current situation. We have done it before.

In the fall of 1957, flush with new world power, Americans were suddenly attacked from outer space by a 183-pound hunk of metal—the Soviet Union's first Sputnik satellite. No bigger than a large watermelon, it whirled cheekily around the earth as if laughing at our national assumption that space travel, and perhaps the planets themselves, were ours for the taking. The Soviets had beaten us to the interplanetary frontier, posing what was then considered to be a serious military threat as well as puncturing our proud self-image as the world's most innovative nation.

It was a wake-up call, and America answered it. We revised school curricula to emphasize the teaching of science and math. We passed the $900 million National Defense Education Act (about $6 billion in today's dollars), providing scholarships, student loans, and scientific equipment for schools. We established the Advanced Research Projects Agency, which became the Department of Defense's DARPA, as well as the National Aeronautics and Space Administration, a monumental thrust toward innovation that culminated in Neil Armstrong's triumphant moon walk on July 20, 1969.

Today we face a challenge without the obvious pain points of Sputnik, a "silent Sputnik" one might say, whose symptoms are eclectic and might be ignored if viewed piecemeal. Taken as a whole, however, they tell a story of grave challenge to our nation's future health and prosperity. Some of the cardinal symptoms, expressed as dismal facts related to our innovation capabilities, are set forth in the following pages. They range from major, earthshaking developments to smaller but telling details. Like all report cards, this one does not aspire to be encyclopedic. Consider it, rather, a snapshot of telling facts.

NOT MAKING THE GRADE

It is the best of times and the worst of times for American innovation. If one were to issue a report card on this topic as of 2006, the situation might appear bright along such dimensions as higher education, funding, start-ups, high-tech innovation, and infrastructure.

Surveys show that we have thirty-eight of the top fifty universities worldwide. We graduated twenty-eight thousand Ph.D.s in science and engineering in 2006. Over $300 billion is spent annually on R & D in this country, two-thirds of it by industry. The federal government itself spends about $30 billion a year funding basic scientific research at universities. Its total spending on R & D through agencies like the National Science Foundation and DARPA amounted to $135 billion in 2006 and the range of funded discoveries was exceedingly broad—everything from more efficient solar cells to new technologies for drug delivery.

Our research laboratories—both corporate and government—actively pursued new opportunities in cutting-edge areas like clean technology and proteomics, the study of protein structure and function that many consider to be the next big thing after genomics. Start-up activity was brisk, with venture capitalists investing over $25 billion in the United States in 2006. The results of our entrepreneurial engine were everywhere to be seen: GPS navigation systems, the Second Life virtual world, nanomolecular materials, unmanned aerial vehicles such as the Global Hawk, next-generation computer chips, and more. Our innovation prowess was on display in other arenas of society, too, from design and architecture to media and social enterprises. Consider the buildings of Frank Gehry and William McDonough, the innovations of Chad Hurley and Steve Chen (creators of YouTube), and the emergence of what some have called netroots participatory democracy, in which political activists organize their constituents and incite their participation through blogging and other forms of online media.

But every one of these seemingly sunny items on our national report card has a dark side—a shadow, if you will. Every "A" pairs up with a "D." Some of these facts are incomplete or the subject of controversy. But taken together, they paint a daunting story of a "perfect storm." Let's consider each in turn.

First, our preeminence in higher education masks the fact that there has been an astounding globalization of higher education in recent years. The result: growing concentrations of well-trained potential innovators all around the world. Australia, for example, has explicitly targeted higher education as a national growth strategy; 250,000 foreign students currently study at Australian institutions and a further 65,000 attend Australian campuses overseas. Most of the students are from China, Hong Kong, Malaysia, and Singapore. India shows signs of deregulating its higher education system so as to open the door to international universities. China's government has an explicit target of bringing at least ten of its universities into the world-class group—it's revealing of China's ambition that the most widely used global ranking of universities is based on research from Shanghai Jiao Tong University.

Meanwhile, the data show that Asian students especially are less likely to seek education in the United States. From 1994 to 1998, Chinese, South Korean, and Taiwanese students who chose to pursue doctorates in the United States dropped 19 percent. An even more telling fact is that the number who chose to get doctorates in their home country almost doubled.

Adding to this global redistribution of higher education, a handful of major American institutions, such as Wharton and Northwestern, which understand the power of becoming global brands, have been opening up shop overseas. Northwestern's highly ranked Kellogg School of Management now has executive education campuses in Hong Kong, Tel Aviv, Toronto, and Vallendar, Germany. There have been reports, officially denied, that patrician Harvard has been studying the potential of having a campus in China. Europe's leading business school, INSEAD, is also globalizing with a Singapore campus that is run in alliance with Wharton.

Then there is the issue of the numbers of students being trained. If we look at the rate of advanced degrees granted, a particularly illuminating statistic comes from China, indicating that its growth curve is beginning to approach and even surpass our own. While China produced just 12,873 master's degrees in 1995, it turned out 63,514 in 2004–2005, leading the United States for the first time.

And while U.S. production of Ph.D.s seems to hover slightly north of 40,000—42,437 in 1996, 42,354 in 2005—China's rate of doctoral production has increased more than fivefold in the past decade, rocketing to 9,427 from 1,784. Absolute numbers alone don't tell the full story. Holders of American doctorates are still generally seen as more employable based on a higher-quality educational experience, which serves to maintain a perception of the United States as solidly in the lead. But at these rates of change, China is becoming a truly formidable contender.

Looking at another metric often used to measure the amount of research being done, our innovation engine would initially seem to be running in high gear. The number of research papers published by scientists, an oft-used measure of a nation's dedication to innovation, puts America handily in the lead. But looking at the rate of growth paints a very different picture: Between 1988 and 2001, the annual production of research papers in China soared from 4,600 to 21,000, up 354 percent. In Asia overall, the increase was 119 percent, with the number of papers published rising to 113,600 from 51,800. "Wait a minute," you might say, the Asian figures simply reflect a low starting point. That may be part of it, but even in Europe the number of research papers went from 143,900 to 229,200, an increase of 59 percent. Meanwhile, in the United States, they went from 177,700 to 200,900, a rise of just 13 percent.

Another important measure of competitiveness is the condition of a nation's talent pool. If demography is destiny, the dire facts cast a pall over our innovation future. Patrick Callan, president of the National Center for Public Policy and Higher Education, put it this way: "The strength of America is in the population that's closest to retirement, while the strength of many countries against whom we compare ourselves is their younger population." A look at one crucial field is revealing. Computer science employment is growing by one hundred thousand jobs annually, according to Microsoft chairman

Bill Gates. But the number of students graduating in computer science is declining. Moreover, the supply of H-1B visas in 2007, which enable foreign scientists and engineers to work in the United States, is so limited that applications were cut off two days after opening day; 133,000 applications were mailed in for 65,000 visas.

The United States is like a company that hasn't yet recruited enough new talent, let alone trained it, even though its best and brightest executives and managers are packing up their mementos and heading to farewell dinners to collect their gold watches. If this nation were a company, the human resources director would be kicked out onto the street.

What about education below the college level? It has been well—and painfully—documented in opinion polls that most U.S. high school students would rather take out the trash, clean their bedrooms, or wash dishes than study math or science. And they seem increasingly indifferent to education. California statistics for 2007 reported that a full 33 percent of high school students failed to graduate, and that was after a decade of costly modifications to education—smaller class sizes, higher education standards, additional teaching training.

U.S. students' low scores on standardized tests are also consistent with these declining trends. The Program for International Student Assessment (PISA) measures the performance of fifteen-year-olds in forty-one countries. American students placed twenty-fourth for math literacy and twenty-sixth for problem-solving; they were below the international average in every component of math literacy.

Then there is the TIMSS (Trends in International Mathematics and Science Study), another international effort. In two consecutive TIMSS reports, the United States had the distinction of having reasonably high-performing fourth graders, who then plunged in the eighth-grade rankings. The latest TIMSS, conducted in 2003, suggests that the performance of U.S. eighth graders has improved, but the overall trend is still worrying.

While our competitor nations focus on educating and training engineers and inventors, our schools are turning out youngsters who are better consumers than they are creators. According to the National Math & Science Initiative, the United States ranks sixteenth out of seventeen nations in the proportion of twenty-four-year-olds who earn degrees in natural science or engineering as opposed to other majors. Worse, we are allowing the vagaries of income disparity to waste generations of potential innovators. In schools serving low-income students, 30 percent of junior high mathematics teachers majored in their subject in college—half the proportion for schools that served the general population. Another telling fact: There are 199 age-appropriate books per household in wealthy Beverly Hills, California, but only 2.7 and 0.4 books per household, respectively, in the nearby poverty-stricken and gang-infested areas of Compton and Watts.

Our growing talent deficit also reflects changing patterns of immigration. For generations, the United States has relied on foreign-born engineers and scientists to fill out the ranks of our homegrown innovators. Emma Lazarus's words "Give me your tired, your poor . . . ," inscribed on the tablets held by the Statue of Liberty, always carried an invisible rider, "your talented." Today, our immigration policies are chasing this talent away. The wait for so-called green cards—they're actually pink and white—now exceeds six years. Meanwhile, nations that once had little or no scientific education or high-tech job opportunities have been transforming themselves. Result: Foreign-born residents are leaving in droves.

The evidence is still anecdotal and reliable trend data have not to date been captured. With that in mind, here are some evocative data points. In 2005 and 2006 alone, for example, thirty thousand Indian-born technology professionals residing in the United States moved back to India, according to Nasscom, a trade group of Indian outsourcing companies. Search firm CEO Anuradha Parthasarathy notes that many Americans of Indian origin working in high-tech fields now regard a return to India as a "career-enhancing move." The strain of resettlement is often eased by the opportunity to live in gated communities with names like Palm Meadows and Lake Vista. And a host of young American executives of non-Indian origin now see a stint in India as a ticket to ride.

Hundreds of Taiwan-born scientists and engineers have been lured away from positions in American companies to the science-based Hsinchu Industrial Park, which was started in the 1980s. In fact, a third of the companies in Hsinchu were founded by so-called repats, who can settle in live-work environments explicitly modeled on Silicon Valley. The same scenario is being played out by the thousands of Irish men and women who have left jobs in the United States to return to the "old sod." And the list goes on.

At the same time, many American-born scientists and engineers are being lured away to other countries with better pay, superior equipment and personnel, and the chance to win the recognition and work environment they feel they deserve. Edison Liu, former head of the U.S. National Cancer Institute and now a division head at Singapore's Biopolis, the country's massive new research center aimed at vaulting Singapore to biotech preeminence in one generation, told me:

> We have been given a paintbrush that is quite broad, with a palette that has lots of color. We're given tools to really do something, draw something nice. That artist in us, that desire to create something beautiful comes out because of the resources and degrees of freedom that are given us.

Other scientists who have made the move include Jackie Ying, formerly of MIT, who now heads the Singapore Institute of Bioengineering and Nanotechnology; Neal Copeland and Nancy Jenkins, who moved from the U.S. National Cancer Institute to Singapore's Institute of Molecular and Cell Biology; Ed Holmes, dean of the

UCSD School of Medicine and his wife Judith Swain, the UCSD medical school's dean of translational medicine, which is the discipline of turning laboratory science into therapies with commercial application.

Welcome to the new world-of-talent war. It is not too soon to start taking seriously the notion of an American brain drain.

The story is no less daunting when we examine the core support for innovation on a national level, such as the funding for basic research and the infrastructure that underpins it—telecommunications and logistics. While other countries are committing more money to research and infrastructure, the United States is dragging its feet.

A global study of R & D tax credits, a major fiscal tool for stimulating research, found that more and more countries around the world are granting generous tax credits to encourage corporate R & D activity. Britain, for instance, introduced a 150 percent tax credit for small and medium-sized enterprises in 2000—part of a major program to boost business innovation. Japan provides a tax credit three times as generous as that of the United States, and for small companies it is four times as generous. China offers a 150 percent deduction on R & D expenses, provided that R & D spending increases at least 10 percent over the prior year. The United States, meanwhile, ranks seventeenth among the thirty countries in the Organization for Economic Cooperation and Development (OECD) when it comes to R & D tax incentives.

These incentives are significant for corporations looking to maximize efficient use of resources on a worldwide basis. Craig Barrett, chairman of Intel, told me that a chip-making facility in Singapore is worth a billion dollars more over ten years than the same facility in the United States, largely because of favorable tax policies, not labor cost advantages.

Those who believe exclusively in the wisdom of the free market may not be concerned about the move to private funding of research, but the progress of scientific and technical innovation depends on the ability to concentrate resources—human as well as financial—in service of large-scale, long time horizon opportunities. It also relies on a talent community's ability to share knowledge, which may run afoul of the private sector's proprietary urges.

The shrinking role of direct government support for research is also part of this story. In the 1960s, U.S. government dollars financed 67 percent of the nation's total spending on R & D overall, with a substantial portion dedicated to basic research—the area from which most major innovations spring. Since then, the government's share has dwindled to 30 percent, the total growing largely in line with U.S. economic growth, not with the pull of new opportunities.

Through the 1980s, the U.S. government consistently spent more than 1 percent of our gross domestic product (GDP) on R & D, but federal spending on R & D dropped to a fifty-year low of 0.68 percent of GDP in 2000. It increased to $93 billion, or 0.8 percent of GDP, in 2004, a level large in absolute terms but one that simply returned us to the standards of 1954 in terms of government commitment. Although the private sector has taken up much of the slack, those resources are directed more toward applied rather than innovation-generating basic research.

With the fading of Bell Labs, Xerox PARC, and the large pharmaceutical company labs, corporate America seems most interested in the kind of innovation that can be obtained through mergers and acquisitions. It is a movement away from homegrown innovation to innovation as transformation of the inventiveness of others. That might be a rational business decision. So-called me-too drugs, which provide minor improvements on existing products, can be quickly profitable after relatively simple trials. But me-too drugs are not going to transform an industry. The turnabout is partly a reflection of the explosive pace of innovation in pharmaceutical and technical fields, which is forcing incumbents to shift their perspective to monitoring developments among a growing constellation of entrepreneurial ventures.

The $300 billion plus that America's government and private industry spend on R & D remains, in absolute terms, far above what most other nations spend. But our foreign competitors are mightily increasing their government investment in research—China and South Korea, for example, by 10 percent or more a year. China has just passed Japan as the second-largest R & D spender, with its $136 billion in 2006 versus Japan's $130 billion. And in terms of R & D spending as a share of the economy, we trail several nations, including Finland, Iceland, Israel, Japan, and Sweden, which are part of an elite group that spends more than 3 percent of GDP on R & D. The United States, which boasts the world's largest economy, is in the second tier, with government and private industry spending totaling 2.7 percent of GDP. When it comes to basic research, we're in eleventh place as a percentage of GDP.

And American companies have been moving their R & D offshore at a rapid clip. Once upon a time, U.S. inventions universally carried the label "Made in America." That is less and less the case. More than 40 percent of our high-tech companies invest in substantial R & D operations overseas, and at least a third of them are intent upon increasing their foreign stakes in R & D capability. While there are obvious benefits to offshoring R & D, including lower cost and more lenient regulatory environments, the net result is a global diffusion of American innovation capability, with long-term implications for our competitiveness.

One of the most stunning migrations of the past decade, though, has been U.S. venture capital's move overseas. The source of such a large share of the funding for innovation is finding its way to China and India in ever greater amounts. In 2006 alone, U.S. venture funds invested $856 million in 71 deals in India and $1.1 billion in 105 deals in China. The second-quarter China investment of $480 million was roughly double the pace of 2005. Part of the attraction was the hot Chinese IPO market; in 2006, there were 155 IPOs in China that raised $53.5 billion, which made China the world's number one IPO market.

Couple the flow of venture capital with negative trade balances in high-tech products that we commonly associate with American industry leadership, and the worrisome scope of our problems becomes clear. For anyone dreaming that our technology industry will save our standing in world trade, consider this: since 1999, America's high-tech trade deficit with the rest of the world has more than doubled, soaring to $96 billion in 2005. What's worse, we are running a negative trade balance—buying more than we sell—in virtually every sector of high tech, not just in a few laggard areas like offshored software development. The chilling list includes optoelectronics, advanced materials, flexible manufacturing, and biotechnology. And the number one exporter of high technology today? In 2005, China exported $406 billion of high-tech goods compared with U.S. exports of $284 billion. Some of this disparity is undoubtedly a function of U.S. companies that are using China as a manufacturing platform; their exports out of China show up as U.S. imports. But according to Robert Atkinson of the Information Technology and Innovation Foundation, stripping those numbers out of the calculation would still leave the United States with a significant high-tech trade deficit.

Furthermore, our slide means we are missing out on the kind of new technology opportunities that often emerge from close engagement with manufacturing and development. Today's exemplar of this close-knit relationship is Toyota, whose R & D on hybrid engines, for example, was rapidly introduced into its products globally. In the Toyota production system, research scientists and engineers work closely with factory managers, marketing teams, and supply-chain wizards. Agility in distribution through supply-chain automation and new concepts of sense-and-respond logistics are also seen as vital. Meanwhile, our wholesale offshoring of manufacturing is depriving us of the ability to generate that kind of strategically invaluable knowledge, which increasingly relies on information technology to create new economies of scale in production.

The story is no better when it comes to high-tech infrastructure. Recent studies show that easy access to information and communication technologies breeds stronger social connections and greater cooperation, which, in turn, spur innovation and new e-business concepts. This is where we should shine. However, with regard to such infrastructure, despite our TiVos and iPhones, the situation is no more promising. In 2006, more than 83 percent of South Koreans had Internet broadband access, while only 45 percent of Americans could make that claim. And "broad" means different things in different countries. The TechNet Innovation Initiative estimates that consumers in other countries have 20, 40, sometimes 100 megabit connections, while broadband usually means speeds of a few megabits or less in the United States.

Traditional infrastructure also figures into this equation. The American Society of Civil Engineers awarded America a "D" grade for its physical infrastructure, which some describe as "decaying." By infrastructure we mean basic stuff—roads, bridges, railways, telecommunications grids, waste- and water-handling systems. The group estimated that $1.3 trillion would be needed just to attain "acceptable" conditions. That's real money. A real "tax" on our ability to invest in the future. And a real problem.

It's worrisome, too, that the United States is lagging in social innovation—the ability to create new institutions and practices that meet social needs and strengthen civil society. Much of the cutting-edge work in this emerging field is being done in Great Britain, while Denmark and Singapore both have government-backed arts programs explicitly aimed at fostering a culture and ethos of innovation on a national scale. The sophistication of these programs is striking. Denmark's government identified the need to deepen the relationship between the arts and business in 2000. The goal was to expose businesses to new creative and artistic skills; encourage new-product development, design, and services; and bring about change in organizational cultures. In the United States, by contrast, political and fiscal pressures have forced cuts in American public arts programs, including those offered in many schools.

Our report card also catalogs deficits in certain other, more global aspects of America's innovation fitness. For instance, what about the physical and mental capabilities of our young? In 2005, while having dinner with the U.S. Army's chief of staff, Peter Schoomacher, I was asked to guess the percentage of America's teenagers who met the army's minimum requirements in these areas. Recall that this was a time when the army was especially interested in boosting recruitment, and its admissions criteria were, if anything, more lenient. The sobering answer was 25 percent.

Our innovation fitness is also based on our ability to understand, speak to, and do business with a variety of different national and ethnic groups. Many of our competitor nations have it, and we basically don't. We certainly undervalue languages: more American university degrees are said to be awarded in parks, recreation, leisure, and fitness studies than in all foreign languages and literatures combined.

For the time being, at least, English remains the lingua franca of science and technology. Thus, it is perhaps not surprising to hear U.K. prime minister Gordon Brown estimate that by 2025 China will have more English speakers than the rest of the world combined. In today's world, people who speak only English are fast losing their advantage. Nonnative speakers of English now outnumber native speakers by a factor of 3 to 1, according to David Crystal, author of *English as a Global Language.* Crystal notes that never have more people spoken the same second language. In Asia alone, the number of English speakers tops 350 million, and an estimated 100 million Chinese children are learning English.

The people of a number of other countries prize what I call cultural intelligence, a crucial asset in their prominent role in peace-keeping, international negotiations, and, of course, international business. It's also a drawing card for top scientists and technologists who used to hang their hats in the United States.

Finally, innovation leadership doesn't come cheap, and America has a hole in its pocket. In the business world, companies struggle to achieve a substantial free cash flow—their net after expenses and taxes. They take their profit from that flow and sink the rest into improving operations and into dividends. If the United States were a business, it would be close to broke. Meanwhile, countries like China, which are saving at a feverish pace, are able to invest in national technology projects, communications infrastructure, and education. The United States is running a vast trade deficit that reached $856 billion in 2006, the fifth consecutive record-breaking year. Our national debt is also spiraling upward. The Treasury Department provides a helpful "debt to the penny" calculation on its Web site. When I checked in the spring of 2007, it had reached over $8.8 trillion. The borrowing needed to cover the trade deficit alone—$2 billion a day in 2006—crowds out more productive investment in initiatives that could spur innovation.

•   •   •

Hopefully, by now you've heard the wake-up call. But my object in drawing up this report card is not to keep score in some kind of zero-sum, global innovation sweepstakes. For the most part, I am happy to see innovation capability spread around the world. I make the fundamental assumption that a world more capable of innovation will be more interconnected and more likely to generate new sources of value that will benefit all humanity.

Data of the kind presented above, however, must be woven into an overall story. Taken piecemeal, it can be hard to assimilate into a true picture of the nation's innovation status. Thus, some argue that the indicators point to serious decline, while others pick out certain bits of data to show that we're in great shape. But the accumulation of data by either camp does not, in itself, make for a compelling, robust vision of what the implications are for the day-to-day lives we Americans might be living in the future if we don't make improvements.

Henry Adams once defined ignorance as the accumulation of inert facts, and, in my experience, true knowledge awaits imagination— the spark of narrative, the power of storytelling to bring facts to life. In my work, I'll do almost anything to keep "innovation" from becoming an abstract word, dead on arrival in my clients' minds. Above all, I like to invent narratives that arouse empathy, levitate people out of their comfortable state, and create alternative outcomes that enlarge their horizons and clarify their choices.

The construction of scenarios—a word that in French literally means screenplay—is a technique pioneered at Royal Dutch Shell by noted futurist Pierre Wack. The technique proved its value in the '70s oil shock by allowing the firm—unlike its rivals—to anticipate soaring oil prices and constricted supply, and to have in place a strategy for seizing advantage. Strategy, as Wack was fond of saying to me during his stint as a visiting scholar at the Harvard Business School, was nothing more than the gentle art of reperceiving what was possible.

The construction of scenarios has since evolved into a disciplined way of spurring the collective imagination to anticipate possible futures, and thereby to identify issues and implications that might otherwise be overlooked. Scenarios are based on well-defined analytics and interactive processes, and their use has been adopted by governments and leading firms worldwide.

In my own work, I use scenarios to drive leadership teams to a more holistic—and often emotional—understanding of plausible futures. Scenarios are a way of recognizing the signs of change and being prepared for them. They are not predictions, but rather a framework of understanding that helps identify potential threats and opportunities. They are an effective means of "connecting the dots" to portray a full landscape, vital when dealing with the inherent ambiguities of the future. Knowledge generated through a well-managed scenario process can then drive the design of action plans and capability building.

In the spring of 2006, I assembled a group of colleagues to look at scenarios for the United States twenty years into the future. They were based on whether or not our talent pool and innovation infrastructure had been allowed to erode, in the process destroying our national competitive capabilities and quality of life. We looked at the global war for talent and the ability to capitalize on new business models for innovation as some of the key factors driving a set of scenarios that, in turn, might define a new global landscape for innovation.

While some of the scenarios told a reasonably positive story, others were deeply troubling in describing what an average American's life might look like if he or she found himself or herself caught in the backwash of a nation that had lost its innovative edge. The short-story-length scenarios, one in this chapter and one in the next, are fictional excursions from our fact-laden narrative. They are meant to activate the heart as well as the head. So, allow me to take you on a trip to the year 2027.

•   •   •

On Saturday morning, Jim Polk awakened to the sound of children playing beside his trailer. For just a moment, he thought he was back in his hometown of Mount Joy, Tennessee, trying to get in an extra hour of sleep while his wife Cindy hushed their two boys: "Your father works hard all week, kids. He needs his rest."

How sweet it had been, the four of them in that little ranch-style house, the love and the laughter. Late at night in bed, after the boys were finally in dreamland, Jim and Cindy would share their own dreams for the future, confident that it could only be better.

Suddenly a rapid-fire series of explosions erupted outside the trailer window. Though still half asleep, Jim instantly reacted, rolling off the bed and across the floor toward the pistol and holster hanging from a nearby chair. By the time he had the weapon in his hand, he realized his error. It was the Fourth of July. The kids were fooling with fireworks.

Jim snorted in disgust and reached for the ever-present bottle of cheap bourbon. The images of his old life returned to haunt him. This was his future, he thought—a decrepit trailer park off Interstate 95 near industrial Bridgeport, Connecticut, a dead-end job, a life without family, without pride, without hope. All he had to show for the passage of time was a growing gut, prematurely gray hair, and that fight-not-flight response to danger he had learned in the army's Third Infantry Division.

He laughed, recalling the words of the snippy woman who had hired him as a security guard two years earlier. "You don't know how lucky you are," she said. "We had four hundred applicants for this job." She was right, too. Up until then, he had scratched out a living doing menial temp work. Now he got to spend ten hours a day, six days a week, pistol on hip, guarding the entrance to Treasure Island.

That's what he liked to call Bonham Reef, a private island in Long Island Sound, just offshore from the metropolis of Stamford. There were dozens of these fortress enclaves scattered around the country. The Reef, once the property of a Rockefeller heir, was now home to two thousand of the new elite—hedge-fund managers, corporate lawyers, heart surgeons, and the foreign executives whose companies kept parts of Stamford prosperous. A four-lane covered highway carried them directly into the city center. On the island, they relied

on Jim and his colleagues to protect them from the crime and growing unrest in the have-not neighborhoods nearby. Except for an occasional ironic salute from a passing teenager, the residents of the
Reef ignored Jim, and he despised and envied them.

It usually took him only a half hour to get to Stamford and the
Reef Highway. The slowest part of the trip was a five-minute crawl
through downtown Norwalk. People told him it had been a bustling
commercial center years before, but now it was a poster child for
urban blight. Naturally, that was where the clamp on his exhaust pipe
had given way on Friday.

Within a minute, a gang of angry-looking men and laughing teenagers had surrounded the car—studying the tread on the tires, checking the interior for a universal communicator or anything else they
could sell. Before they could make their move, Jim pulled his pistol
and fired a shot over the head of the man he took to be the leader.
After that, he was able to reattach the clamp and escape without
harm.

As he sat in his trailer the next day, thinking back over the inci-
dent, he wondered how much time he had before the gangs took over
entirely, before the Treasure Islands and the protected corporate
centers were totally isolated in an ocean of anarchy. Some of the men
he drank with, Iraq vets all, were members of the Sons of Liberty,
one of the militia groups now springing up all around the nation.
They wanted Jim to join—ex-army snipers were always welcome—
but he turned them down. Angry as he was, he could not bring himself to be party to the armed "demonstrations" they were planning
for some of the heavy-crime neighborhoods of Bridgeport. "I'm a
real Mr. Nice Guy," he told himself, with a self-denigrating hoot. "It
must be in my blood."

Jim was born in Mount Joy, Tennessee, in 1980 to a family of lawyers, including his namesake, the eleventh president of the United
States, James Knox Polk. Jim's dad was a dentist, the first male non-

lawyer Polk in seven generations, and Jim's mother taught ninth-grade math at Mount Joy High.

When Cindy got pregnant in their senior year, Jim insisted that they marry. He found a job in a local accounting firm—he'd always been top of his class in math and science—and began work on a B.S. degree in engineering at a nearby college. To earn some extra money, he joined the army reserves. All that, and some parental help, enabled the young couple to buy their first home just in time for the birth of their first son, James.

Then Jim's reserve unit was activated and dispatched to Baghdad. He served three tours there, each worse than the one before. The war's death and destruction took its toll on him. He saw his wife just long enough to father another son, Knox, but he and Cindy no longer spoke the same language or shared the same dreams. In her loneliness, she found another man and sued for divorce. By then, Jim hardly cared. The platoon had become his only family.

The America Jim had returned to was a far cry from the nation he had once known. *Fortune* magazine wrote of the "hollowing out" of society, the disappearance of any real middle class. The trend was already evident back when Jim was first called to Iraq. Five percent of the population was paying 57 percent of the taxes (and earning 33 percent of the income), and half the population was paying only 3 percent of the total. Now, that 5 percent had shrunk to 3 percent, and they were paying 75 percent of the taxes. Effectively, there were only haves and have-nots in the country, a first-world elite and an increasingly restive third-world underclass. Meanwhile, countries like Brazil and South Africa, once completely split across social class lines, were enjoying a new, innovation-fueled renaissance along with a resurgent middle class.

Jim was no scholar, but he could not avoid the headlines. The economy was in terrible shape; the Dow had been flat for years. American products had become so notorious for their poor quality that they had virtually no overseas market. The country was constantly in danger of defaulting on its gigantic foreign debt, and the dollar had sunk to a new low, replaced by the euro as the international currency of choice. Foreign governments and companies, stuck with billions of dollars that no one else wanted, were using them to buy up U.S. corporations, land, and housing at fire-sale prices. General Motors was now a division of Toyota, churning out low-cost versions of Toyota's high-tech vehicles in an American wrapper and strictly for the U.S. market. The film industry, the quintessential American cultural icon, had been completely taken over by foreign conglomerates and was churning out derivative entertainments based on European game shows and Japanese avatar technology. Even basic national transportation infrastructure, the network of trains and highways, was crumbling—Jim had been late to work twice in the last month because of repairs on the interstate to Stamford.

As he knew only too well, the standard of living for most Americans had sunk abysmally low. So had their educational level, with 50 percent of their children never finishing high school—compared to 30 percent in 2006.

His older son, James, had been on the losing side of that statistic. After Cindy's second marriage fell apart, she found a job in telemarketing in Nashville and settled with the boys in a high-rise federal project. In short order, James joined a gang, became addicted to whiz, the new super-cocaine designer drug, and dropped out of high school. Cindy tearfully told Jim she didn't know where James had gone or what had become of him.

Knox had done better—much better. He inherited his father's mathematical bent and won all sorts of prizes in high school. Even so, he had trouble getting into the leading colleges. Their ranks were filled with the well-tutored children of the elite, both American and foreign. Knox was still in his sixth-choice college, majoring in engineering like his dad, when he and Jim reconnected.

According to Knox, who poured out his heart to his dad one

evening, his future in the United States was strictly limited. He was determined to operate on the cutting edge of technology, and America's top companies by and large were not interested. To start with, science and technology were the purview of the privileged classes. And their companies mostly specialized in global logistics, design, rapid prototyping, intellectual property, and the like— they served as a kind of systems integrator to the world by branding, processing and repackaging other people's ideas. Breakthrough technology—nanomolecular materials and life-extending pharmaceuticals, for example—was mostly coming out of China, India, and Europe these days.

Jim could hardly believe his ears. He remembered how, in his day, the United States had been at the front end of innovation while the rest of the world bought or copied our great ideas and products. Dozens of U.S. universities offered a world-class education. The best and brightest of the world came to the United States to study, and many of them stayed to help power the American innovation factory. Other nations complained bitterly about losing their top talent to the United States.

Not any more, Knox told Jim. The brain drain was working in reverse. Yes, there were still foreign students in America, but now they were mostly going back home right after graduation, at least the best ones, while the rest waited for a chance to access the best jobs abroad. America's top universities had established branches abroad, and cutting-edge technical schools were sprouting all around the world. The result: More and more would-be American engineers and scientists, as well as their foreign counterparts, were studying abroad and making their careers there. No need to come to the increasingly xenophobic United States. Knox had met a Finnish girl at his school, and he was talking about settling in Helsinki—just as Jim was getting reacquainted with his son.

"Why not stay in the States?" Jim wanted to know.

"Are you kidding?" Knox replied. "It's what you used to call a no-brainer. Look around you. If I got lucky, I could get a job in a lab in some fortified city like Stamford and get pigeonholed in some routine product work. My family could hunker down on Treasure Island and pretend we didn't notice all the poverty and rage around us.

"In Finland, the sky's the limit, every which way. What Roosa and I want to do is start our own lab—we've got an idea for a next-generation PDA with a revolutionary new user interface—and there's plenty of venture capital out there. We wouldn't have a chance in hell of getting that kind of backing here."

Jim did not even try to argue with his son. It really was a no-brainer.

• • •

Not convinced that this is a plausible scenario? Do you find it hard to believe that the United States could get so far off its game? As we consider whether or not we might face this sort of future, it's vital to consider not only the dulling of our own competitive edge, but also the remarkably vibrant innovation that can be seen in so many hot spots around the world.

The next chapter tells the stories of other countries that are not only starting to get it, but starting to get it done. There is much to make us nervous, but even more from which we can learn.

THREE

THE NEW GEOGRAPHY OF INNOVATION

Innovation and imagination give an economy or a company that extra edge. Today, wealth is generated by new ideas.

**—Goh Chok Tong,
former prime minister, Singapore**

At the end of World War II, a single nation stood atop Mount Innovation, and it was the United States. Now, powerful new climbers have emerged to challenge U.S. supremacy across a broad front of innovation. Some may be surprising—Brazil, Denmark, Estonia, Finland, New Zealand, Singapore, Taiwan—while others, such as China and India, are more familiar. The bottom line? Today, the map of innovation has been profoundly redrawn.

As an adviser to governments and organizations on almost every continent, I have occupied a front-row seat as a sometimes exhilarating, sometimes disturbing story has played across the world stage. In one country after another, I have seen innovation woven into national purpose to form a linchpin of public policy that influences national priorities, infrastructure investments, and the development of human capital.

This chapter looks closely at the assertive policies and achievements of some key countries, analyzing both what they've done and how they've done it. Business models, strategies, and the underlying mechanisms of innovation will come under the glass. My hope is that in learning more about those who have embraced the innovation imperative, unsettling though it may be, the United States will embrace a revitalized innovation agenda.

Certainly, America is home to a number of the largest, most vibrant centers of innovation in the world. No other country performs at our level today. But, to use Clay Christensen's term in *The Innovator's Dilemma*, we are the incumbents. Our consciousness is etched with business models of discovery, distribution, and governance that evolved over long periods of time. Countries like Singapore and the People's Republic of China are examples of insurgents; the former founded in 1965, the latter in 1949. They are hungry, willing to experiment, and have little downside to investing in new opportunities as compared with the United States. And Christensen puts forward a sobering observation, namely that innovation tends to come from insurgents, not incumbents. It comes from those who are willing to invest in finding new sources of demand, new customer needs, and new social trends on which to place bets. China, which is adopting the ethos of fundamental discovery, is destined to become a powerhouse in basic science, for example. Meanwhile, other nations are basing their business models on outsourcing or their ability to bridge cultures.

Ratcheting up the stakes is the fact that today's technology-enabled entrepreneurs are lighter and faster than ever before. An increasing number of ventures are global from the outset, as well as fast, economical, and in my words "weightless." So the competitive race is accelerating at an ever-faster pace at the same time that the nature of the race itself is changing. If we merely stick to our knitting, we will soon find ourselves surrounded by agile competitors who have learned to play a different set of standard-setting games.

To begin with, let's take a look at two relatively small countries that have made enormous strides in innovating the actual process of innovation and in becoming world-class centers of innovation. First is the tiny city-state of Singapore. The country is a testament to the notion that a nation doesn't have to be big to be a leading competitor in the global innovation race.

Singapore is an island nation the size of Chicago but with twice as many people—4.4 million to be exact. Its innovation ambition, however, is continent sized. Lee Huntsman, who during his tenure as president of the University of Washington negotiated a number of joint ventures and partnership programs with Singapore, calls it a "venture capital company masquerading as a government."

One of Singapore's strategic thrusts (along with digital media and clean technology) involves competing in the global economy as a leader in biotechnology. Like many other Singapore-watchers, Huntsman, himself a well-known bioengineer, particularly admires Biopolis. The huge new research center's strategy for achieving life-science dominance in just one generation is all about nurturing and leveraging human capital in a twofold approach: first recruit world-renowned scientists and arm them with the tools they need to find cures for major diseases. And second, educate a generation of native and immigrant Singaporeans to carry on that highly specialized work.

In the United States, which has seventy times more people than Singapore, approximately four thousand Americans receive Ph.D.s in the biological sciences each year. In Singapore, where the government pays their way, more than five hundred students are currently on track toward doctorates and the goal is to double that number by 2015. That would mean that a population one-seventieth the size of the United States was achieving a quarter of what we have been able to accomplish in cultivating talent—an astonishing disparity.

Biopolis already has two thousand scientists working in more than 2 million square feet of super-tech bliss. Additional facilities will eventually support a total research force of ten thousand. By comparison, the long-established U.S. flagship, the National Institutes of Health in Bethesda, Maryland, with its twenty-seven centers and institutes, employs six thousand doctoral-level scientists.

It is noteworthy that Biopolis was explicitly modeled after Silicon Valley, both in its business model and its ambitions. A monograph on Biopolis presents its vision: "(It) had to be an icon, every stick and every stone of it. In a way, it would be the biomedical world's equivalent of California's Silicon Valley." To add to its edge, Biopolis was designed by a group of young talents, not the old guard. Principal architect Kok Poh June was twenty-eight when the project started, project leader Goh Kok Huat was thirty-five. Youth translated into speed. When authorities in Cambridge, England, told them it would take fifteen years to develop a world-class life sciences center, the team buckled down and delivered Biopolis in just two and a half years.

The result is a $300 million complex, the master plan for which was developed by noted architect Zaha Hadid. It encompasses seven architecturally distinctive buildings with evocative names such as Helios, Proteos, and Nanos, interconnected by a network of sky bridges. They contain a mix of government research institutes and biotech start-ups as well as pharmaceutical multinationals. At full capacity, the lineup will include contingents from Eli Lilly, GlaxoSmithKline, Novartis, and a dozen other leading pharmaceutical firms.

The numerous foreign luminaries now working at Biopolis, in addition to those mentioned earlier, include Alan Colman, the Scottish scientist who ran the Roslin Institute, where Dolly the sheep was famously cloned in 1996. Colman rejected job offers from the United States and Britain in favor of Singapore, where he feels freest to pursue his goal of finding a cure for diabetes. When he left Scotland, he said, "I'm a scientist and the type of science I want to do is expensive, and I'll go where the investment is made." Biopolis's American recruits include Sidney Brenner, a Nobel Prize winner from the Salk Institute, and Mark Seielstad, who quit the Harvard School of Public Health because the "environment was better" at Biopolis.

One big draw is the center's resource-sharing program. All researchers get to use its state-of-the-art equipment instead of having to buy their own. Still another enticement is Singapore's liberal policies toward stem-cell research. Long a major supplier of cells to U.S. scientists, whose work has encountered political obstacles, Singapore has some of the world's most liberal laws governing therapeutic cloning and banking of human stem cells for research. Such embryonic stem cells may eventually play a crucial role in regenerative medicine and tissue replacement, as well as in therapies for cancer, Parkinson's disease, and spinal cord injuries. And Biopolis's cultivated pool of laboratory mice is also said to be an advantage compared with places hamstrung by regulations regarding animal experimentation.

Biopolis does not scrimp on quality of life, either. It boasts day care, laundry services, even a bar. And a new entertainment district, intentionally situated nearby, is under construction. It will include Singapore's largest concert venue, an extreme sports center, high-end shopping, gourmet restaurants, and more.

Biopolis is part of One North, a "city within a city" project, so named because Singapore is located one degree north of the equator. Fusionopolis, aimed at further enhancing the appeal of the complex to the new media talent community, is the second major element of One North. Housed in a futuristic high rise designed by Japanese architect Kisho Kurokawa, it will combine elements of New York's SoHo and California's Silicon Valley. Fusionopolis is emblematic of Singapore's push into what it calls IDM (interactive and digital media). As one local news report put it: "Arts, business, and technology will hopefully become bedfellows, and researchers may be able to rub shoulders with moviemakers to create, say, better digital films or cybergames."

Additionally, One North is adjacent to a large tract of undeveloped real estate set aside for "future agendas." So Fusionopolis and Biopolis may be just the beginning for a country that believes in using advanced principles of urban design to create national white space that can in turn further its innovation ambitions. It is also a place for dreams: an exhibition at One North presents a history of the future with such headlines as "2015—a Singapore research team develops a new compound using structural genomics to target the proteins responsible for leukemia." The arts are also included; the exhibit envisions that a One North–based filmmaker will someday win the Palme d'Or at Cannes.

The concept of One North was articulated by JTC Corporation assistant CEO and early instigator Philip Su, who told me, "We wanted to build a gifted community where the relevant metrics would no longer be GFA [gross floor area] built out, but the quantity of intellectual property created over time—a future metric as opposed to a present metric."

And Tan Chin Nam, chairman of One North as well as permanent secretary of the Ministry of Information and the Arts, points to the importance of a fusion among the arts, science, and business in going beyond the traditional science park model. He describes One North as a "new ecosystem and huge national experiment—a next generation live, work, learn environment and talent center."

When Singapore first set out to attract world-class scientists and technologists, its informal brand identity might have been called "China done by the Swiss." Its reputation was also that of a buttoned-up, Confucian society that imposed strict and well-publicized penalties for misbehavior. Pragmatism intervened, and the country changed course. Its current crop of technocratic leaders, schooled at elite universities in the United States and Britain, recognized that a more open culture, not a restrictive one, was what was needed to entice creative talent. Accordingly, they commissioned a veritable parade of thought leaders from around the world to offer advice about how to transform Singapore from an exemplar of efficiency to an enabler of innovation. These days, creative skills are taught in the public schools in an effort to instill mental agility, while government-backed investment companies fund the development of cutting-edge megamalls and nightclubs. Public-sector tolerance for freewheeling entertainments—including massive beachside raves that draw Bohemian types from all over Southeast Asia—has also increased.

Besides raising a new breed of homegrown talent that is better equipped to practice innovation, this more tolerant and creative climate has helped attract some of the world's best scientists and engineers, on either a full-time or time-share basis. Singapore's various advisory boards now read like a Who's Who of the world's senior talent in such areas as digital media and materials science. The list of stars includes Paul Saffo, thought leader on digital technology from Stanford University; John Seely Brown, former head of Xerox PARC; Peter Schwartz, chairman of the Global Business Network; Curtis Carlson, head of the California-based research powerhouse SRI International; and Rita Colwell, former head of the National Science Foundation and professor of biological sciences at the University of Maryland.

The Singapore government's commitment to innovation was never more evident than in the formation in January 2006 of the National Research Foundation (NRF). Its specific charter was to extend the nation's research thrust beyond biomedical sciences into two additional areas—environmental and water technologies and interactive and digital media—that were seen as "poised for rapid growth in Asia and the world." The NRF was given a five-year budget of $3.3 billion—a budget that, taken together with other government initiatives, means little Singapore's spending on R & D will total 3 percent of GDP by 2010. Recall that the United States spends 2.7 percent of its GDP on R & D, ranking it sixth among countries that devote resources to research and development.

Now consider Denmark. Shrugged off by many as a nanny state hopelessly hamstrung by the taxes that pay for its social largesse, Denmark is sending the naysayers scurrying for shelter. Long ranked among the world's most prosperous countries, Denmark now comes in sixth in terms of GDP per capita. And with a remarkable combination of hardheaded realism, energy, and creative thinking, the country has managed to nurture a lively, highly competitive capitalist economy—all without sacrificing more than a fraction of its social benefits and while retaining tax rates that would boggle American minds. Denmark's top tax rate—63 percent—applies to all incomes over $60,000.

The key to Denmark's success lies in a common eagerness to ignore pessimists and, instead, to apply creativity and question conventional wisdom in fields ranging from energy and education to urban planning and public transportation. For instance, the Danes, who lack the offshore oil that has enriched nearby Norway and Britain, turned their country into a world leader in wind power. Denmark exports super-efficient windmills to customers across the planet, and its wind-power industry, led by Vestas, the world's largest turbine manufacturer, controls nearly 40 percent of the global market. It's all part of a remarkably successful thirty-year effort for the country to hold down energy consumption and increase self-sufficiency. Over three decades, energy use has stayed remarkably constant in Denmark while its GDP has doubled.

Significantly, the evolving wind power industry was shepherded by a powerful combination of intelligent government incentives, targeted technological innovation, and a broadly supportive culture. Spurred by the energy crisis of the early 1970s, the Danish government sponsored a major energy research program that included wind power; from that initiative emerged innovative turbine designs crafted by Danish companies. The government then provided a powerful market incentive by requiring power companies to pay 85 percent of the retail—not wholesale—electricity price for power generated by privately owned turbines, many of which were built and operated by local business associations taking early advantage of Denmark's capital subsidy for construction. With premium prices guaranteed by the government, the new breed of turbine manufacturers found a ready market.

With their penchant for ingenuity, the Danes have also demonstrated that social problems can be solved without throwing money at them. Case in point: the government figured out that the country could save money—and combat pollution—by simply giving senior citizens cab fare rather than building fleets of vans to haul them around.

Crucial to the Danish success in innovation has been a joint effort by the government, private sector, and powerful trade unions to find new ways of gaining national competitive advantage through innovation. And, as I saw firsthand during a 2005 trip, all three stakeholders work cooperatively to achieve that advantage. My brief visit included trips to the prime minister's Innovation Council, a public-private sector alliance that fosters society-wide dialogue and stewardship for innovation; the education ministry's Learning Lab, which bridges the world of emerging best practices and the education mainstream; and the economy ministry's MindLab, a creativity incubator for government officials.

But what, you may wonder, are all these committees and consortiums actually accomplishing? Well, for one thing, they are building innovation infrastructure. Few countries can boast a comparable infrastructure, let alone nations of Denmark's size.

Just as with Singapore, the role of social innovation has been especially important in Denmark's evolution into an innovation leader. Take, for example, the impressive manner in which Denmark has swung from agriculture to industry to innovation, what my friend Uffe Elbaek, the head of one of Denmark's leading business schools, describes as a "rugged transformation." As Elbaek reports, "Eighty percent of the population was living in the countryside, and a few decades later most of them had moved to the city. So how is it that every time you make a list of the ten richest nations, Scandinavian countries come up again and again?" The answer, he suggests, is social innovation, and he offered a down-to-earth example.

Denmark is famous the world over for the quality of its agricultural products like bacon, butter, and cheese. That happened, Elback explained, not because the nation had a big agricultural industry, but because a lot of small farmers joined forces to create cooperative organizations that could maintain high-quality standards. They had realized a crucial truth: there was no long-term future in producing agricultural commodities, but they could carve out a niche in high-tech food processing. And Denmark had effective mechanisms for making the transformation. "We are very smart in our social fabric," Elbaek said. "In our worker system we are able to stress cross-training and the value of learning together as a community that makes us different from many other countries."

This is consistent with what Denmark calls a "flexicurity" model— a combination of flexibility and security. Compared to many European countries, it's easy to hire and fire workers in Denmark. But instead of being ensured job security, Danish workers have employment security; if they lose their job, the government provides well-funded retraining.

Elbaek's message is this: the social innovations needed by the modern world today will come from a high level of collaboration and cooperation. They will require new skills and new social mechanisms that include continuous learning, agility, and a willingness to reinvent the nature of competitive advantage in a cooperative, as opposed to a winner-take-all, manner.

The school my friend runs, KaosPilots (no relation to me; *kaos* is Danish for "chaos"), is a freewheeling, private, three-year graduate school that exemplifies a consciousness among Danish thought leaders about the need for a new breed of business people who can facilitate social innovation. The school describes its mission as training managers to transform chaos into innovative social and economic change and to develop an "entrepreneurial lifestyle." The curriculum embraces concepts such as social responsibility, handling change and creative processes, motivating action in unknown terrain, working through public-private partnerships, teamwork, intrapreneurship, and entrepreneurship.

Singapore and Denmark provide proof that small can be beautiful. They are great examples for the United States of the role ingenuity and aggressiveness play in nurturing innovation.

But there is no shortage of big competitors pursuing national innovation policies either, and chief among them is China. From a standing start in 1979, the country has already become the world's fourth-largest exporter; by some estimates, its economy will surpass that of the United States by the middle of this century. Never before has a nation created so much wealth so rapidly. Recent estimates place the number of Chinese millionaires at over 300,000, compared with 2 million in the United States. What is most significant is that China had no millionaires just a few short decades ago. Its recent pace of wealth creation has been truly revolutionary. A real-estate development outside Beijing boasts mansions with indoor swimming pools and stained-glass windows; prices start at $2 million. What would Mao say?

China's growth is impressive both for its scale and its focus on spurring innovation. For example, the city of Shanghai has been developing itself into a "digital harbor" since 1994. In 2002, it advanced a "digital city Shanghai" strategy that envisioned a wide range of intelligent, Internet-delivered services in such areas as education, finance, health care, and tourism. The city plans to fund R & D using 2.5 percent of the metropolitan Shanghai GDP, an unusual example of a city using metrics more commonly applied to nations. More than 140 international R & D laboratories have already been established in Shanghai, supported by a huge educational infrastructure of fifty-nine colleges and universities.

Beijing is not to be outdone. Not far from the Emperor's Summer Palace, for instance, in the northwest corner of Beijing, the Zhongquancun district has mushroomed into a mighty technology center. Just as California's Silicon Valley benefits from its connections to Stanford and Berkeley, so Zhongquancun feeds off Tsinghua and Peking universities (this top Chinese university has quixotically clung to the old transliteration of the city's name). There are said to be some twelve thousand high-tech companies in the district, with over a half-million employees. Small local companies thrive alongside such international giants as NEC, Microsoft, Siemens, and Sun.

In the center of the district, the Tsinghua Science Park has been taking shape over hundreds of acres. A huge and still growing complex of sleek modern buildings, the park includes research facilities that spur work in biotechnology, energy-related ventures, information technology, and materials science, but it also houses venture capitalists, legal services, and other kinds of business support. Tenants benefit from special tax breaks and the park has offices to help companies navigate the Chinese government bureaucracy. In short, everything the aspiring entrepreneur might need is close at hand. And I mean everything—a first-class hotel, health clubs, and even support groups for those who are having trouble handling the inevitable problems and stress of early-stage capitalist life.

Meanwhile, the Chinese government speaks more and more explicitly about its national innovation policies, developing intellectual property regulations, emphasizing science and engineering education, and streamlining business processes formerly hamstrung by bureaucratic inertia.

Significantly, innovation and enterprise have always been part of the Chinese character. In a *Harvard Business Review* article I wrote some years ago entitled "The Worldwide Web of Chinese Business," I pointed to Chinese culture as an enabler of the kind of global networking, agility, and pragmatism that can support a wide range of global business models. The traditional family orientation of Chinese businesses has been transformed with remarkable agility into globe-spanning networks of trusting relationships.

Certainly, China has had no shortage of creative breakthroughs in the long sweep of its history. The country invented the compass, gunpowder, the mechanical clock, rocketry, and the paddlewheel boat, among scores of other firsts. Scholar Joseph Needham's magisterial history of science in China totals some twenty volumes. And China's ambitions today—to establish bases on the moon, for example—are only one sign of its growing vision for science and technology.

•   •   •

As I've acknowledged, the United States has a range and depth of innovation centers—from Silicon Valley to the MIT-Harvard centered nexus to the Research Triangle in North Carolina. But my point in introducing the examples of Singapore, Denmark, and China above is how rapidly innovation centers have sprung up elsewhere. There are four principal driving factors behind this global evolution:

1. *Silicon Valley is now everywhere.* As the old saw has it, imitation is the sincerest form of flattery. For decades, governments and educators around the world sought to re-create the conditions

that originally propelled American science and technology to breakthrough innovations. Physics Nobelist Steven Chu, director of California's Lawrence Berkeley National Laboratory, says that wherever he travels in the world, university teachers and administrators ask him how they can nurture an American-style environment for learning, thinking, and innovation. "They are catching up quickly," he reports.

Once upon a time, not so long ago, there was nothing like Silicon Valley anywhere else in the world. Its convergence of world-class universities, venture capital, permissive culture, great weather, supportive corporations, and first-rate infrastructure was unmatched. A recent monograph even referred to a Silicon Valley "habitat" for innovation. Now, Silicon Valleys are sprouting up everywhere, perhaps most notably in India.

On the grounds of an ornate palace where a maharaja once reigned, the man of the hour on May 30, 2006, was Samuel J. Palmisano, chairman and CEO of IBM. He had traveled to the city of Bangalore to announce that his company was planning to triple its $2 billion investment in India over the next few years. A large portion of that sum would be spent by and for the ten thousand IBM employees, many of them software engineers, who labor in Bangalore, an Indian technology center with the greatest concentration of scientists and engineers in the country. In recent years, IBM has increased its employee base in India from nine thousand to forty-three thousand, while laying off thousands of employees in the United States and Europe.

After 1947, when India won its independence, Bangalore developed into a center for the defense and aerospace industries, but over the last decade, these enterprises have been overshadowed by an influx of new high-tech companies, particularly in information technology and biotechnology. The area hosts 47 percent of India's biotech companies, and accounts for 35 percent of the country's software exports. Some two hundred thousand workers labor there in one thousand two hundred companies. Infosys and Wipro, two of the world's largest software firms, are based there. A few years ago, these and other Indian companies carried out lower-value, back-office work, but today the leading Indian firms have moved into the high-value realms once reserved for engineers, technicians, and other types of professionals in the United States and Western Europe.

The tech boom in Bangalore has been supported by both the government and leading universities, including the century-old Indian Institute of Science (IIS), which has more than two thousand researchers on staff. The advantages of having the IIS in Bangalore were amplified when the government created the first Indian Institute of Information Technology in the city and improved the city's telecommunications, power, and transport infrastructure.

The government has also provided funding for the Karnataka Information Technology Venture Capital Fund (Kitven). Supported by the state of Karnataka and the Small Industries Development Bank of India, the fund started with only $3.5 million in 1999. Though small, Kitven was a pioneer among Indian venture capital funds, fueling the Bangalore boom before many recognized what was happening. It runs just like a private venture fund, with an ever-changing portfolio of start-ups. Kitven—which now has a second, $11 million fund—has posted a 30 percent rate of return, which compares nicely with any high-profile fund.

Thousands of miles and cultural light years away from Bangalore, little Finland also has a story to tell. The research and industrial district of Otaniemi, some five miles from downtown Helsinki, is home to Northern Europe's premier concentration of biotech and information sciences companies. One of the district's main features is the Otaniemi Science Park, a peninsula on the Gulf of Finland that combines a technical university, a business hub, and ninety technology and service companies with eight thousand professional researchers. They receive a wide range of incubation and business-development assistance, including partner search and international contacts.

The Otaniemi cluster also encompasses a number of Finnish research and technology organizations, ranging from the Technical Geological Survey to the Technical Research Center. The major institution, though, in this Silicon Valley–like development is the Helsinki University of Technology, which moved here more than forty years ago. The university, which has more than eleven thousand undergraduates and two thousand six hundred graduate students, is home to six research operations, including the National Physics Research Institute and the Helsinki Institute of Information Technology. Its labs and research projects soak up more than half the money Finland spends on high-level technological research. Leading-edge research is being conducted on everything from materials science and wireless technology to innovations in how the forest industry— traditionally a bulwark in Finland—deals with timber handling, mill operations, and harvesting.

Otaniemi has also become a world leader in research into micro-electromechanical systems (MEMS), a technology that combines computers with tiny mechanical sensors, valves, gears, mirrors, and actuators embedded in semiconductor chips. For example, MEMS enable the clever Nintendo Wii controllers and tell car airbags when to inflate. Otaniemi also boasts Innopoli, a unit that offers start-up advice and support to hundreds of young, high-tech companies.

Just for the record, in addition to Otaniemi and Bangalore, the Siliconia Web site counts 105 Silicon Valley–like places worldwide, all of which will, almost surely, continue to develop—some quite rapidly.

2. *Talent is now everywhere.* We in the United States have a tendency to judge ourselves based on the accomplishments of others much like us. Connecticut high school seniors, for instance, rejoice at outscoring their California peers on SAT tests, or a Brooklyn school district wins plaudits for outperforming its Manhattan rival. Meanwhile, we pay scant attention to the fact that math and science education standards of many of our overseas competitors are higher than our own, as is the performance of their students.

For a dramatic example, consider the Chinese educational system, where the emphasis on science and technology is strong. As a recent report by the Asia Society points out, a rotating group of science specialists starts working with students as early as the third grade, something we in the United States might associate with high school, not primary school. And once in high school, Chinese students must successfully complete mandatory courses in biology, chemistry, physics, algebra, and geometry before they can graduate. By contrast, 40 percent of U.S. high school students take no science beyond introductory biology.

As for the teachers, the vast majority of Chinese math and science teachers have advanced degrees, whereas less than 60 percent of U.S. eighth-grade science teachers have completed a major in a science-related discipline and only 48 percent of math teachers have completed a math major. Throughout East Asia, about 90 percent of eighth-grade science teachers have science degrees as well as science education training.

A nation's talent pool doesn't only include who it trains, but who it can attract. In the past, we have benefited by importing talent. Nearly 40 percent of the Ph.D.-level scientists and engineers in the United States are foreign born, for example. However, these days, with research blossoming and economies rocketing in country after country, many foreigners who are well established in U.S. corporations or academia are returning home. Fully 54 percent of the staff at Beijing's Chinese Academy of Engineering, for example, and an amazing 81 percent of the scientists at the Chinese Academy of Sciences, are repatriates. The Chinese call them "sea turtles"—partly as a pun, since the word for sea turtle—*hai gui*—sounds like the word for someone coming back from abroad, and partly because both turtles and researchers may wander for a while before eventually returning to the nest.

Time was when America was, by far, the world's most powerful talent magnet, attracting the best and brightest of other nations to our universities and research labs. But, as noted in the previous chapter, the tide is beginning to turn away from our shores.

Not all those heading to centers overseas are foreigners. A former student of mine, Tom Melcher, now lives in Beijing with his wife and two daughters, both of whom are fluent in Chinese, by the way. Tom, who boasts a world-class résumé—Yale, Harvard Business School, McKinsey & Company, IBM, and a raft of Silicon Valley start-ups—says he prefers Beijing to Palo Alto, his previous home, because of the professional opportunities there as well as the educational opportunities for his children.

The sea turtles—Chinese and otherwise—are on the move the world over.

3. *Capital is now everywhere.* Another transformative feature of the new geography of innovation is easier access to funding every-

where. If innovations are to blossom from idea to full-blown enterprise, they must be showered with cash—from corporate parents, the state, or venture capitalists. In the United States, far more than anywhere else, venture capitalists have played a pivotal role in backing the fledgling companies that have become our innovative corporate powerhouses. More than $25 billion of venture funding flowed to new companies in 2006 alone. Amazon, Apple, FedEx, Google, Intel, and Starbucks are just a handful of the enterprises originally financed by venture capitalists. All told, companies in which VC firms have invested provide jobs for 10 million Americans and over $2.1 trillion in revenue since 1970.

But now, the rest of the world is catching up. Venture capital pools are operating all around the globe. The availability of European venture capital is comparable to that in the United States, although investment is skewed away from the risky start-ups often funded in America and directed to investment in more mature enterprises. Asian venture capital, in particular, is growing rapidly, not least through funds established by major U.S. firms in China and India.

The prototype of the new-era, VC-backed, global company may well be Skype, the toll-free, Internet-based phone service. It was founded by a Swede and a Dane who used software developers from Estonia and start-up capital from a mixed bag of European and U.S. venture capitalists. It was headquartered in Luxembourg, with offices in London and Estonia's capital of Tallinn. From its launch in August 2003, Skype grew to 1 million daily users in just one year. Within three years, it had over 100 million registered users and 9 million users a day. Skype was acquired by America's eBay in 2005.

The increased flow of VC money overseas is still relatively small compared with the rate of domestic investment, but it is growing at warp speed. According to the *Asian Venture Capital Journal*, for example, capital flowing into China-oriented VC funds rose to $4 billion in 2006 from just $325 million three years earlier. Few people are unfamiliar with the massive investments being made in China today. Each year, it attracts over $50 billion in foreign direct investment, making it one of the world's top investment destinations.

Indicative of China's rapidly growing stature is the following on-air exchange between James B. Rogers, noted investor (cofounder, along with George Soros, of the Quantum Fund), author, and world traveler, with the talk-show host Charlie Rose. "I have a baby girl who is twenty-months old," Rogers told Rose. "She has a bank account, and all of her assets [are] outside of the U.S." China is the focus of her allocation strategy. In fact, Rogers said, he is so convinced that China will be the "next great country of the world" that he has moved his family to Shanghai and hired a Chinese nanny for his daughter. The nanny speaks to her only in Mandarin, because that will be the "next language of her lifetime," Rogers said.

I'm not sure which Chinese investments were the recipients of Miss Rogers' money, nor does it much matter. My concern is not with the oft-noted foreign dollars going into infrastructure and corporate buyouts, nor the billions in direct investments by the United States and other Western industries that are building their own Chinese factories and sales outlets. No, what I would like to know is where the venture capitalists will land next.

Just as American logistics companies like FedEx set up shop in China to ease the transportation snarl, some stateside operators are establishing beachheads there to make venture capital more easily available to innovative companies. SVB Financial Group, based in Santa Clara, California, is one of them. As SVB senior vice president Daniel Quon explained, "We will try to be the gateway to connect entrepreneurs with an ecosystem of business opportunities."

Then there's Thomas Tsao. He runs a Shanghai-based VC firm called Gobi Partners, specializing in digital media companies. As he told *Business Week*, a few years ago no one was interested in contributing to his fund. Now, "everybody wants to come in." In Tsao's case, everybody includes IBM, McGraw-Hill, and the Japanese telecom giant NTT DoCoMo.

The United States has led the Chinese VC parade. Sequoia Capital launched a $200 million China fund in 2005. That same year, IDG and Accel set up a joint $250 million China Growth Fund, which is operated by Chinese partners. GSR Ventures has a $200 million venture fund sponsored by Silicon Valley's Mayfield Fund, and Kleiner Perkins Caufield & Byers opened its offices in Beijing and Shanghai with a $360 million fund in 2007.

Many other nations, particularly India, are also benefiting from the wave of international investment. A major attraction there is the booming market for Internet and wireless applications. Cisco, IBM, and Microsoft have been building up substantial R & D operations in India. Cisco now has two thousand engineers there, and by 2009, IBM will pump another $6 billion on top of the $2 billion it has already invested. And Bill Gates announced in 2005 that Microsoft would invest $1.7 billion in India.

4. *Government investment in military and aerospace is now everywhere.* Considering the global security environment the United States operates in today, this is a particularly thought-provoking aspect of the changing geography of innovation. America's capabilities for innovation have long been powerfully expressed through the military and aerospace R & D that is supported by govern-

ment funding. Today, other nations are successfully following
our lead.

In April 2006, the U.S. Department of Defense raised the
curtain on its annual selection of leading-edge technologies,
forty-two of which were chosen for evaluation and possible
adoption by the U.S. military from a pool of 120 candidates. At
this rite of spring, no one rose to complain that twenty of the
chosen forty-two projects were based outside the United States.
In fact, no one seemed to think there was anything particularly
unusual about it. And why should they when the Pentagon program for evaluating the entries was actually called Foreign
Comparative Testing?

The competition featured vehicle-mounted systems to clear
land mines that were designed by Croatia, Denmark, Norway,
and Britain. From Italy came a high-frequency combat radio.
Sweden entered a tandem warhead for shoulder-fired muni-
tions, so called because it uses a first charge to power through a
wall and a second to destroy whatever or whoever is behind the
wall. Germany offered advanced weather forecasting and analysis software.

Many military innovations still emerge from our fifty states,
but the competition from abroad is impressive. When *IT Week*
selected its top fifty Technology Innovators of 2005, for example, high on the list was Columbitech of Stockholm, Sweden, a
six-year-old specialist in developing wireless software products. As *IT Week* put it, the company provides the "de facto standard in wireless security" for both military and civilian
applications.

A sobering case study of how military innovation has gone
global is that of the helicopter. In 2004, a Pentagon report
clearly stated that the Defense Department's plans to modern-
ize its vertical-lift forces were at risk because of a "lack of inno-

vation" in the U.S. helicopter industry. As a result, the report warned, the three major American manufacturers—Bell, Boeing, and Sikorsky—could very well lose business to overseas competitors.

Guess what? In June 2006, the Pentagon announced that the army's $3 billion competition for a new light utility helicopter had been won by Eurocopter, a division of the European Aeronautic Defense and Space Company (EADS). The winning craft, the EC 145, was jointly developed by Eurocopter, which includes French, German, and Spanish companies, and Kawasaki Heavy Industries of Japan.

Other than jawboning, the U.S. government has given the domestic helicopter industry little support for greater innovation. NASA no longer finances basic vertical-lift research, and it has closed down its full-scale wind tunnel and crash-test facilities. All science and development for military aircraft is now in the hands of the Pentagon. And as Steve Thompson, a Pentagon aide, told *National Defense* magazine in 2005, decisions about research funding are based on near-term considerations: "We don't have the resources to pursue technology for the sake of technology." This should disturb you if you believe, as I do, that innovation and competitiveness depend on supporting the frontiers of R & D.

• • •

The globalization of innovation and of the capital to fund it are, in my estimation, great positives overall for both the United States and the rest of the world. But the United States must begin ratcheting up its own innovation capacity to stay ahead of the curve. The big questions are, of course, can we do it? And if so, how? The rest of this book will lay out my vision for how to proceed.

But first, another scenario of the Polk family, this one designed to offer a vision of what it might be like to live in a revitalized United States and showing how the ideas laid out in
the pages ahead might actually be lived. The Polks, in such dire
straits the last time we met, now find themselves in a happier
scenario. It is 2027 in the United States as Innovation Nation.

•　　•　　•

"Sweetie," Cindy called from upstairs. "Are you ever coming to bed?"

Jim Polk rubbed his eyes. He must have dozed off, he thought, as he
took in the pile of midterm papers on the desk, the pen that had
slipped from his grasp, the tumbler of melted ice and watery bourbon.
Then the pleasant details of his dream returned: the little ranch-style
house in Mount Joy all those years ago, his sons fast asleep, Cindy
sharing her hopes for their future. He smiled to himself as he thought
how drastically their world had changed over the preceding two decades in ways the two of them could never have imagined.

"I'll be right up, honey," he yelled back.

Jim's year in Iraq had been hell, culminating in a firefight that cost
him a kneecap and months of replacement surgery and rehab at a
Veterans Administration hospital in New Haven. Cindy and the
boys camped out with a relative in Bridgeport. By the time Jim recu-
perated, they had come up with a whole new plan for their lives.
They sold the house in Tennessee and bought one just like it in north
Bridgeport, not far from the boys' nursery school. With the help of
an updated GI Bill, Jim was able to enroll full-time at a decent local
university, while Cindy took a part-time job in a radiologist's office.

Perhaps in reaction to his ordeal in Iraq, Jim found himself less
interested in machines and engineering—and more interested in
people. The idea of teaching held great appeal, and math was a natural subject. He might have signed up with a suburban high school,
but Bridgeport High was a greater challenge, and he accepted it.

Back then, Connecticut's largest city was an urban disaster with soaring unemployment, a DMZ of a downtown, corrupt politicians, and gang wars worthy of Los Angeles. Climbing the stairs, Jim chuckled. Amazing what a difference sixteen years could make.

After rising early to finish going over his students' midterm papers, Jim set off for school in his American-made hybrid, a 110-mile-per-gallon winner. It was a pleasant drive these days, past tastefully restored two-family houses and manicured parks, through a clean, bustling business center. Since being designated as a Federal Innovation Community (FIC), Bridgeport had prospered mightily.

Back in 2010, the government had established twenty of these centers around the country. They were intended to jump-start the U.S. innovation engine to address the global challenges of disease, energy, and the environment. The goal: a nation dedicated to continuous invention.

Bridgeport was the sentimental favorite for a ground-transport FIC, having been the place where pioneering autos such as the Locomobile had been manufactured a century before. Washington had put up the seed money to lure the most advanced transportation labs and test facilities to the area. As some of the world's top designers and engineers moved in, they began to take a hand in local politics, and within a few years Bridgeport had a master plan for rejuvenating the city. Evidence of its success was everywhere Jim looked, including the high school itself. An ancient firetrap had been replaced by a straightforward, energy-efficient building wired with the latest teaching aids.

Of course, Jim thought, the real educational revolution had taken place inside the minds and hearts of the teachers and students. The danger posed by America's slide toward technological and scientific mediocrity back in the century's first decade had finally inspired the nation to undertake a kind of Manhattan Project for education. Research labs, financed by twenty-five major foundations to the tune of a hundred million dollars each, carried out large-scale, action-oriented practical experiments to develop best practices in education. The results were spread throughout the public school system by the federal government with the active support of state and local officials, as well as the teachers' unions.

In Jim's own school, the impact of these new approaches on the teachers and students had been electrifying. He felt he himself was doing a far better job, especially in challenging students to think independently and practically. And creative and entrepreneurial skill development was woven into the basic curriculum from an early age.

The national education initiative, particularly in the areas of math and science, had also dramatically improved teachers' standing in the community. Suddenly, Jim and his colleagues were being treated with far greater respect by their students, allowing them to spend their time teaching instead of disciplining. Teachers' salaries rose 40 percent in the course of a few years. And the applicant pool for teaching slots once again included the best and the brightest.

The renewed emphasis on innovation also reinspired long-neglected university departments of science and engineering. Once again, Washington began financing extensive basic research projects on university campuses. Hundreds of new scholarships and fellowships were created for gifted youngsters. Jim's older son, James, who had been uncertain whether to go into business or science, was studying physics at the Massachusetts Institute of Technology on just such a scholarship.

"I absolutely did not tell him what to do," Jim told Cindy, after James made his decision. She laughed. "I heard you talk to him about how great the teachers are at MIT," she said, "and about all the terrific people he'd meet there from all over the world." Jim groaned. "What did you want me to do? Lie?"

One of the results of the educational upgrade and the FIC program was a reversal of the brain drain. Now, American technical and scientific students definitely wanted careers stateside, and more and more foreign students were once again settling in the United States after graduation. The government helped that process along by revising immigration policies to welcome overseas talent. Every foreigner who got a Ph.D. in the United States was given an expedited pathway to a green card, for example.

Once America's venture capitalists saw the nation's scientific renaissance gather steam, they began to vote with their checkbooks by trimming their foreign commitments in favor of the homegrown variety. At the same time, the federal government renewed its commitment to funding basic research. Jim and Cindy's younger son, Knox, and his Finnish wife, Roosa, were able to open their own lab in Bridgeport to develop a new wireless teaching tool, backed by a local, Connecticut-based venture firm and government grants. They had sounded Jim out about eventually hiring him as a consultant, but he told them he was nowhere near ready to leave Bridgeport High.

With the country's innovation factory turning out a host of new products, and unemployment at historically low levels, the economy looked strong. Jim's TIAA-CREF account was building nicely with the Dow at an all-time high—and, marking the pace of innovation, more than half of the companies on the Dow hadn't existed before 2000. For a change, tax surpluses were being used to dig the nation out of its huge debt.

Once the boys were out of the house, Cindy had embarked on a career of her own as the manager of a new art museum. The whole country was experiencing a groundswell of public interest in every form of culture, from architecture to music to the theater, and she wanted to be part of it. Jim said he was proud of her, though he complained when she had to work during part of his long summer vacation.

In the evening, over an after-dinner drink, Jim and Cindy often acknowledged that they were leading the "good life." Their sons were well and happy. Their income was more than sufficient. They thoroughly enjoyed their jobs—and each other. But beyond that, they felt comfortable with themselves as contributing to a decent, honorable society.

The nation's renaissance had not been limited to technology. There had been exciting advances in space exploration and the life sciences—alternative fuels, for example, had greatly reduced U.S. dependence on petroleum. But the focus on the innovation process itself had also helped resolve some seemingly intractable social problems common to the United States and the developed world.

With universal Internet access and new teaching tools, for example, average citizens were able to gain a clearer sense of complex issues and to better vote their interest and their conscience. In America, the turnout in presidential elections rose 20 percentage points above its 51 percent level in 2000. And new approaches to health care quickly brought forth new and cost-effective, not to mention life-saving, treatments to fight disease around the world.

As the United States confronted its problems and found responsible solutions, its relationship with the world at large evolved. Once again, America was a leader among nations, but this time around there was no effort or intent to pursue an imperial destiny. Rather than imposing its will upon other countries, the United States supported international initiatives, provided a supportive platform for all forms of innovation, and freely shared its knowledge with other lands.

•   •   •

That happy ending for the Polks and the United States reflects what our future can be. But fixing these problems will not be easy. Forget about the default strategies and incremental solutions of the past: extending the school year, assigning more homework, or hiring more teachers; providing more bandwidth, beefing up the R & D staff, or sinking more money into basic research. I approve of such steps, but they are the all-too-familiar kinds of incremental initiatives that we should be doing on a routine basis—mousetrap 2.0, 2.1, 2.2. Such incremental improvements will likely make things better, but they are not the game-changing innovations that will alter the fundamentals or lead us toward a desired future. That will require a thorough rethinking of our country's approach to national innovation.

In the chapters to come, I will describe the steps we must take in order to bring about this kind of renaissance of American innovation, and then bring those insights together to put forth a plan for a transformative national innovation strategy.

FOUR

MAKING TALENT

You have to have a talent for having talent.
                                    —Ruth Gordon, actress

When Finland trumpeted its global business ambitions twenty years ago, the world yawned. The Finns had been also-rans ever since their ancestors slogged west from Russia's Ural Mountains. Speaking an obscure language akin to Hungarian, they settled on a desolate peninsula at the frostbitten head of the Baltic Sea. For twenty centuries, little Finland was a killing field for warring Russians and Swedes. Not until the 1950s was it truly independent; not until the 1980s was it ready for the global big time. Even then, it had few natural resources, scant arable land, and little to sell beyond herring and timber.

Finland has since blossomed into a true global winner, the little country that could. Smaller than Montana, it has the same population as metropolitan Atlanta. But today, it is a world leader in technology, symbolized by Nokia, maker of the planet's most ubiquitous cell phones, with 35 percent global market share and revenues equivalent to 3 percent of Finnish GDP. At the 2005 World Economic Forum in Davos, Switzerland, Finland won acclaim as the most competitive economy on earth. How did Finland accomplish this miracle? Largely by investing in human capital—people with talent, ideas, and knowledge; people with entrepreneurial zeal, vision, and organizational ability.

How does a country get this capital? Well, you can cultivate your own people or you can seduce them from abroad. Make or buy. And, it should be noted, "make" takes time. "Buy" can be as fast as the time it takes for the ink to dry on an employment contract.

Theoretically, the talent behind Finland's rebirth could have been attracted from other countries. But the Finns didn't bother trying to lure sun-loving innovators to a frigid nation with only fourteen people per square kilometer, most of them crammed into one city—Helsinki—trying to stay warm in winter. Instead, with remarkable self-confidence, starting in the 1970s they set about planting and harvesting their own talent, converting their schools from mediocrity to excellence, and motivating their own scientists and entrepreneurs.

It didn't take barrels of money, either. Finland spends 6.4 percent of its GDP on education, compared to 5.7 percent for the United States. But that spending places the Finns only twenty-third on the global league charts in terms of percent of GDP devoted to education. When it comes to results, though, Finland consistently places in the top rank of countries.

Attitude even more than money is behind the Finns' achievement. A vast cultural shift has accompanied the new national approach to education. Learning is very hot in frigid Finland.

A little more than thirty years ago, Finnish children were required to attend school for only six years. Today, 95 percent of sixteen-year-olds are enrolled in secondary education and the government is not shy about conveying its desire to make that figure 100 percent. Youngsters who go to work instead of school at sixteen are ineligible to receive unemployment payments until they are twenty-five. And financial need is no excuse for leaving school, since none of Finland's schools charge tuition. Even books and school supplies are free at the lower levels. University students receive financial grants, housing allowances, and government-guaranteed loans. No wonder the majority of secondary school students go on to higher education.

What is more, many of the brightest students become teachers. Finns have come to cherish gifted educators as Texans do ace quarterbacks. The country's teacher training schools have ten applicants for every opening, and their graduates routinely earn master's degrees even to instruct first graders in schools. Overcrowding in schools is a nonissue in Finland; it's rare to find a public school with more than five hundred students or more than ten students per class.

These are also schools without custodial headaches. Indeed, Finland is now widely credited with producing the world's best students in the world's best schools. Example: In examinations of fifteen-year-olds in thirty-nine industrial countries, Finnish students won first place two years in a row. As for the American contestants, they weren't even in the top ten, nowhere near it, in fact; They ranked twenty-fourth.

What can we in the United States learn from Finland? Begin with this: Human capital is the primary key to a national success strategy. Smart, sophisticated, and globally savvy people are the sine qua non of the business world. And right now, just when a global war for talent is being waged, making it an asset harder to come by than capital, our nation is depleting its stock of ammunition. But, as little Finland illustrates, you really can grow your own talent, an area in which the United States used to excel.

HOMEGROWN TALENT I: OVER THERE

Finland is not the only national competitor intent on cultivating its own talent. Singapore, for example, has had phenomenal success in attracting foreign talent. But, at the same time, Singapore has no intention of squandering its own fine young intellects or letting them bolt for better opportunities abroad. The country with a brand identity for education—"Thinking Schools, Learning Nation"—has worked hard to establish quality curricula, reward high-performing teachers, and experiment with new learning technologies. With its relentless focus on education, it will come as no surprise that one of Singapore's most important national icons is not a 120-story skyscraper, but its futuristic National Library. Even the country's leaders are models of educational excellence: two-thirds of government officials have advanced degrees, and the correlation between senior government service and a degree from Cambridge, Harvard, MIT, or Oxford is very high.

Singapore's Economic Development Board set out a plan in 2002 for the country to become a "global schoolhouse," with a cluster of the world's best educational institutions to draw top academics, researchers, and students. The goal was to attract at least ten world-class institutions by 2008, and it met that target—five years ahead of schedule, in 2003. Among the big names now found in Singapore are the University of Chicago's Graduate School of Business, the Massachusetts Institute of Technology, Duke University's School of Medicine, the Culinary Institute of America, and New York University's Tisch School of the Arts.

Singapore's university students are eligible for plentiful scholarships that enable smart competitors, for example, to earn doctorates in life sciences at top international universities. And, get this, you don't even have to be a native Singaporean to enter the race. The only condition is that winners agree to come back to work in Singapore for at least six years. Those who win scholarships to study at Singaporean institutions are bound to government service for four years. Former prime minister Goh Chok Tong said, "We systematically set out to identify what we call the best people." He likened his government to a "headhunter," with the prime minister serving as "chief headhunter."

Students who satisfy the rigorous eligibility requirements to be sent abroad for Ph.D. studies receive even more substantial financial support—in excess of 1 million Singaporean dollars over the life of the fellowship. A twenty-something student could easily cover basic expenses like tuition and rent, and with even a bit of frugality, he or she could stash away six-figure savings that might be used for a starter condo or a new BMW.

When Philip Yeo took over Biopolis in 2001, he told me that the emphasis was on bringing in foreign scientists. "That was okay," he said, "but I wanted to know, 'Where are the Singaporeans?'" In short order, he developed a program to help bright youngsters acquire overseas Ph.Ds. "My most important job is taking care of the kids," he told me. "I don't interfere with the researchers; they know what to do." The scholarship program has produced more than 570 Singapore Ph.D.s, all within the last five years.

Yeo is a fascinating man. Short, slim, and hyperenergetic, he paces around a huge, ultramodern office furnished with floor-to-ceiling racks full of journals and books as well as dozens of photos of the young people he has mentored. In addition to his Biopolis position, he is chairman of A*STAR, the government agency for science, technology, and research, which encompasses twelve research institutes. In both capacities, he is the premier cheerleader for his brilliant kids, constantly lending his name and person to programs that praise and promote their achievements.

For instance, Yeo puts on a lunch for scholars named to the chairman's annual honors list and those whose three consecutive years of honors have earned them a permanent spot on the A*STAR Roll of Honor. The names of the latter group are engraved on a huge marble tablet in the lobby of one of the main Biopolis buildings. He also sponsors a special chairman's tea for participants in the scholarship program and presides over the annual graduate scholars' symposium, where the kids' projects are "showcased and celebrated."

In addition, Yeo has initiated a national science challenge, which crowns a grand champion after seven weeks of intensive science quiz competition. And he makes sure the challenge and other events are widely publicized, both within the academic community and by the public media. When I suggested that he was turning the young scientists into rock stars, he nodded in agreement. It is all part of stoking a dynamic, talent-driven innovation machine.

Singapore's ability to innovate in education stems in significant measure from an ethos of collaboration at the most senior levels of government and also from its ability to think outside the confines of traditional disciplines and bureaucratic silos. Singapore's cabinet-level permanent secretary of education works closely with the nation's Infocomm Development Authority (IDA) to explore the cross-fertilization of advanced, over-the-horizon digital technology and link it with current as well as future educational needs.

In the spring of 2006, an IDA official, accompanied by the permanent secretaries of the education and the information and arts ministries, the chairman of the Economic Development Board, and representatives from the Singapore National Science Foundation, paid an extraordinary visit to my office. The group was touring the United States to help formulate Singapore's digital media strategy, one of the major focal points in its National Science Foundation investment plan, along with biotechnology/life sciences and environmental technologies. All had their senior-level antennae tuned to what was going on elsewhere in the world. There is no question that Singapore is positioning itself on the frontier of interactive and digital media for education and a host of other fields. I try to imagine what a comparable American delegation would look like and rue its improbability.

Singapore illustrates that the impact of talent on national strength is nonlinear, not at all a function of absolute numbers. It's an old story: size yields to skill and intelligence. By any obvious measure, Goliath should have made mincemeat of David, but the shepherd boy had the talent and the motivation. By making the most of its human resources, Singapore has sprinted ahead of far larger countries that lack the island nation's disciplined commitment to innovation leadership.

Now let's consider another island of educational excellence: Ireland. Its economic resurgence over the last few decades has been striking—and there is universal agreement that the transformation of its educational system has been a key ingredient.

Ireland used to be one of the poorest nations in western Europe; it is now among the wealthiest. Since 1985, its GDP has tripled, employment has risen 75 percent, productivity has almost doubled, and the volume of its exports has increased eightfold.

When Ireland first announced its intention more than two decades ago to become a knowledge economy, skeptics scoffed at its audacity. Where, they wanted to know, were the Irish engineers? Where was the educational infrastructure to support major industry? "From 1922 to 1970, we invested nothing in education while the rest of Europe did," John Fitz Gerald, an economist at Dublin's Economic and Social Research Institute, told *Fortune*. Then the government woke up. Over the last thirty years, every educational level, from primary grades through graduate school, has seen major improvement. Nine regional technical colleges were established and new universities were opened in Limerick and Dublin. Scientific and technical training became far more sophisticated. The government made outsized investments in scholarships and fellowships as well as in bricks and mortar.

The results have been impressive. As of 2003, 85 percent of the Irish population between the ages of twenty and twenty-four were high school graduates, just a single percentage point behind the United States. Thirty-seven percent of 25-to-34-year-olds were college graduates, compared to 39 percent in the United States. A whole generation of highly trained and educated Irish-born engineers and scientists has emerged to help power the nation's economic miracle.

Ireland's bootstrap campaign to develop a knowledge economy, built on developing its talent, has done the job. The success of its strategy was evident to me as I traveled around the nation and saw firsthand leading-edge companies such as Google, Intel, and Microsoft hard at work there. I also noticed advertising that featured icons of Irish creativity such as rock legend Bono with captions, like "The Irish: creative, imaginative and flexible. Agile minds with a unique capacity to innovate without being directed."

Generally speaking, I am of the quality-trumps-quantity school, but when it comes to technical talent, there is no denying the power of the bell curve. Let's assume that 1 percent of a nation's population has the innate potential to become a productive scientist. By that measure, Singapore, no matter how great its success in cultivating its talent pool, could never match the number the United States turns out. The 3 million or so people in our top 1 percent are an abundant asset base, the same order of magnitude as Singapore's entire population.

And by the same token, in absolute numbers of top one-percenters, America is never going to match China and India with their outsize populations. These are also countries that have learned how to make the bell curve work for them. In fact, the two together already turn out some 6.5 million college graduates a year, five times as many as the United States, and nearly 1 million of them are engineers, versus around seventy thousand U.S. engineering graduates each year. And according to *Tapping America's Potential,* a report recently published by fifteen major U.S. business organizations, if current trends continue, more than 90 percent of all scientists and engineers in the world will be living in Asia by 2010. (To add insult to injury, virtually all well-schooled Chinese students speak some degree of English, which has become the de facto international language of business and science.)

To be sure, the top American graduate schools are still at present the world's best, and their graduates are still going to be the best of the best. In fact, the United States still has a fourfold lead over any other country in the number of engineers qualified to work for multinational organizations. But the enormous growth of well-educated, lower-paid technical talent in other countries will surely have a negative impact here at home as cost-cutting U.S. companies outsource many more thousands of increasingly skilled jobs. Consultants at McKinsey & Company estimate that up to 52 percent of engineering jobs and 31 percent of finance and accounting positions globally could ultimately be outsourced. And people with lower value-added skills will be hungry to climb the ladder to the realm of higher value-added jobs.

HOMEGROWN TALENT II: OVER HERE

Harvard professor and education authority Howard Gardner told me that he views education's core challenge as getting people engaged in the "right things." He means that inculcating a sense of respect for knowledge and ethics is as important as improving cognitive abilities. In other words, educators have to establish an ongoing linkage between learning and purpose. Were we to pursue a national strategy for innovation, the necessary debate about methods and strategies would help us to articulate national priorities based on a vision of our desired role in the world, and that, in turn, would drive our education agenda. Sadly, we are deficient in all these areas.

It is worth noting that secondary education in America began as a privilege for the wealthy, and even after the first public high school appeared in 1822, few teenagers attended. Until the Great Depression, America's labor force was loaded with fifteen-year-old breadwinners handling full-time jobs and adult responsibilities. Hard times changed all that. To protect their adult members' jobs, trade unions sought to remove teenage workers from the labor market. They did it by lobbying for child labor laws and compulsory school attendance. These pressures, plus the growing need for vocational training, drove huge numbers of newly jobless teenagers into the shelter of our free public high schools.

Elsewhere in the world, only a relative handful of the wealthy and/ or talented received a free secondary education, much less a shot at a nearly free state university. Other developed nations focused almost entirely on the education of an elite cadre of superbly trained graduates. Such systems led to individual breakthroughs in the arts and sciences, while deferring the benefits of education to society as a whole.

America chose a different tack, putting its faith—and educational resources—in the potential of its burgeoning middle class. As the 1940s began, the United States was the world's best-schooled country in terms of the education of all its citizens. Some 25 percent of adults in this country were high school graduates; six percent had college degrees. The postwar G.I. Bill of Rights and the National Defense Education Act (NDEA) of 1958 helped push those numbers even higher.

President Franklin Roosevelt and his advisers clearly understood the importance of education and science. In November 1944, as World War II was entering its final phase, FDR wrote: "New frontiers of the mind are before us, and if they are pioneered with the same vision, boldness, and drive with which we have waged this war, we can create a fuller and more fruitful employment and a fuller and more fruitful life." His science adviser, Vannevar Bush, in turn observed:

> The responsibility for the creation of new scientific knowledge—and for most of its application—rests on that small body of men and women who understand the fundamental laws of nature and are skilled in the techniques of scientific research.

We shall have rapid or slow advance on any scientific frontier depending on the number of highly qualified and trained scientists exploring it.

President Roosevelt signed the G.I. Bill into law in 1944, shortly before the Normandy invasion. Intent on righting the wrongs inflicted on World War I veterans, whose long-promised bonuses had been delayed until 1936, Roosevelt backed a multibillion-dollar education and housing commitment to returning veterans. Myopic heads of premier U.S. universities joined conservative Republican lawmakers to rail against the perceived giveaway to the unwashed and unqualified. The veterans proved the naysayers wrong on all counts.

Eager young veterans poured onto college campuses. The G.I. Bill was covering living expenses for half the country's college students by 1947. At Syracuse University, veterans swelled enrollment to over nineteen thousand from three thousand at war's end. At Rensselaer Polytechnic Institute, surplus tank landing ships were modified to house six hundred veterans on the Hudson River. Benefiting from one of the largest investments in human capital that the United States, if not the world, had ever made, more than 8 million veterans took advantage of the opportunity presented by the G.I. Bill to become scientists and engineers, doctors and teachers, thus paving the way for the boom years that followed.

President Dwight D. Eisenhower continued the revolution when he signed the National Defense Education Act in 1958. Congress reached into the nation's coffers to support almost any kind of training that could be shown to contribute to the security of our country, from vocational instruction to the training of the highly skilled scientists vital to national defense. The legislation authorized federal help to establish low-cost student-loan funds and fellowships aimed at increasing the number of students in graduate programs.

The G.I. Bill and the NDEA laid the groundwork for what *Time* magazine's oracular founder Henry Luce proclaimed "The American Century." They created the educational apparatus that nurtured the talent that built the great post–World War II American innovation machine.

Today, there are also some heartening signs of innovation in our education system. For example, two veteran not-for-profit organizations—the College Board and the International Baccalaureate Organization (IBO)—are having a major impact on the nation's educational prospects by exposing high school students to more rigorous courses than the typical curriculum offers.

The College Board's advanced placement (AP) program, which enables students to win university credits for college-level classes they take in high school, emerged in 1951 from a gathering of educators from elite institutions. The number of students taking AP courses has doubled in the last decade to more than a million. And the variety of courses offered has continually expanded to almost forty. One especially good sign: the first AP exam in Chinese language and culture was offered in May 2007.

Another encouraging development is that more and more low-income minority families are prodding their kids to tackle the courses. "Only 17 percent of our parents have attended college," according to Brian Rodriguez, the AP coordinator at Encinal High School in Alameda, California, "but AP has had a tremendous impact here—we regularly send kids to Stanford, Brown, Dartmouth, Harvard, Berkeley, and UCLA who never would have had a chance to go there even six years ago."

Less well known in the United States is the program of the IBO. Based in Geneva, Switzerland, the IBO was founded in 1968 to provide a private-school, universally recognized, portable education for youngsters whose parents are diplomats or some other variety of world wanderer. Having greatly enlarged both its target audience and its scope, the IBO offers a full schedule of academic courses at three age levels—three to twelve, eleven to sixteen, and sixteen to nineteen. To help teachers and schools maintain its high standards, the organization provides a large menu of workshops and conferences.

IB courses are generally more rigorous than the usual public school fare, and there is greater focus on testing students' mastery of the material. Those who do well on IB high-school-level tests are usually permitted to take advanced classes in college. The IB curriculum has won the praise of many educational authorities, including Howard Gardner, who told the *New York Times* that it is "less parochial than most American efforts." For example, material from French and British sources is an integral part of a lesson on the American Revolution—not just the view from the rebel perspective. Gardner and other experts also admire the program's focus on connecting disciplines and the requirement of fluency in at least a second modern language.

Near Birmingham, Alabama, for instance, is the Jefferson County IB School, which has just 325 students. Imagine yourself a sixteen-year-old newcomer, taking your first class in European history. After a rapid-fire introduction to triumphs and tragedies you've probably never heard of, like the Magna Carta and the Black Death, you get your first assignment—memorize the map of Europe tonight and show up tomorrow ready to draw every country, along with ten capitals, ten rivers, and ten bodies of water. That's day one, the easiest; a dozen equally tough courses lie ahead. Not surprisingly, after examining scores of top candidates across the country, *Newsweek* named Jefferson the best high school in the United States.

More and more American schools are signing on to IB: 682 now offer one or more of the three curricula, with 72 providing primary level, 168 middle, and 520 high school level. But only a fraction of our schools participate in the IB program.

However, despite these forward-thinking and undeniably useful programs, American talent is suffering a gradual, insidious erosion in the middle of the educational process, a "hollowing out" of sorts. For example, millions of young Americans—one-third by some estimates—are not even finishing high school, while jobs demanding technical competencies are growing at three times the rate of jobs in general. In 2006, California, for example, reported its lowest high school graduation rate in ten years at 67 percent, which was a 4 percent drop from just the year before. And this despite a decade of costly modifications to the classroom experience: smaller class sizes, higher academic standards, additional teacher training, and so on.

Furthermore, for those who do make it through high school and on to college, technical training is not popular. The seventy thousand engineering degrees awarded in the United States each year represents a 20 percent plunge from the peak year of 1985. It's more than ironic that a generation that celebrates the iPod, can't live without its cell phones, and shares its most intimate videos on YouTube is increasingly turning away from the technological fields that enable today's youth culture.

The United States still spends more per student on education than most of the world's more advanced economies. At the primary level, according to figures from the Organization for Economic Co-operation and Development, the United States spends an average of $7,560 each year on each student. Only Denmark, at $7,572, and little Luxembourg, at $7,873, spend more. We are similarly in the very top rank in spending per student at the secondary level. The problem is that the United States has less to show for it. We are losing ground in the global competition to cultivate domestic talent, in large measure because our public elementary and high schools are simply not making the grade.

What are we doing about it, and what more can be done?

THE GATES EXPERIMENT,
AND OTHER ALMOST ANSWERS

Experimentation is urgently needed as a forerunner to educational reform. Since 2000, the Bill and Melinda Gates Foundation has been answering the call, in part by spending $1 billion to establish one thousand small high schools throughout the United States. Just as the Gates had hoped, the more intimate, welcoming environments and the greater student-teacher interaction afforded by small schools have reduced dropout rates, one of the couple's prime concerns. But there's been bad news as well: the students at their small schools have, to date, scored little better in English and reading improvement, and much less improvement in math than their peers at traditional big schools.

The Gates experiment is an admirable piece of a complex and confusing mosaic of efforts by individuals and private organizations, as well as federal and local governments to come to grips with the wicked problem of our education crisis. There are some basic reforms that most experts can agree on, others that are controversial, and still more that have yet to be discovered. I'm very much afraid that the most important solutions reside in that third category. In other words, we are going to have to innovate innovation in education to make real headway. It's the classic innovator's dilemma: should we choose the path of incremental improvement in education or seek disruptive innovations—game changers—in the form of financing schemes, faculty development approaches, curriculum design, or adoption of technology that can change the nature of the education enterprise?

Obviously, we need both the incremental improvements and the game changers. We can start with some widely accepted semi-solutions—no-brainers, in my book. Take the role of teachers in our society. We desperately need to rethink it, drastically improving the way they are recruited, trained, and rewarded. Bumping up annual salaries for some into the six-figure range, creating incentive compensation based on new kinds of metrics (student retention, academic performance), and bringing a cadre of retirees and volunteers into our public schools to bolster flagging capabilities would all make a difference.

It's a crime against our children that half of the math teachers in the United States have no formal training in mathematics and are sometimes recruited from the bottom third of their high school graduating classes. As a result, their ability to convey the exhilaration and the fundamentals of math is limited by whatever minimal instruction they received in the subject at a teacher's college. To attract better, and better-educated, teachers to our schools, we have to pay them well and find ways to regain prestige for them and the jobs they do. They deserve respect, recognition, community standing, bonus pay, and chances for continuing education and enrichment. In a world of more and more standardized testing and standardized curricula, the unique skills and knowledge that teachers can bring to the classroom are given little currency, and we must find a way to reverse that misappraisal.

Secondary to that goal, we need to develop rigorous curricula that excite and challenge our children at every level. As it stands, a cloud of special interests within and outside of the educational establishment—everyone from school managers to state legislators to religious organizations—slows the pace at which curriculum is revamped. Some would argue that the No Child Left Behind Act, with its focus on mandatory testing, has only worsened the problem, forcing teachers to spend time "teaching to the test" while increasing the perceived risks of using more creative or tailored material in the classroom. One of the problems of education innovation is that results need to be measured, yet measurement can be a core piece of the problem. Robert Sternberg, dean of the School of Arts and Sciences and professor of psychology at Tufts University, summed up the situation: "The increasingly massive and far-reaching use of standardized testing is one of the most effective, if unintentional, ways we have created for suppressing creativity."

Another roadblock to curriculum reform is the enormous power textbook publishers wield over schools that are dependent on the publishers for course materials. Teachers who lack expertise in their subjects have no choice but to teach from the textbook. Content to continue turning out millions of copies of only incrementally improved materials year after year, the publishers discourage teachers from experimenting by not developing new materials for them to use.

Besides being slow to change, schoolbooks are costly. As a result, students in thousands of classrooms around the country are using textbooks held together with duct tape and rubber bands—books written ten or fifteen years ago that still talk about the "Soviet Union" as our major enemy in the world and make no mention of cell phones or the Internet. And in a 2002 survey by the Association of American Publishers and the National Education Association, more than 16 percent of the teachers surveyed didn't have enough textbooks of any caliber to provide one for each student. (Presumably, not much homework is assigned in those classes, either.)

Just how far do we have to go these days to find answers for our schools? Perhaps all the way to China, according to a 2005 report prepared for the Asia Society by a delegation of American educators and business leaders who observed that country's educational system. In "Education in China: Lessons for U.S. Educators," the group recommended that U.S. leaders and school administrators adopt some best practices from the Chinese—an astonishing turnaround. Their recommendations:

- Make American high school curricula more globally attuned by adding more history, geography, and international economics while also increasing international content in required core subject areas.

- Foster global student exchanges.

- Increase language study with the goal of having at least 5 percent of U.S. high school students enrolled in Chinese language courses by 2015.

- Benchmark U.S. educational policies against other high-achieving systems.

Even implementing all the no-brainers won't turn the tide, however. Incremental innovation is just not enough. Yet, because education in the United States has become a political football, any effort to make decisive changes in the way schools operate runs head on into a wasp nest of competing interests. Bill and Melinda Gates discovered that in implementing their small-school idea, as they struggled to convince local school districts and states to agree on the need to break up big schools. It was no slam dunk. Each level of the education bureaucracy is jealous of its prerogatives and inclined to resist change.

Instead of tinkering with ways to make a test-based, one-size-fits-all approach to education meet our country's needs, we should ask: How do we get our best minds and most motivated talent into teaching? And what will make kids eager to learn and keep them coming back to school? One answer is to promote creative diversity as a goal and to build our schools around learners and learning processes rather than around the bureaucratic convenience of a model of scheduling still optimized more for agricultural production than for the information age. Put another way, we can either guarantee that creative teachers will continue to be frustrated by a rigid system that allows them too little room to introduce new ideas and initiatives or we can encourage their efforts to expand our children's horizons.

Further complicating any attempt to reform our educational system is the frustratingly glacial pace at which change is implemented. Right now, workable solutions are being found, but it often takes fifteen to twenty years before the results of important research are widely applied. Society's inability to keep up with innovation, technological and otherwise, is what sociologists call a cultural lag. There is a void between the education academics and thought leaders conducting the research on one side, and the textbook publishers and classroom teachers interacting with kids on a day-to-day basis on the other. Isolated in their respective milieus, the two camps seem unable to find a collaborative and more integrated approach to the wicked problem of education.

To prevent further erosion of our education capabilities, we must build a new model of stewardship for a transformation process, one that brings all of the stakeholders to the table—not just the policy makers and education professionals, but parents as well—and engages them in the work of bringing innovation to education. To solve our wicked problem, all parties must open their minds to new and innovative ways of teaching (some of which you will read about below) that demonstrate how real progress can be made if ingenuity is applied.

I believe we should consider launching a national program to glean and evaluate the lessons to be learned from a host of effective state and local educational initiatives, not to mention international best practices, that are aimed at both program and curricula development so that we can consolidate the best practices for implementation all around the country. Doing so would help us address the "we don't know what we know" problem. And above all we need to invest more resources. The U.S. Department of Education's 2006 budget appropriation for its Office of Innovation and Improvement was $936 million, a modest sum given the importance of the issue at hand and the crying need for experimentation and prototyping across a broad array of education agendas.

In terms of national programs, Singapore offers an example to be envied. The city-state boasts a national Learning Sciences Laboratory renowned for its excellence. Its research overview report, "Signature Models of 21st Century Learning," reads like a mouthwatering menu for education innovation. It focuses on five areas: promoting new literacies, science as systems, mathematics and problem solving, knowledge-building communities, and emerging research and teaching methods. Of course, research in all of these fields occurs in the United States at great institutions such as Columbia University's Teachers College and at the Stanford and Harvard schools of education. But unlike in Singapore, there is no strong, seamless bond in the United States among our state and national policy makers, private sector players, and such centers of educational excellence.

If we are to build the talent we need, we have no choice but to get better at innovating education. One promising avenue for disruptive innovation lies in our mastery—at least for now—of Internet-based technologies, which Nina Zolt has used to advantage in her groundbreaking In2Books program. But there were plenty of doubters back in 1997 when Zolt, a retired entertainment lawyer in Washington, D.C., proposed her idea.

As a volunteer in her children's schools who grew impatient with the progress she was seeing, Zolt devised a program to improve the educational process by connecting "under-resourced" primary-school children with adult mentors. Mentors and kids would read the same books and exchange digital letters about what they had read, with teachers overseeing the correspondence on both ends.

From its beginnings in a third-grade classroom in Arlington, Virginia, Zolt's In2Books program has since reached more than sixteen thousand students in grades three through five, primarily in Washington. The results have been impressive. Students using the In2Books approach for two years scored significantly higher on the Stanford reading test than those without the program. Mentoring programs are nothing new, of course, and more than a million adult volunteers already work with students. Such programs have been shown to improve students' attitudes toward school and reduce discipline problems and absences. What they generally do not accomplish, though, is a major improvement in the kids' academic achievement.

The In2Books program broke the mold by recognizing that books and classroom drills are boring for many children—the assigned materials lack any immediate relevance to their lives. It fills that gap by requiring children to share their thoughts about a book with a mentor. As Joann Cornish, a third-grade teacher in Washington, explained to the *Washington Post*, the children "are looking forward to receiving the pen pals' letters, and it makes them write." And the Internet reinforces the sense of purpose by opening up new opportunities for communication between the mentors and the children. No youngster has to be convinced that learning how to use a computer is relevant. To my mind, the Internet is the most significant learning tool to appear since Gutenberg invented moveable type in the fifteenth century.

If teenagers don't see the point of being in school, if they don't understand how their schoolwork connects to what they care about or what they will be doing in the outside real world, they're not likely to stay around long enough to graduate. In2Books president Linda Dozier believes that changes in the structure of the school day—fewer but longer instruction periods, for example, instead of the current succession of hour-long classes—could help make schools, in her words, "stickier." She also emphasizes the need for teachers to have enough expertise in their subject matter to create a "real life sort of context" for their students. At the innovative Park Day School in Oakland, California, for example, a seventh-grade math teacher introduces students to the notion of a minimum wage and the cost of living to help teach statistics—and much else besides.

Another example of technology-based innovation in education is ePals. A year before In2Books was born, Tim Discipio, a pioneer in online media and ecommerce, plunged into the education business. He created a Web site where teachers and their classrooms could connect with other classrooms to engage in joint learning exercises. The project, called ePals Classroom Exchange, began with just four schools, but it rapidly developed into a significant cross-cultural learning tool. As of early 2007, it was reaching 7 million students in almost 300,000 classrooms in 191 countries.

The ePals' SchoolMail program provides a suite of online tools that make it safe and easy for students and teachers to communicate online. Language translation is built into discussion boards and file sharing. Another program, SchoolBlog, makes it possible for students to get to know each other across barriers of space and language. Using ePals' Safebrowser software, teachers can build so-called walled gardens to house educational Web sites that children can safely access and use.

In business as in romance, two organizations that complement each other so well simply couldn't remain apart. In January 2007, In2Books and ePals announced their merger. The new company, which kept the ePals name, will introduce In2Books' curriculum and mentoring techniques to the company's huge online membership around the world.

In2Books and ePals are part of a growing effort to add more rigor and vigor into American schools. Many schools are actively seeking curricula and textbooks that develop students' critical-thinking abilities, as opposed to the tendency in far too many U.S. schools to bury students in quickly forgotten details. A teacher of a tenth-grade science class in Michigan, for example, assigned students to select a consumer product, describe its impact on the environment, and then come up with a way to change the product's design and/or manufacture to make it greener while still retaining its consumer appeal. In the process, the students learned not just about earth science, but also about chemistry, commerce, and design. Harvard's Howard Gardner has long advocated such an approach, using, for example, a detailed study of Darwin's finches to tease out the concepts of evolution. And these integrative approaches are supported by new curriculum materials. Roy Pea, codirector of the Stanford Center for Innovations in Learning, points out that "countries from Germany to Singapore have extremely small textbooks that focus on the most powerful and generative ideas."

One of the most exciting new educational approaches comes from what, at first, may seem an unlikely source. Scott McNealy, the chairman of Sun Microsystems, couldn't find a lively Web site where his third-grade son could learn about electricity. So McNealy, whose company was an early advocate of open-source software, decided to create a free Wikipedia-like site to answer any question a student might have. Curriki.org went live in January 2006 and quickly proved itself. Students began asking questions and taking the courses offered. Educators began sharing their successful experiments in classroom techniques and content. It was something new in the world, an educational town hall. A year after launch, Curriki had thirty-five thousand members and three thousand posted items of teaching material, ranging from a curriculum on the history of computers to an animation of battle tactics in the American Revolution.

Another Silicon Valley denizen, polymath John Seely Brown, is also involved in new models for education. He argues that the rapid pace of change in technology and the way business is conducted means that students must have the capacity to learn independently, work comfortably on cross-disciplinary teams, and know how to use multiple methods for thinking through problems—mathematical, linguistic, artistic, and so on.

JSB, as he is often referred to, advocates a number of very different learning environments, such as the classroom as architecture or design studio. He describes it this way: "All work in progress is made public . . . every student can see what every other student is doing; every student witnesses the strategies that others use . . . and there is public critique, typically by the master and perhaps several outside practitioners."

Education environments need not necessarily be physical. JSB reckons that today's high school and college-age generation may have a deep love of learning and problem solving that comes alive especially in conjunction with video and computer games, not the classroom. Success in these games, he avers, requires "extremely good pattern recognition, sense-making in confusing environments, and multitasking . . . Continuous decision-making in conditions of uncertainty is the essential skill."

In2Books, ePals, Curriki, and JSB's different learning environments are the kind of experiments that we must look to for help in framing the future of education in this country.

THINK LOCAL AND SCALE UP

In our system of government, one of the trickiest issues of education reform is how to implement improvements across our country. National talent policies must be organized at the federal level, but defenders of states' rights currently stress the importance of letting the states have their say in how policies should be implemented to work best for them. Indeed, the states can serve as laboratories—experimenting with ideas, testing them, and honing methods to make them work as well as possible for the whole country. And given the inherent competition among the states to attract families on the move, their educational systems are, or should be, of crucial concern. As such, the states might therefore be inclined to aim higher and take on greater risk in devising new teaching methods than Washington would. There are disadvantages to having education reform managed at a state level, of course, but they can be outweighed by the benefits of diverse perspectives, approaches, and findings—if, that is, we have the ability to coordinate, fund, and pursue experimentation on a national level.

With so little to show for our many years of discussion about educational reform, many may be skeptical about how much progress can really be made, even at the state level. But the fact is that many states have impressive entrepreneurial drive. Always seeking new job opportunities and more tax revenues, they have learned how to lure hot companies and industries to their communities. The shrewdest among them have also come to recognize the shortcomings of pursuing grand projects like costly sports arenas, hardly known as primary magnets for talent. They are focused instead on raising capital for the cutting-edge facilities that innovators need, including medical schools and academic research centers.

Take North Carolina, for instance. In so many ways, it epitomizes the up-and-comers. It is known as a great place to do business, thanks to its stress on education and job training. But interestingly enough, that perception dates to the 1930s, when, during the Great Depression, North Carolina's General Assembly became the only state legislature in the country to continue full economic support for its public schools. That image had become blurred, however, by 2001, when Governor Michael Easley took office. With hard times squeezing traditional businesses (farming, furniture, textiles), state revenues plunged.

Looking ahead with clarity, Easley promised to reform schools to give North Carolina a workforce trained to thrive in a high-tech global economy. Among his early efforts was More at Four, the nation's first statewide pre-K program for "at-risk" four-year-olds. Another Easley initiative, dubbed Learn and Earn, offered students an associate's degree if they stayed for a fifth year of high school, giving them an advantage in the job market. A third incentive for staying in school—started with $11 million from the Gates Foundation—was the governor's plan to launch one hundred new high schools with topic-specific curricula divided between college prep and outside work experience.

North Carolina also has a thriving and innovative community college network serving eight hundred thousand students at three hundred sites. As the economy of the region has changed, so has training at these schools, providing a steady flow of graduates with skills that match the needs of companies in the state as well as those who might settle there. In fact, if a company wants one or more of its employees trained in a subject not taught by the colleges, the system will create a program to do the job—so long as the company pledges to add at least twelve jobs in one year. With state funding, such programs are free to both student and company, though the degree of support the colleges provide varies with the skill level required and the number of new jobs involved, among other things.

Easley's stress on education has paid off handsomely: North Carolina ranks first in the nation for its overall number and its percentage share of national board-certified teachers. It also ranks seventh in *Education Week*'s national listing of state efforts to improve teacher quality.

The state's crown jewel is Raleigh-Durham's Research Triangle Park, a seven thousand-acre technology center containing one hundred facilities and surrounded by three eminent research partners: Duke University, North Carolina State University, and the University of North Carolina. All sorts of innovations, but most notably in biotechnology, have flowed from this powerhouse, making North Carolina the country's third-ranking biotech state (behind California and Massachusetts) in a recent Ernst & Young report. Although the triangle is now recognized as a national innovation center, it came about only through three decades of conscious effort by state and regional policy makers.

Among the leading-edge companies that call the triangle home is pharmaceutical services provider Quintiles Transnational. Founded in 1982 by UNC professor Dennis Gillings, now its chairman and chief executive, Quintiles has grown into a multinational with sixteen thousand employees and a record of helping to speed nine of the world's ten leading biotech products to market. "This is where the action is," Gillings recently told *Fortune*. "North Carolina is where we find people with the right business, financial, and legal skills—and some of the best scientific minds in the business." What better testament to Michael Easley's innovative vision for education.

As the North Carolina success story shows, the diversity found in our fifty states can be a strength, not a weakness. And no plan to reinvigorate America's capacity for nourishing talent can be complete without tapping their creativity. But as the states forge ahead with experiments, the federal government must put in place effective mechanisms for knowledge sharing and assessment of overall results.

The portfolio of ideas that follows does not constitute a grand strategy for education. Rather, it is an attempt to spark experimentation with multiple creative approaches that can be rapidly prototyped, tested, and communicated as part of a more definitive national innovation strategy. I propose that we:

- Recruit America's brightest junior high school students as full-time apprentices to leading innovators, a form of national early mentoring by the country's best minds. If we accept that mastery of the innovation process comes from proximity to master practitioners, as exemplified by the early guilds and today's design studios, then replicating those successful dynamics becomes an interesting approach to consider. That means forming intimate groups to encourage interaction between people with vastly different levels of expertise and immersing them in practical problem solving. I envision creating a brood herd of the best and brightest, highly sophisticated young disciples who would be given a chance to work with top innovators much earlier in their careers than is now possible.

In this regard, we can enlist leading scientists, engineers, and entrepreneurs to make regular visits to our schools—particularly public schools in disadvantaged neighborhoods—to excite an up-and-coming generation about learning and achieving in those fields.

- Market the importance of education to the American people in order to galvanize them into action. In April 2007, Bill Gates teamed up with another philanthropist, Eli Broad, to create a $60 million single-issue effort to vault education to the top of the political agenda for 2008. Strong American Schools, the name of the project, calls for three things: stronger, more consistent curriculum standards nationwide; lengthening the school day and year; and improving teacher quality through merit pay and other measures.

- Mobilize the talent of mass media to make innovation as compelling as becoming a singing star. Why not an *American Idol*–style competition for young entrepreneurs or inventors? Why not a television series or feature film based on the achievements of smart kids?

- Create and support alternative avenues for learning that are complementary to schools. Among the creative programs that already meet these aims is the nonprofit organization called FIRST (For Inspiration and Recognition of Science and Technology). FIRST was founded in 1989 by the entrepreneurial inventor Dean Kamen. Its avowed mission is "to create a world where science and technology are celebrated . . . where young people dream of becoming science and technology heroes."

The organization is probably best known for the FIRST Robotics Competition (FRC), a varsity sport of the mind for high school students (although there are also other FIRST programs for kids as young as six). Teams of young people and their mentors have six weeks to solve the annual FRC challenge, using a standard kit of parts and a common set of rules. The 2007 competition featured over one thousand teams playing "rack 'n' roll," a game that required remote-controlled robots to place different kinds of tubes on a spidery rack placed in the center of a playing field. Let's turn our national fixation on competition and medal winning into a learning and intellectual achievement to create more FIRSTs, whether funded by foundations, states, or local governments.

- Enable a network of talent brokers and entrepreneurs to identify national goals, organize leadership teams by field, launch partnerships with business and academia, and lobby for support at every political level—from the West Wing of the White House to city halls across the country.

- Ballyhoo the wunderkind generation of high-powered, high-tech innovators as role models. Examples: Jerry Yang, founder of Yahoo; Sergey Brin and Larry Page, of Google; John Lassiter, of Pixar; Steve Jobs, of Apple; Bill Gates, of Microsoft; and Michael Dell, of Dell Computer.

  In addition to these rock stars, there is a much larger contingent of equally significant contributors who can also serve as inspirations. If we promote them the way we idolize screen actors and fashion models, they'll take on an allure all their own that will inspire our young people, but in a different, arguably more important direction.

•　　•　　•

In my visits with Biopolis' Philip Yeo in Singapore, he often spoke of the younger generation of his country as being "hungry," by which he meant eager and ambitious to do great things. If that should happen, I asked, what would he do? "Easy," he replied. "We would import hungry people. Otherwise, we would stagnate."

Yeo raises an important issue. Not only must we find ways to better train our homegrown talent, but we must start focusing on doing a better job of luring foreign talent to our shores. In the past, the United States relied heavily on talent imported from other nations. Why that flow has dwindled and what we can do about it is the topic of the next chapter.

FIVE

SEDUCING TALENT

If you don't have the horses, you can't run.
—Arnie Katz, video game pioneer

Anyone still complacent about the preeminence of America's scientific talent would have been shocked back to reality in a hurry not long ago. It was April 2006 in San Antonio, Texas, scene of the world finals of the ACM International Collegiate Programming Contest, with computer teams competing from colleges and universities around the globe.

Time was, a decade or so ago, when U.S. students had a lock on this competition. But this time, only one American team—from MIT—scored in the top twelve. The winners, from Saratov State University in Russia, solved six arcane puzzles during the grueling five-hour contest. Teams from Eastern Europe and Asia grabbed most of the top scores. Duke University's three programmers solved only one problem, stumbling out of the competition dazed and depressed. When coach Owen Astrachan tried to console his team by reminding them that this was a contest among the "best of the best," twenty-year-old Matt Edwards replied, "Yeah. We're the worst of the best of the best."

As the previous chapter explained, it isn't time to give up on raising homegrown talent that can compete with the world's best in science and engineering. But, at the very least, the outcome in San Antonio demonstrates that the international talent competition is wide open. Any country, company, or high-tech center that hopes to stay in the race will have to snare top recruits from wherever they happen to reside in the world. And since no one, with the possible exception of North Korea, gets away with kidnapping talent these days, that means practicing the art of seduction.

Technology, to be sure, is only a part of America's innovation story, but it is a critical one. As Franklin Roosevelt's science adviser, Vannevar Bush, once remarked, "A nation which depends upon others for its new basic scientific knowledge will be slow in its industrial progress and weak in its competitive position." In the United States, the diminishing allure of the sciences and engineering for students is a major concern. According to the U.S. Labor Department, the number of jobs for "computer/math scientists" will jump by 40 percent, to 3.5 million, over the ten years ending in 2012. But a 2006 survey of 1.3 million full-time college freshmen by the Higher Education Research Institute at the University of California at Los Angeles showed that only 1.1 percent planned to major in computer science, less than a third the number who entered the field five years earlier.

If it lasts, this retreat from the race could cost our country dearly. "If our talent base weakens, our lead in technology, business, and economics will fade faster than any of us can imagine," warns Richard Florida, a George Mason University economist and the author of *The Flight of the Creative Class.*

For years, foreign scientists and engineers, drawn by the freedom and opportunities the United States offered, have broadened that base. The flow of immigrants during and after World War II provides a striking example of the influence geopolitics has on the movement of talent. Migration fueled by anti-Semitism caused the crown for "most Nobel Prizes won in science" to pass from Germany to the United States. In the 1940s, European scientists gave America an edge by making major contributions to the Manhattan Project and in such fields as aviation, petrochemicals, and optics. And in subsequent decades, foreign talent greatly expanded in this country. A study by scholars at Duke University's engineering school found that one-quarter of companies started in the United States between 1995 and 2005 had at least one founder who was foreign born. All told, these businesses produced $52 billion in sales and employed 450,000 workers. In Silicon Valley, according to the Duke study, over one-half of start-ups had at least one immigrant as a key founder. And to add to the picture, half of America's computer scientists, 45 percent of our mathematicians, and a third of our physics teachers today are foreign born.

At the same time, our universities have steadily drawn top students from abroad, and they have assumed a vital role in the life of our graduate schools. Their studies have increased our collective knowledge, their teaching of undergraduates has inspired each new generation of our homegrown talent, and their participation in university research projects has greatly added to American science.

Today, foreigners represent 17 percent of our 1.4 million graduate students and—more to the point—half of all graduate students in engineering and 40 percent in the physical sciences. Without them, the research conducted in our academic laboratories would be crippled. Nor do the contributions of foreign students stop there. Many settle in the United States after graduation, representing a crucial segment of our scientific and technical talent base. In the United States today, according to the National Science Foundation, 40 percent of doctorate-degree holders working in science and engineering are foreign born, as are the majority of doctorate holders in computer science and electrical, civil, and mechanical engineering.

Yet, just when a looming shortage of homegrown scientific talent makes it imperative that the United States hold onto the foreign-born stars we've got and entice even more into our constellation, exactly the opposite is happening, as noted in Chapter 2. Countries promising greener pastures are stealing away some of the talent that might once have been attracted here.

If talent as global currency sounds vaguely familiar, perhaps it's because science-fiction writer William Gibson has presciently described a future world in which war is fought not over territory or natural resources, but over the services of experts in such areas as nanomaterials and life sciences. The real world hasn't reached that point, not yet at least, and the United States remains a huge attractor of foreign talent. But the hot competition is starting to cost us stars in science, technology, and other fields that we can't afford to lose. There is an as yet small but still noticeable reverse brain drain.

Globalization and the easy movement of people, companies, and cash around the world are partly to blame. But superheated economic development in nations such as China, Ireland, and Singapore is also a major factor—along with bold public efforts by these nations to bring their long-lost talent home. I've already detailed the repats in Taiwan, the new inhabitants of Silicon Valley–like housing developments in Bangalore and the sea turtles in China.

Now, the reverse brain drain of technological talent is being aggravated by America's waning ability to attract and hold onto the best and brightest students from abroad. For example, U.S. graduate school applications from foreign students living abroad fell 28 percent in 2004, and they dropped another 5 percent the following year—largely because of expanding choices, the increasing difficulties of obtaining student visas, and the often higher cost of American education compared with international competitors. At the same time, many foreign-born graduate students who once would have remained in the United States are, like their professional elders, returning to their native lands. Improved quality of life and greater career opportunities than in the past are often the deciding factors.

Kshipra Bhawalkar, a nineteen-year-old member of the Duke

programming team mentioned earlier, is a case in point. Recognized as a math prodigy in her sixth-grade class in Pune, India, she decided to become a scientist, thus fulfilling the prophecy of a palm-reading family friend. And where will Bhawalkar's future be? She has no doubts. "In the past, people from India stayed here after they got their degrees," she told *BusinessWeek*. "But now India is at a turning point. It's getting to be a leader." She's going to return home after graduation.

As for the falloff in U.S. grad school applications from abroad, competition from fast-growing foreign universities is turning the tide. In times past, the choice was simple: any student hoping for a top-flight scientific or engineering degree had to go to Germany, England, or the United States. And the United States drew twice as many foreign graduate students as the other two countries combined. Today, that picture is changing. Our competitors have created impressive educational alternatives at flank speed.

The European Union is investing heavily in improved college and postgraduate instruction. China has spent billions of dollars on one hundred new universities, with plans to make them world class. India is not far behind. The time is fast approaching when foreigners yearning for world class engineering and science degrees will have a cornucopia of schools from which to choose. And if they happen to live in Shanghai or Bombay, the chances are greater that they will enroll close to home—not at faraway Stanford or Harvard. When the number of Indian students applying to U.S. universities drops by 28 percent in just one year, as happened in 2006, the writing is on the wall.

Worse yet, when the new universities being built overseas get up to full speed, they won't be siphoning off just the foreign students who might otherwise have chosen U.S. schools. They will be corralling some of our own top scholars, too.

There's another, even more unsettling reason fewer foreign students—and established scientists as well—are coming to America: Our restrictive post-9/11 immigration policies are driving them away. If ever there were a time when the United States should be wooing much-needed foreign students and talents, it is now. Instead, we're barring the doors. Tighter restrictions since 9/11 on student visas and green cards for skilled workers have hamstrung companies and colleges hoping to import top-tier talent. Bill Gates got it right in March 2006 when he warned Congress that these restrictions diminish American global competitiveness "as other countries benefit from the international talent that U.S. employers cannot hire or retain."

It's an Alice-in-Wonderland scenario. We desperately need to entice more foreign students to settle here after they graduate. But when would-be students apply for visas to study in the United States, they are turned away unless they can prove that they do *not* plan to stay on after graduation. And they must do so in the course of an interview, often of only a few minutes' duration, with an official in an American consulate who may have no idea whether they are telling the truth. The deck is clearly stacked against the foreign student. So while other nations around the world are aggressively recruiting foreign talent for their universities, we are scaring it away.

Just as wrongheaded is our policy regarding the admission of skilled foreign workers. We have put a strict annual limit on the number of work visas available to these talented people and stiffened the application requirements. In the 1990s, two hundred thousand H-1B nonimmigrant work visas were available annually for people with special technical skills who had a company sponsor. After 9/11, the number was slashed to fewer than seventy thousand a year. Not surprisingly, the low quota is now exhausted in a matter of days, denying untold numbers of talented individuals even the chance of coming to the United States. And this at a moment in history when American companies are facing a growing shortage of knowledge workers as well as top-flight technology and engineering talents.

Even if the quotas were to be increased, the number of students and skilled professionals coming to the United States might still decline. Why? Because many of them are so turned off by our national policies that they aren't even bothering to apply. According to the previously cited Pew Global Attitudes survey, many foreigners are losing faith and interest in the United States.

Foreign-born scientists and students are not the only bright minds slipping from our grasp. As noted elsewhere in these pages, many of our own top people are taking jobs abroad. Noted marketing professor Ronald E. Frank was lured away from American academia to serve as president of Singapore Management University, the city-state's first private university. Others who have decamped to Singapore include Edison Liu, the former division director at the National Cancer Institute, who told me he moved in part because he felt a renewed sense of purpose in Singapore for connecting science to the needs of society. Comparing the atmosphere at Biopolis to the heyday of the Manhattan Project or MIT's Lincoln Labs, the site of major breakthroughs in America's air defense system, Liu relishes the opportunity to work with students who are suffused with the same sense of purpose.

What is more, our shortage of homegrown technical talent is about to be greatly magnified by the aging of the country's 76 million baby boomers, the first of whom will reach retirement age in 2011. Then, as the decade unfolds, a growing economy and the stepped-up pace of retirement by the boomers will increase the need for workers in the 35-to-45 age group by 25 percent. But the number of Americans in that cohort will actually shrink by 15 percent. Meanwhile, nations ranging from China and Russia to Israel and Italy will be scouting for managers, scientists, and creative thinkers to drive their economies. The collision of interests will be as jolting as it is inevitable, with the outcome determining which nations remain in the top ranks and which will be called up to the majors.

As we chart our strategy for competing in the recruitment race, Singapore's playbook once again offers a model to study. No nation is more successful than this tiny competitor in attracting skilled foreign talent—including our own.

Several years ago, the Singapore government ran a striking advertisement in a number of life sciences journals. Showing a variety of scientists and technicians drawn from a rainbow coalition of backgrounds, the tag line was short and to the point: "If you are a world-class life scientist, you are a Singaporean." The campaign was spectacularly successful. More than three-quarters of the two thousand scientists now working in Singapore's Biopolis research center were recruited from abroad, and sixteen multinational pharmaceutical companies plan to send their own scientists from around the world to join Singapore's research effort.

Philip Yeo, the head man, personally directs the Biopolis recruiting effort. He exults in his nickname, "serial kidnapper," sparing neither time nor expense to get the talent he wants. For openers, Yeo seeks out eager, young high-tech students, who come to Singapore from all over the world, and offers them scholarships to the best U.S. and European universities. He interviews the candidates himself, exercising an eye for talent so keen that of his 108 students in the United States in 2005, fully 45 percent scored grade-point averages above 3.95, while another 41 percent ranked between 3.8 and 3.95. Only 14 percent failed to make the ambitious 3.8-point cutoff that qualifies them for continuing government support to study for a Ph.D.

Making that cut is like winning the lottery. In addition to full tuition, the doctoral students, as noted previously, also get tax-free living allowances. The $1 million Singapore dollars ($750,000 U.S. at current exchange rates) they receive over their five years of study lifts them out of the ranks of typically struggling graduate students. Already affluent, they can cover their needs and also save money for a start in life—especially if, as frequently happens, they marry each other. "I'm in the matchmaking business, too," Yeo jokes.

Singapore is equally lavish in luring senior talent from top jobs around the world, with salaries that can reach $1 million a year or more. So far, the recruiting bill has come to more than $1.7 billion for some one thousand five hundred ranking scientists. The top scientists privately acknowledge a financial premium in their compensation packages compared to what they could get at home. But money is only part of the attraction. A bigger factor, Yeo tells me, is freedom to do the work they want to do.

If you're a senior scientist in the United States, he says, "You have no freedom. You spend your time writing grant proposals for money. You are a professional beggar." In addition, he points out, the U.S. government makes it difficult for scientists who aren't citizens to travel to other countries. That's another handicap for the United States in the competition to lure talent.

"In the past, America was like a Golden Mountain," Yeo told me. "Now, it is very forbidding. Every foreigner is a threat, and the whole atmosphere is changing." Yeo's own diplomatic visa, once good for five years, was reduced to two years, then one, then three months. Other scientists have been refused admission or have even been briefly detained because their names resembled some on watch lists of possible terrorists. In sharp contrast, he notes, Singapore is operating on what used to be the U.S. model: bring us your talent, and we'll set it free.

That freedom includes the total absence of political strictures on research—a sharp contrast to the U.S. government's restrictions on the use of embryonic stem cells. Marie Csete, a cell biologist at Emory University, said the restrictions on research are "so odious that many scientists just do not try." John Gearhart of Johns Hopkins University, one of the scientists who first isolated human stem cells, said, "I am not as concerned about where the science will go, as about where we will be permitted to go." He continued, "How do you build a research base if you don't know from president to president what the policy will be?" It's difficult to overstate the chilling effect that policy has had on scientists. One of the prime requirements in any creative discipline is the freedom to follow any lead, no matter where it takes you.

Just as scientists like Gearhart want and need the freedom to pursue different paths, so too do talented individuals seek places that are free from restraint. The United States owes part of its previous success in innovation to the nurturing of locations at which the right resources were joined with the right business and cultural climate.

Foreign talent—and domestic, too—increasingly ends up living and working in communities perceived to be "really nice." To a surprising degree, a city's social, cultural, and even political ambience takes precedence over its industrial and academic environment—particularly among that most-coveted demographic, the 24-to-34-year-old college graduates. That age cohort was weaned on computers and is the most up-to-date on the latest scientific and technological developments. And it's a population much in demand, not just in the United States but around the world; there are simply too few members of this demographic to fill available jobs. When the baby boomers begin retiring at the start of the next decade, the American economy will be losing two workers for each one added. Europe and Japan will feel the pinch even sooner.

Remember all the talk about the electronic future, when the world would be linked by video communications and the Internet? We imagined that we would live essentially in cyberspace. But for the talented, location matters more than ever. Young graduates tend to select a community to live in before they even find a job. Right now, the hot ticket on American business school campuses may be a job that leads to Shanghai. And if not Shanghai, graduates still prefer big-city excitement to the charms of small-town life. They want to settle in downtown areas, where they can easily access public trans-portation and enjoy cultural attractions and night life. And once a city begins to pull in these young scientists and engineers, it creates a snowball effect. The talent hot spot itself becomes a prime attrac-tion, eventually creating what smart young people see as an ideal situation—a critical mass of high-powered minds dreaming up in-novative ideas that they can bounce off one another.

Like attracts like, and that magnetism has greatly accelerated in recent years. One study a number of years ago found that 11 percent of the population over twenty-five had a college education, and these young graduates were spread evenly across the United States. Today, their numbers have grown by more than 100 percent, but Richard Florida has shown that the spread is far more uneven—toward the coasts and away from the center of the country.

Major corporations are well aware of these trends as they look for new sites on which to set up shop. "Keep your tax incentives and highway interchanges," a Silicon Valley executive told a panel of gov-ernors not long ago. "We will go where the highly skilled people are."

Inspired by the evidence of thriving communities of entrepre-neurs, artists, scientists, and engineers in places like the San Fran-cisco Bay Area, Boston, or San Diego, city fathers now understand that a successful talent hunt demands a major effort by national, re-gional, and metropolitan communities. Not surprisingly, a new breed of consultant has emerged to help tailor towns to the tastes of brainy innovators. Here are some of the characteristics they are promoting:

- Quality of life.

Since top innovators generally have no problem finding universi-ties and companies eager for their services, they can afford to be picky about things like the cost of living, the social scene, the cultural atmosphere. They want to know about after-hours clubs and mosh pits, about museums and the local symphony, about the personality of the place—lively or laid-back, friendly or stuffy.

One winner in the talent hunt is Atlanta, Georgia. Between 1990 and 2000, it saw a 46 percent rise in the number of 25-34-year-old college graduates living there. As a local booster commented, "The jury of the most skeptical age group in America has looked at Atlanta's character and likes it."

The city is especially popular with young, educated African-Americans like twenty-seven-year-old Tiffany Patterson. She was interviewed by the *New York Times* at a new downtown bar-restaurant filled with the talk and laughter of upscale young people—the kind of scene, she said, that convinced her to settle in Atlanta rather than return to her hometown of Dallas. At home, she said, "Women my age are looking for a husband." After college, she worked in finance for a while, then started her own business as a marketing consultant. "I thought, 'I can break out and do it myself,' " she said. "It really is the city of the fearless."

Portland, Oregon, too, has seen a big jump in young college graduates, and it's no accident that the increase has come at a time when formerly rundown areas like the Pearl District have been rejuvenated with art galleries and elegant restaurants. Along with its natural attractions, such as snowboarding on nearby Mount Hood, Portland offers such urban amenities as a network of bike paths used by thousands of residents to commute to work.

• Opportunities to specialize.

Many cities that have successfully attracted top people, whether in the United States or abroad, have developed an affinity for a particular cutting-edge industry. Edinburgh, Scotland, and nearby Dundee, for example, have become a mecca for the computer-gaming industry, boasting such pioneers as Real Time Worlds and

Rockstar Games, the creator of Grand Theft Auto. The University of Abertay at Dundee offers a computer-gaming degree, the world's first, and local banks and the Scottish government provide gaming companies and other digital media outfits with start-up capital.

A lively art scene is a plus for Montreal, but many of its young engineering graduates are lured by the city's role as a center for companies specializing in animation and 3-D digital imaging. The list includes Digital Dimensions, Softimage, and Toon Boom Animation. Creative companies also receive substantial financial help from the city, and the province of Quebec provides rebates to game makers equivalent to up to 37.5 percent of the cost of the labor used.

Design of all kinds is big in Portland, providing yet another lure for hundreds of foreign settlers. Just ask Sohrab Vossoughi, founder of the industrial design firm Ziba, which hires twenty young designers a year. "The values of this generation are in line with the DNA of this city," he says of his adopted Oregon home. Vossoughi, who emigrated with his family from Tehran when he was fourteen, took a design job in Portland with Hewlett-Packard in 1980. He started Ziba, which means "beautiful" in Farsi, four years later. His company has designed everything from the Microsoft Natural Keyboard to garbage cans for Rubbermaid, winning a number of prestigious design awards.

- A reputation for tolerance.

Winning cities in the hunt for innovative talent are tolerant of diversity and welcome all sorts of newcomers, from immigrant foreigners and convention-flouting artists to entertainers and the gay community. Such diversity makes for a lively, interesting, and fun-to-live-in community, with a flow of ideas that not only entertain but spur creativity. Richard Florida, who first singled out acceptance of gays as a factor in the talent competition, sees no one-to-one relationship between the gay community and high-tech growth. Rather, a strong gay presence is an "indicator of a place that is open to many different kinds of people," he explains, and that's the kind of place talented young people prefer.

And again, Atlanta, with its large international and gay populations, fills the bill. "Atlanta's just one of those mixes," says T. J. Ashiru, a thirty-year-old Nigerian who was thinking of going to college in New York City but opted for Atlanta after it hosted the 1996 Olympics. He likes the city so much that he stayed after graduation and found a job in finance. "The Olympics," he points out, "was basically the catalyst for what Atlanta became."

The power of diversity and the right climate for innovation are gaining currency with community leaders around the world. They are rapidly moving to win over both outstanding foreign students and senior technical people. Take Kyoto, Japan, for instance. The city has long been the Asian nation's cultural capital, famous for its Buddhist temples (one thousand six hundred of them) and its shrines, palaces, and gardens. Unlike so many other Japanese cities, Kyoto was spared from bombing in World War II, leaving its ancient architectural splendors intact. But it is also a rapidly growing modern city with a population of 1.5 million and a sizable commercial and industrial base.

Home to Nintendo, Omron, Kyocera, and other high-tech companies, Kyoto has developed an ambitious plan to bring in foreign talent. The strategy calls for boosting the "international competitiveness" of its universities and improving the "daily living environment" so that "foreigners will want to settle down." The national relaxation of immigration rules will make it easier for foreign scholars to visit. And to entice overseas students, the city plans to create an "experience Kyoto" program and an "overseas student passport," theorizing that once young people sample the city's attractions, they will want to enroll at a local university.

To attract and retain young rising stars in science, engineering, and other talent-driven fields, companies are paying them higher and higher salaries. Of course, you see that happening all through our economy, from sports to films, from Wall Street to academe. Yes, even top professors are getting extra pay, not only because they're good but also because they attract others of their ilk to the university—again, serving as a talent multiplier.

One downside of all this generosity is that it breeds social and financial inequality. Between 1980 and 2004, the share of income going to the best-paid 1 percent of Americans doubled. As *The Economist* put it, "The talent war is producing a global meritocracy." This is because companies feel they simply cannot lose their leaders and innovators to better-paying competitors, particularly at a time when young stars are in short supply. The result is that hot spots are increasingly seeing a hollowing out between the high-talent elite above and ill-paid service workers below. It is a hollowing out not of industrial capability, as was the case with Japan in the 1980s, but of talent. Those who previously occupied the middle—including vital constituents like teachers—can no longer afford the soaring cost of downtown living, especially housing, so they move away to less dynamic areas. And the cycle is being repeated in developed nations around the world.

For cities as well, the hunt for innovation stars is a zero-sum game. Every scientist a city snares is one that other cities won't win over. And innovation cities develop a powerful momentum as the existing cadre of creative talent lures more and more kindred souls. Conversely, cities that start to lose their creative young people are hard put to halt the brain drain.

• • •

During one of my visits to Philip Yeo's office at Singapore's Biopolis, I noticed a striking poster featuring an attractive young woman. Upon closer inspection, I saw that a tattoo in the shape of the double helix of DNA encircled her upper arm. In fine print were written the words: "Got a passion for science? We'll take it to a higher level." And in still smaller print, I read the words: "International Science Fellowship, A*STAR Foundation." Behind me, Yeo asked softly, "You like her? She's a model—Chinese father, Norwegian mother. We make science sexy here!"

Clearly, other countries are raising the bar on seduction as an art form in the global innovation race. For the United States, the key lesson to take away is that talented individuals are drawn to these hot spots because they know they will flourish there. They crave environments that are conducive to creativity and the free exchange of ideas, and they are attracted by communities designed for a better quality of life.

To get the most out of our talent, both homegrown and imported, we should also apply these insights at the more basic level of where their work takes place. Talent needs an environment where it can do its best work. Therefore, we also have to be innovative in looking at workplaces with an eye to encouraging creative interaction and supporting the inventiveness of those we recruit. The chapter just ahead describes the kind of work environments that best serve that purpose, and the design principles that underlie them. I predict that you'll find yourself wishing you worked in one of these innovative work spaces.

SIX

THE IMPORTANCE
OF PLACE

**And the space in between, all the comets and stars
will be ours.**

—Frank Zappa

When I was eighteen years old and a budding professional pianist, the looking glass opened up, and I fell through. I wangled an audition with Frank Zappa, legendary musical disruptor, and he invited me out to Los Angeles for a summer of studio recording with his band, the Mothers of Invention, as well as to have some good clean fun.

After waking up in the early afternoon (recording sessions were often all-night affairs), I would drive down to Sunset Highland Studios to watch, listen, and play as the wild and wonderful Zappa decided how the recording space for his band would be set up for the night. It was always different, depending on who was going to perform on Zappa's latest whim and inspiration.

Some nights, Sugercane Harris would electrify everyone in earshot with his blues violin solos. Current and future stars like Alice Cooper and Captain Beefheart stood in the wings while the Mothers recorded. Sometimes, two large grand pianos would be set up cheek to cheek, and I would play one or even both at the same time. Sometimes, voice tracks would be rerecorded behind bunker-like acoustic baffling, or a mountain of percussion instruments would be raised to support the Mothers' legendary backbeat. This was Mr. Zappa's eminent domain, his place of innovation, and he rocked in it.

Years later, but just a few miles away, I encountered another such place, a movie studio in Hollywood. Its huge, warehouse-like rooms were called sound stages, though the name misleads: these were the magical spaces where sets are built and films are shot. And they, too, were different from one week to the next. Now you see Stuart Little's New York apartment, tomorrow it might be Captain Hook's ship or the bridge of the starship *Enterprise*. The sense of place was completely variable, awaiting the inspiration of director, producer, set designers, and actors to bring it alive.

These experiences have stuck with me for the duration. Those places were completely at odds with where most organizations seek (and fail) to inspire creativity and inventiveness. And this is just as true at the national as the corporate level. If this country is to reinvent its innovation capabilities for a new era, we are going to have to rethink and redesign our innovation environments. The Lakota Indians have a saying that "wisdom lives in places." So does the kind of innovation that comes from talented people working in the right environment with the right tools.

We tend to think of the design of place and organizations as separate agendas, when they are in fact intimately connected. If an organization wants to morph into a radical new form—say a flat management structure composed of constantly shifting work groups—then giving people a place that is conducive to that way of working is essential. And environment shapes not just the structure of our organizations but the way in which what MIT collaboration expert Michael Schrage calls our "shared minds" work together—

how we discover, experiment, and learn in a collaborative manner. In turn, innovation arises not only from the nurturing and attracting of talent but also from the way we facilitate talented people's ability to work. In short, the design of place is part of a larger agenda of redesigning the work of innovation.

This chapter focuses on work spaces because talent increasingly desires (and demands) an environment in which it can excel. Current work space design generally reflects the ethos of the industrial era, when the goal was to maximize efficiency, control complexity, support the existing pecking order, and eliminate uncertainty. It called for rigid, stable, hard-to-change structures, what you'd want if you were in a business focused on economies of scale and long production runs. Privacy was nonexistent, as employees were constantly scrutinized to make sure they were delivering the proper number of levers pulled, papers pushed, or widgets assembled. Obviously, workers had little if any latitude in how they used their space or organized their time.

Our current approach to work space design isn't so much chosen as inherited, and its underlying agenda is often hard to see, hidden as it is in plain sight. Because it's so familiar, we hang onto it. For the most part, leaders have no idea how asphyxiating these work places can be—despite the best efforts of actor Steve Carell and his castmates in *The Office* to clue them in. One company I know of actually measures the square feet by which executives' offices may be expanded when they receive a particular promotion. They also get to choose new furniture: plastic veneer, make way for wood-grain plastic veneer.

If an organization of any kind is to inspire optimal creativity and collaboration for innovation, it needs much looser habitats. Environments for innovation must be designed differently from those intended to maximize efficiency; we can't force-fit people into one-size-fits-all places. Quite the opposite. In an imagination-driven economy, we must learn to adapt places to people. For a century or more, our work environment has been a slave to the demands of industrial processes. It is long past time for form to yield to function.

To accomplish this, we must learn to think of place as a variable, not a given. We must open ourselves to a host of new concepts of interior design, furniture, and workflow that enable idea generation, development, prototyping, testing, and deployment. The key is that we must reperceive our physical spaces as media through which people can collaborate and learn.

Think of the difference between a symphony hall and a jazz club. When you arrive at the symphony, you walk in holding a program of the pieces to be performed. You know the identity of the performers, approximately how long each piece of music will take, and pretty much what will happen. The occasional surprise in the form of an encore or a particularly wonderful or unforgettable performance in no way diminishes the pleasures of predictability. Symphony halls are closed systems. What you receive is a linear function of what you put in.

Jazz clubs, in contrast, are open systems. What you take out may bear only a vague and nonlinear relationship to your input. You don't know what the jazz musicians will play or how long the program will last. You know who the headliner is, but you don't know which other musicians might wander in and take the stage. And the music itself is always a surprise because the performers themselves don't know what will emerge until they jam with each other—blending a bit of the known (the tune) with the unknown (improvisation). Who could have foreseen that pianist Keith Jarrett, giddy with sleeplessness after a cross-Europe car trip, would get up on a concert hall stage in Germany and deliver two seamless solo improvisations that lasted twenty-six and forty minutes, respectively? Thankfully, his immortal 1975 Köln concert was recorded and is widely regarded as one of the great jazz recordings of all time.

Most businesses and governments have been set up like symphony halls. Physically, they are temples to a rigid and predictable method of working. In that model, innovation occurs incrementally—an experimental piece of music may occasionally be juxtaposed with a more familiar Beethoven symphony. I believe we need to study the jazz club in order to design more effective work spaces, and in turn, better methods of working together to produce more disruptive, game-changing innovation.

PLACE POWER

There is a wisdom of place.

Since time immemorial, humankind has been drawn to special places where, it is believed, one can tap into the mysterious unknown. Human beings have long believed that certain places—the Grand Canyon, Mont Blanc, Devil's Tower in Wyoming, the Ganges River—hold a mysterious power to enlighten the mind, inspire creativity, and awaken the soul to its true purpose. In many of these places, people have erected temples or other ritual structures: think of Delphi, Machu Picchu, Stonehenge, and the Pyramids. What makes these places special—in addition to their inherent qualities— is the fact that when we go there, we open ourselves to absorb what we don't know. We free ourselves of our preconceptions. Instead of talking, we allow the "wit and wisdom of the place," as an old Chinese saying puts it, to speak to us.

In today's world, these special places may also be separated from headquarters by geography to create a desired level of insulation from the main stream. Xerox, located in the corporate hub of Connecticut, chose to locate its advanced research facility in Palo Alto, in order to underline the importance of longer time horizons (and, possibly, longer hair). The Rand Corporation chose sunny Santa Monica as the site for its think tank. And the faculty of the U.S. Naval

Postgraduate School, which is located in Monterey, California, are said to relish their distance from Washington, D.C.

The notion of physical place as an architecture for knowledge is not new. In 1595, the Italian Jesuit Matteo Ricci went to China to spread Catholicism in that largely Confucian country. The priest realized that before he could even begin to persuade educated Chinese to abandon their traditional faith for his, he would have to prove the general superiority of Western culture. So, drawing on a tradition that dated to the ancient Greeks, Ricci told his students to arrange their knowledge—ideas, inventions, and wisdom—in an imaginary "memory palace."

Rooms became clumps of knowledge: The kitchen held X, the hallway held Y, the banquet hall Z. Every piece of knowledge was ordered according to volume, character, and juxtaposition to another. So dazzling was Ricci's method to the Chinese that he had the honor of becoming the first westerner invited into the imperial compound of the Forbidden City.

A SPACE, PERCHANCE TO DREAM

None of this is meant to suggest that we necessarily have to subscribe to mystical notions about the power of place. Rather, it is to note that if one wishes to tap into the unknown, it helps to work in a place where the imagination can soar. Most of us hunger at times for an unstructured place in which to dream. We tinker in our garages, play in our home-recording studios, and retreat to our dens.

Recently, I saw this hunger in that most practical and decidedly unmystical human creature, a navy admiral. His corner berth at the Office of Naval Research in Arlington, Virginia, was piled high with confidential documents. Aides waited in the corridor to do his bidding. At one point, he wearily leaned back in his chair. "You know what we need most around here?" he asked me. "We need something like Starbucks."

He was right. The navy needed what you might call a dream space—a space that was neither home (where one eats, sleeps, and raises children), nor personal office (where one works), nor conference room (in which formal agendas run the show). Cafés like Starbucks are just such a space. When one wants to dream, write poetry, foment a revolution, or fall in love, one goes to a café. There, all kinds of diverse elements are in play—the staff, the other customers, the ambience, the world beyond the windows—to help inspire your ideas and dreams. The interplay of personal and public space, combined with a sense that anything can happen, makes a café a great place for innovation to happen. No wonder the Office of Naval Research built its own version of Starbucks.

The great Dutch architect Herman Hertzberger saw the importance of a dream space forty years ago, when he designed the headquarters for the Centraal Beheer insurance group in Apeldoorn. Instead of a vast open plan or a maze of corridors with closed offices, Hertzberger took his inspiration from Italian hill towns. The group's offices included "streets" for circulation and every corner had informal spaces for meetings, coffee, or conversation. (Hertzberger was so disheartened by the determination of most companies to take a "managerial" approach to their offices that, later in his career, he turned almost exclusively to designing schools and cultural buildings.)

Organizations need a place where specific opportunities and projects can be explored in a freewheeling, no-intellectual-holds-barred manner. They need spaces designed to elicit questioning, discovery, experimentation, and prototype development. They need spaces that expand the mental boundaries, that balance openness with intention. Talent also requires the right blend of public and private space—the openness of a brainstorming room coexisting with the shelter of an individual studio environment. Obviously, employees also need time to perform this type of creative work. Having the right kind of setting can free up more time to be in the "zone."

What I have in mind is a kind of studio for innovation that re-
sembles the so-called skunk works some companies have set up, sites
where creative staffers can work in an environment with the exhilarating flavor of a start-up. There they have the freedom to generate
off-the-wall ideas, insulated at least temporarily from the immediate pressures of deadlines, standard-issue metrics, and corporate
oversight.

That was the modus operandi of the original Skunk Works, an
elite product development unit begun by Lockheed in 1943. Because
the Burbank, California, operation was downwind of a foul-smelling
plastics factory, staffers were reminded of the backwoods moonshine
still that was christened the "skonk works" in the then-popular *Li'l
Abner* comic strip. Over the years, the Lockheed Skunk Works
achieved miracles, including the creation in only 143 days of the first
prototype of the P-80 Shooting Star, America's first operational jet
fighter.

Skunk works are notable for the way they orchestrate activity in a
physical environment adapted for the purpose as well as for their
ability to insulate an embryonic innovation agenda from corporate interference. A skunk works is an elegant solution for an organization that needs to be—in the term devised by Stanford's Charles
O'Reilly and Harvard Business School's Michael Tushman—
ambidextrous. This involves staying focused, on the one hand, on
the operational realities of efficiency such as deadlines, metrics, and
accountability, while still reserving enough time for the white space
activity that activates the collective imagination and nurtures new,
valuable possibilities.

One of my favorite recent examples of a skunk works arose within
Motorola in 2003. At the time, the company was in the doldrums; its
leadership of the cell phone market had been challenged and then
erased by Nokia. But the company's engineers had come up with the
dream of a phone that might restore Motorola's fortunes. It was sup-

posed to be much thinner than any existing model and lovely to look at, like a piece of jewelry. But because of the corporation's deteriorating fortunes, the new phone had to be ready, in engineering terms, virtually overnight—twelve months.

An elite group of technical people and designers was assigned to create the new product. They set up shop in an unprepossessing office north of Chicago and miles from corporate headquarters, where they created a world unto themselves. It soon became evident that the team's twenty engineers could not accomplish their mission by simply aping existing phones in terms of design, materials, or circuitry. They rebelled against Motorola's usual business procedures, including the practice of consulting with the wireless providers that would sell the new product, and they kept their experiments secret from the rest of the organization. They sometimes fought with each other over proposed solutions, but they worked twelve-hour days to iron out their differences.

The team missed its one-year deadline by a few months or so, but they produced a phone that was supremely elegant and impossibly slim, with its backlit keypad and aluminum finish. They talked about calling it *Síliqua Patula*, Latin for razor clam, but settled for RAZR. It was as close to the company's dream phone as anyone could wish, and it was a commercial success. As of the end of 2006, Motorola had sold more than 100 million of the now iconic RAZRs.

Motorola's success with the RAZR, however, was a double-edged sword. Rather than capitalize on its breakthrough with further exciting innovations, the company chose instead to turn out pale incremental improvements of the RAZR—a new color, a new finish, a minor new add-on. Other companies quickly aped the RAZR style and produced their own innovations in a hypercompetitive free-for-all. The speed of competition in this industry is no joke; industry leader Nokia estimates that its new models enjoy no more than a thirty-day marketing window before being imitated. By early 2007, the once premium-priced RAZR was a cheap commodity and Motorola's share price was again on the skids.

Too often, companies think of the process of innovating a bold new product like the RAZR in terms of a big breakthrough, rather than as an ongoing mode of doing business. But if a small working group could come up with the RAZR in a little over a year's time, then why couldn't such a group perform similar feats of ingenuity again and again? We should be striving for more than a cosmetic change of workspace or a temporary shift in venue. We should want nothing less than a fundamental reshaping of our workspaces and a reframing of our organizational style.

One of the first bona fide dream spaces I discovered was at Oticon, a Danish manufacturer of hearing aids. In the early 1990s, I visited Oticon's lovely, three-tier loft space in an old Tuborg beer factory outside Copenhagen. The then-CEO, Lars Kolind, told me the company was focused on changing the way its 150 employees spent their days. His philosophy went something like this: "To succeed, we must be innovative. To be innovative, we must change the way we work." Kolind's vision was more than a whimsical ideal. When he became CEO in 1991, Oticon was a failing local manufacturer of analog hearing aids. Organizational transformation was intimately tied to revamping the company's performance, and Kolind correctly perceived that the design of the company's physical environment should be crafted to assist in that goal.

The company operated on a project basis. Teams were formed; they worked together; then they disbanded when the project was completed. The inventor of the project idea became the team leader and competed with other leaders for the people and resources needed to pursue the project's goals. A member of the ten-person management board advised but did not supervise the leader. As many as one hundred projects might be under way at any given time, and the CEO himself described the company as nothing more or less than a bag of projects supported by a thin layer of corporate resources.

But Kolind envisioned the company operating as a flat organization that could tap the creativity and efficiency of all his people in what he termed a "spaghetti" structure. The company's headquarters and its furnishings were tailored to accommodate that vision. Work stations and other office elements were set on wheels so that employees could move their work spaces around in response to the collaborative needs of the moment. Kolind himself was notorious for rolling his office about, locating opposite the marketing staff one week, hovering around technical developers the next.

Because their offices were on the move, employees relied on the intimacy of in-person conversation, the time-shifting e-mail, or the place-shifting mobile phone to get their messages and contact their colleagues. And since Kolind stressed the importance of direct contact, paper was virtually banned. Employees went each morning to a so-called paper room on the second floor, where they checked incoming snail mail. Discarded paper was tossed into a transparent tube that passed through the company canteen and ended at the shredder, a constant reminder of Kolind's anti-paper message. All other communication was in person, by phone, or digital.

As a result, Kolind told me, Oticon began creating new products at twice the speed of its competitors. It was the first company to launch a digital hearing aid and went from near-failure to a highly profitable corporation that boasted a quarter of the world market.

A similar approach to encouraging informality and collaboration can be seen in the recent Clark Center, which houses Stanford University's Bio-X program. Bio-X is interdisciplinary, bringing engineering, computer science, and physics to bear on biomedical issues. British architect Norman Foster designed its building with large, open laboratories containing benches and desks on wheels so new projects and lab equipment could be accommodated quickly. Bridges and balconies throughout the building help groups intermingle—in fact, people are required, by design, to get to know others outside their lab group. A large coffee bar and restaurant also ensures human circulation and increases the chance of collaboration across disciplinary boundaries.

An organization with employees numbering in the hundreds is one kind of management challenge. But can you apply these lessons to very large-scale enterprises? The answer is yes, as I learned in my work with the U.S. Navy's aircraft carrier program. Carriers bear a fabled history and legacy, yet that can be part of the problem as incumbent thinking clashes with the insurgency of new ideas.

Early on, I concluded that the organization lacked a space big and inspiring enough to host the kind of intense conversations that take place between shipbuilders and ship designers, for example, or between nuclear engineers and naval aviators. The solution was the design of the OASIS, which in our acronym-heavy government stands for Organizational Acceleration and Systems Innovation Space. The acronym is actually an accurate description of the room's function—to inspire creativity—and it truly became an oasis of creativity for those in the carrier program.

The space was spartan by the interior-design standards of business; it offered few creature comforts like expensive ergonomic chairs, flat-panel displays, or motorized projection screens. It did, however, have what is probably the biggest whiteboard in service in the military, measuring 40 feet by 9 feet. No matter how many people were working in the space, there was no problem making sure everyone knew what ideas were being hatched so long as they were entered on that board. And like the Oticon work spaces, OASIS was equipped with wheeled furniture that could be easily moved to create appropriate groupings of participants in brainstorming sessions. It has served as a safe place for considering a variety of challenges pertaining to the design of a physical and technical system as complex as a next-generation aircraft carrier.

BUILDING A DREAM SPACE

Think of your own dream space as a kind of internal marketplace in which resources such as capital, knowledge assets, enabling technology, best practices, access to Internet-based tools for search and collaboration, raw ideas, and people can be brought together and recombined in novel ways. It's a place where traditional corporate procedures collide with unconventional innovation techniques to create something new from the deconstructed parts—perhaps a fresh design for a familiar product or a master plan for reorganizing a company. It is a place in which public and private work coexist, albeit in sometimes new and fluid ways.

It starts, naturally enough, with a physical container: a floor of a building, an old warehouse, a repurposing of an existing community space such as a conference room. It is often more interesting to use a found space than to try designing a full-blown innovation studio from the ground up.

Dream spaces should be customized to particular applications and communities. A next-generation so-called fusion center for acting on military-grade intelligence, for example, will look different than the next iteration of a customer-experience and product-development room in a major advertising agency. Dream spaces, as innovations in themselves, should also be set up to evolve over time. One size definitely will not fit all circumstances. Much will depend upon the number of people who will use the space, the nature of their relationships as they carry out their work, the culture of the organization they work in, and the particular purpose to which the space is dedicated.

In most of today's offices, the furniture and the floor space are designed to box us in and keep our eyes, hands, and brains focused on the work in front of us, whether that work is on our computer screens, in our in-boxes, or sitting on the chairs in front of our desks. In a dream space, the furniture, tools, and partitioning of the environment via flexible or fixed elements are crucial to providing what you might call a "put-everything-on-the-table" environment. This can greatly enable the kind of integrative collaboration that can address wicked problems.

Instead of hiding behind an executive assistant, the desks, chairs, work surfaces, and other office elements might be put on wheels, à la Oticon. Or desks might be arranged in a circle so that everyone faces everyone else. Participants might be asked to sit in beanbag chairs or even, temporarily, on the floor—anything to move them away from their "normal" way of thinking and interacting. The result? Teams feel freed to jump on emergent agendas—ones half-formed or unclear—and develop them with more speed and flexibility, with less need to wait for approvals from above. They can immerse themselves in the work of discovery and allow projects to unfold over hours, days, or weeks without having to obey the scheduling dictates of the conference room. They can bring in the right people for the right tasks, just in time. And they can bring in all relevant viewpoints, no matter how divergent, to consider all aspects of a problem. They can also exploit the ability of a dream space to support rapid learning and collaboration by sharing their experiences with others and bringing them up to speed. In this fashion, form follows the need to imagine, rather than the dictates of efficient production.

Such design principles have always been characteristic of military situation rooms, air-traffic control centers, and Wall Street trading floors. But in today's fast-paced environment, it was no accident when New York mayor Michael Bloomberg decreed that his leadership team work in a similarly unstructured environment. Bloomberg calls it the bullpen, and it's bustling, open set of desks where everyone has a line of sight to everyone else. The mayor is right in the middle of the hubbub, a far cry from the typically grand and hushed mayoral suite.

Though it may seem somewhat implausible, simply finding the

right kind of furniture may be enough to break people out of their rigid, assigned roles and expectations, and may even render roles invisible. I remember the day the secretary of the navy and his entourage of fifteen people visited one of my previous innovation spaces. We put everyone—from the most junior to the most senior—in bleacher seats. It disrupted the status hierarchy, usually expressed by having the most senior person sit front and center, and it led to the possibility of a different, more informal and collegial conversation.

At the same time, the furniture and the whole physical ambience of the dream space should not be so "different" as to make participants feel uneasy or threatened. They have to feel comfortable enough to come forward with their thoughts. In this vein, I have always had offices that looked like living rooms. And David Rockwell, a pioneer in dazzling "event" design (he "papered" one wall in the Las Vegas branch of the Nobu sushi restaurant in dried seaweed), is legendary for going to flea markets to provision the spaces of his corporate clients with homey touches like oversized sofas and antique armoires.

Along the same lines, many of my M.B.A. students at Harvard remember that I festooned my office coffee table with a hundred Japanese windup toys. It was hard not to pick up and play with them, so the visiting student and I would share some version of a back-to-childhood experience. I would also sometimes glean valuable data about my visitors' personal style and state of mind. In the course of our play, their wary, watch-what-you-say, visiting-the-professor frame of mind would ease, and we would be able to communicate on a different, more meaningful level.

As ideas are generated, I find it immensely helpful to make them a visual part of the dream space environment. This allows the participants to see connections among ideas they might otherwise have missed. In my sessions, I see to it that innovative thoughts are writ large on huge sheets of paper and stuck up all around the room. The knowledge itself becomes part of the physical space—and, at the same time, available for others to manipulate and comment on. It becomes a graphic pathway to understanding what learning has taken place. David Sibbet, the father of graphic facilitation, refers to this as the ability to encourage the literal phenomenon of "I see what you mean." It is a way of sharing with newcomers and affirming accomplishments with existing participants. Everyone sees more and, in seeing more, is able to do more.

As a group moves toward consensus about a particular idea, it is vital to make assumptions and implicit ideas explicit—that is, public and shared. If I tell you an idea, you may not see all of the assumptions I am making—and to complicate matters further yet, you may insert a number of your own. But if I draw you a picture, build you a model, show you a computer-generated simulation, I am making our assumptions explicit so we can address them. By finding a concrete language to express our ideas, we prototype our possibilities, transforming abstract, intellectual, and private understandings into something concrete, something you can see and touch, comprehend and work with, on a different, deeper collective level.

A San Francisco–based company, Grove Consultants, founded by David Sibbet, has built a business model based on creating physical templates in the form of wall charts, which, once filled in, allow teams to visualize their collective understandings around such agendas as action plans, strategy, vision, mission, and desired future state. Such visuals could be considered a form of what I call "conceptual prototyping." For example, the client might visualize a new building design, organizational structure, workplace, or even a business model, supply chain, or set of customer relationships.

So a dream space should come equipped with facilitation expertise, as well as the media and expressive tools needed to make ideas concrete and visual, all housed in an environment that allows such tools to be flexibly deployed. Trained facilitation professionals can help teams make full use of dream space capabilities. In fact, all participants can benefit from facilitation training to enable the optimum use of these sophisticated tools, which are useless without sophisticated people who know how to use them.

At every juncture of the effort to loosen the imagination, whether it's in the early idea stage (when I sometimes display participants' suggestions on really big Post-it Notes scattered around the room) or in the prototyping (when I might form a clay model of the product design a group has arrived at), I firmly believe that the simpler and more straightforward the tools are, the better.

I recently suffered a bout of taxpayer heartburn when I looked at a catalog certified by the General Services Administration (GSA) for government procurement of office equipment. What I saw were $2,000 whiteboards and $1,000 pushpin surfaces. This is not only a potential waste of our money; it's also a wonderful way to keep the wings of imagination pinned down. Throwing money at the idea process smacks of the old way of using fancy tools to bring extra pressure on people to come up with a fancy idea. Personally, I like to use a thick marker and a lot of butcher paper.

On the other hand, there are times when I do rely on technology. Tools more frequently found in a preschool, like a roll of paper and thick marker pens, can be an excellent starter kit, but the insightful use of technology can lead to a qualitatively heightened and infinitely expandable form of collaboration. People may only be available to meet in person from time to time, but cyberspace is always on, enabling innovation collaboration to occur 24/7. We used to think that sending an e-mail to the person sitting at the next desk was exotic. Now we take it for granted. Indeed, the state of digital art now resides in chat rooms and social spaces—and not just those inhabited by hackers, antique car fanciers, and lonely hearts in Cleveland.

In the dream centers I've designed, technology is appropriately applied in support of a desired level of shared creativity. The large, computer-filled conference room can include groupware systems for electronic brainstorming, digital polling technology to track team opinions on various matters, and electronic whiteboards connected to high definition videoconferencing equipment enabled by effortless Internet access via a wireless network. You don't have to schedule a meeting through the video department. You can dial a number on your phone list, see colleagues in real time, and exchange ideas on the fly. With a budget of near-zero, you can use Skype to hold a multi-country videoconference.

And that's just the beginning. We can now create virtual worlds, building innovation-dedicated communities that can link with knowledge and other assets in new and unpredicted ways. I have built several bespoke innovation centers, for example, in the 3-D virtual world known as Second Life.

Just imagine: A dozen corporate executives need to meet to hash out some new topside directives, but they're located in offices all over Asia, Europe, and the United States. Instead of traveling to corporate headquarters, instead of videoconferencing, they all sign on to Second Life. All of them have previously designed their own avatars, animated personas that represent them in this virtual world. The avatars can be easily moved about to meet people, attend events, and buy everything from a T-shirt to a house using virtual money. With a little practice using a simple computer programming language, you can actually, as the Web site promises, "Sculpt a butterfly, then write a short chunk of code that lets it follow you around as you walk."

Sounds like science fiction, right? Well, a host of companies are using Second Life as a new environment for experimentation. American Apparel, the Los Angeles-based clothing manufacturer with one hundred forty retail stores, has a virtual store where virtual versions of its T-shirts and leggings are sold for virtual dollars. Starwood has set up a concept hotel and invites avatars to take a tour and let the company know how they like its features. And Toyota opened a virtual car dealership in Second Life to spark both interest and creativity with its youth-oriented Scion brand. In the futuristic, gritty Scion City, avatars spend about three hundred Linden dollars for a Scion (about $1.08 at current exchange rates) which is then completely customizable—Scion's designers in turn get a window into a host of weird and sometimes viable user-created ideas.

IBM and other companies have also explored the business potential of virtual worlds in Second Life. What are they doing in this virtual playworld? They are experimenting with interaction models of relationships among their suppliers, customers, and employees. Unlike mathematical simulations that could be carried out using conventional tools, IBM uses Second Life to simulate entire ecosystems, each one changing as streams of data flow in from the real world to the virtual and back again. Listen to Irving Wladawsky-Berger, IBM's vice president for technical strategy and innovation (whose avatar in Second Life is Irving Islander): "We are poised for the next major step. We can now bring these exciting capabilities . . . into the worlds of business, education, health care, and government . . . Could we be at the onset of v-business?"

Elsewhere, new software is enabling simulation and gaming with vast production value (*Lord of the Rings* meets military-grade software) that can greatly facilitate innovation. Complex simulation enables us to peer into the realm of what we don't know we don't know. For example, Alok Chaturvedi, an associate professor of management information systems at Purdue's Krannert Graduate School of Management, began working with Pentagon war-gaming experts to develop business simulations for the school. Chaturvedi and his colleagues came up with SEAS, for Synthetic Environments for Analysis and Simulation. They have spun off SEAS into a commercial company, Simulex, which now works with businesses like pharmaceutical group Eli Lilly and defense giant Lockheed Martin, as well as a host of military clients. Give Simulex three weeks for research, and

it can build an artificial world for an entire industry. Up to two hundred players can compete in the games, each representing a different
company. An agribusiness simulation designed by Simulex, for example, includes product seeds, crop-protection service warranties,
financing, and interaction among competitors and their channels of
distribution.

Complex simulations are also part of Singapore's national agenda.
The government team responsible for digital media has commissioned a complete digital rendering of the island republic, intended
as a test bed for new business models in commerce and tourism, for
example. Companies could use digital Singapore to explore, say, novel
approaches to traffic management or to examine the impact of a new
high-tech zone. By layering rich data over what we observe in our ev-
eryday environment, Singapore is in an excellent position to experiment with what I have called "blended reality," in which the physical
landscape and digital objects are seamlessly layered together.

Novel simulations aren't just for business. The United Nations
World Food Program (WFP) developed Food Force, a free, downloadable game, to teach users about the intricacies and challenges of
food assistance programs. Mike Harrison, the designer, describes
Food Force as "somewhere between a game like Tomb Raider and a
lecture from the WFP." Food Force opens with a short movie that
explains a crisis in an imaginary country due to drought and civil war.
Players are required to complete a series of missions, ranging from
dropping food parcels from the air to a Sim City–type game where
players use food aid to rebuild the country's economy. The lessons
are driven home by a short video at the end of each mission explaining how the WFP would have handled the situation. When Food
Force was launched on Yahoo Games in 2005, it became the number
one game, with 1 million downloads in two months.

These kinds of technologies allow users, regardless of location, to
collaborate in such a way that knowledge and processes are shared

rather than dictated. And they contribute to what MIT's Michael Schrage has called "hyperinnovation," the ability of organizations that have mastered digital simulation to reap the rewards of being able to experiment, prototype, and iterate at a speed inconceivable in the physical world.

The well-known technology researcher, designer, and writer Brenda Laurel, who works in the field of human-computer interaction, has observed—and I think accurately—that the computer screen is a theater with a proscenium stage defined by the computer cabinet. Now, the day is coming when our dream spaces will be fully architected, completely immersive virtual worlds that will serve as digital containers encompassing and supporting our people, our resources, our processes, and our emergent ideas.

However, with all this, I don't want to leave the impression that technology is the only or necessarily the best route to innovation. It does however provide organizations with a much broader palette of tools for conceptual prototyping, mental rehearsal, and what knowledge management expert David Snowden calls "sense-making"—the collective application of individual intuition to identify changes in existing patterns. And the power and scale of these tools is evolving at the speed of Moore's Law.

While physical rehearsal and simulation will always be vital, the availability of digital simulation tools also allows for enhanced experimentation and learning. This is especially true in a world in which the silos of learning, operations, and research are merging. The model for what we are evolving toward might be the F-16 pilot, someone who is simultaneously gathering information relevant to a mission (learning), integrating that knowledge into a mission plan (operations), while the information streams back to an integration center for analysis (research) to tease out patterns and insights that will guide a next wave of strategic decision making and investment.

Once the work of inspiring innovative ideas is done, the dream space, ideally, can also serve as a publishing and media production center. It's no good having new ideas without powerful tools to disseminate them, and the communications department in most organizations is boxed into conventional, outmoded practices. Put the idea generators in your dream space together with constituents from throughout the organization and allow team members to tell their imaginative stories, which can also be captured on the fly via digital video, streaming Internet media, storyboards, or graphic recording. That will give you the potential to generate a lot of passion as well as alignment throughout the organization and beyond.

As described in these pages, dream spaces can also be the engines that link networks of innovation facilities to enable the sharing of learning experiences, best practices, and breaking news in a distributed mode of collaboration that is indifferent to the effects of geography. And as our ability to store knowledge assumes an increasingly compact form, the simplest spaces can be the twenty-first-century equivalents of the ancient Library of Alexandria and twentieth-century media studio rolled into one.

In fact, the logarithmic improvements in information storage technology suggest that we will be able to carry a significant part of the world's entire store of information around on a pendant-sized device at some point later in this century. With such immense resources available, each node of a network will have greatly amplified power, and the capabilities of the network as a whole will be hugely augmented.

Creating a practical and inspirational dream space should be thought of as a continuous improvement process. It inevitably involves trial and error—there are just so many imponderables. You need to be agnostic and experimental, assuming that there will be elements that will be inefficient, messy, even counterproductive. Above all, the place of innovation should represent freedom for those who go there—an ultimate jazz club for ideas, a place where participants can breathe.

The more collaborative, flexible styles of working I've been discussing in this chapter are in fact coalescing—thanks primarily to the Internet—into a truly radical new form of production that is fundamentally challenging the notion of top-down management. This is the brave new world of bottom-up, social Internet, social networking, and social innovation, which we will explore in the next chapter.

SEVEN

THE "US" IN USA

In a world of many eyeballs, all bugs are shallow.
—Eric Raymond, open source pioneer

You've probably never heard of Yuri Maslyukov. He had the distinction of being the last leader of Gosplan, the huge organization devoted to drawing up the Soviet Union's five-year plans. Teams of experts high up in the bureaucracy at Gosplan meticulously combed over every statistic and report from industry and agriculture before issuing their directives to the masses below. Surely a collection of brilliant minds with access to oceans of data was a foolproof recipe for economic success. Yet, the former Soviet Union, among other followers of central planning, came to realize that a closed, top-down planning approach was a recipe for disaster.

History shows that closed societies like Stalin's Soviet Union, Franco's Spain, and Hitler's Germany seldom survive much beyond their ruler-driven story lines. Airless throne rooms—whether at Enron or the Kremlin—breed rot and complacency. Soviet music students, a colleague told me, often transcribed a soloist's improvised notes as they listened to jazz records, then studied them as if they were pieces of music composed in advance by Bach or Chopin. But their rote reproduction completely went against the essence of jazz, which celebrates the free expression of musical talent in the moment. No wonder the centrally planned Soviet Union couldn't compete with decentralized market economies; the jazz of capitalism simply couldn't be reproduced in a closed system that relied exclusively on Politburo-dictated five-year plans.

This chapter argues that the nothing is more inimical to the United States' national innovation agenda than opacity and the belief that those organizations prosper best that control most and hide their knowledge from outsiders. The truth lies almost always precisely in the opposite direction. Thanks in no small part to extraordinary changes wrought by the Internet and related communication technologies, we have discovered that innovation and sizable profits can flow from adding openness to your business model.

Open businesses are increasingly trading ideas with their competitors, customers, and other outsiders, showing a mutual receptivity to new ways of thinking and multiplying innovation and benefits for all participants with unprecedented speed. Companies that know how to encourage the bubbling up of ideas, internally or from an outside community of experts, advisers, or opinionated consumers, will expand their base of imaginative assets. Nokia, Procter & Gamble, Salesforce.com, and Google are just a few of the practitioners of openness as a business model. The mainstream is not far behind. In fact, in a recent study by IBM, CEOs surveyed considered their employees to be the most significant sources of innovative ideas, followed by business partners, customers, consultants, competitors, and trade associations. Internal R & D came in a distant eighth.

Openness, as we now know, is also an essential component of the creative climate that produces national growth and vibrant societies—and it is a climate in which American ingenuity thrives. We have a lot of historical and cultural experience with what might be called "open-source innovation," the kind that can come from anywhere in a meritocracy of talent.

The literal meaning of open source is this: cooperatively produced software with source code that is free, open to the world, and continuously improved by users. Legendary hacker Richard Stallman defines the "free" in the sense of free speech, not free beer. By any definition, it's an approach that competes with proprietary operating-system providers like Microsoft. It is also the inspiration for the transparency this book endorses, an environment that allows many peers to operate freely in the marketplace, to access information and collaborative opportunities with and among organizations, unhindered by top-down direction based solely on the bureaucratic status of those in charge.

It would be naive to proclaim that the end of top-down business and society has arrived, or that bottom-up is all good and top-down all bad. All organizations have to maintain a balance between the two models, a balance that tends to shift as they evolve. Military futurists John Arquilla and David Ronfeldt use the term "guarded openness" to refer to the balancing act that is required to keep some things guarded, while others can be shared. In their view, the art is figuring out which is which.

How open or closed an organization's models are also depends to some extent on their level of development. At their birth, organizations are likely to be flat with a minimal chain of command and simplicity of intent. However, as they become more complex, with additional lines of business and greater numbers of people, they need direction and more ways of integrating a widening array of agendas. Ultimately, a much longer and involved chain of command comes into being. In other words, the top-down model is, in an organizational sense, a response to the need to deal with complexity. And from that need has emerged the complex, formal, command-and-control systems of management that have for so long ruled the corporate and government roosts.

But today's reality is that innovation process must blend top-down *and* bottom-up approaches. What's essential is how well the new blend meets both the need to make complexity manageable and the need to harness an organization's full ability to generate creative variety, and to bring the fruits back into the mainstream to create value. In that regard, disintermediation has become a business model. In the case of the rapidly changing music industry, for example, how about going directly from artist to fan, bypassing the traditional lineup of music publishers, record companies, and distributors—all with palms extended, waiting to be greased? New models can be crafted by taking out the middleman and reducing the traditional layered complexity of systems that may slow down the business process with their "friction" and overhead.

Such innovation requires a dogma-free environment that is characterized by transparency and equality of opportunity, qualities that are woven into our American ethic. This, I believe, is one of the main reasons we have a serious shot at creating Innovation Nation, which will thrive in the kind of open-air culture that favors the success of grassroots ideas and entrepreneurs. In fact, successful innovation today is profoundly democratic, and it is enabled by the kind of technologies I'm about to describe—technologies that largely originated in the United States and, if harnessed and fully exploited, can significantly add to our national innovation capabilities.

SURFING THE FIFTH WAVE

The digital era, already nearly a half-century old, has been divided by technology writer Michael Copeland into five "waves," starting with the 1960s, when huge mainframe computers became part of the corporate arsenal. Minicomputers succeeded those first ugly monsters in the 1970s; personal computers followed in the 1980s; and the Internet, with all its potential for networking, in the 1990s. But if hardware generally dominated the first four waves of computing, the current fifth wave is quite different. Fed by three big changes—

falling computer prices, increasingly pervasive broadband, and the move to social software that opens up new collaborative possibilities—the fifth wave vastly magnifies everyone's access to nearly limitless content, whether it be online information, community opinion, services, or entertainment.

The fifth wave has brought with it a world in which a huge percentage of people in any public place are either massaging laptops or chatting on cell phones, often driving others crazy with unedited effluvia of unearned intimacy. But all this cyberchatter reflects a profound change in human relations. Like it or not, more and more of us are unavoidably connected to each other by chain reactions of digital interactions that—through the power of growing networks—generate more connections between people, more perspectives brought to bear on problem solving, and, most important, more opportunities to consider.

The driving force here is openness. Unlike most previous innovators, fifth-wave leaders see far greater profit in sharing their savvy than in hoarding it. And users are quick to grab the opportunities presented. Sharing can attract a like-minded community of developers whose desire to create can coexist with the self-interest served by adding additional layers of value. The result can be a huge efflorescence of follow-up applications and related products created by lead users and other tinkerers, as companies like Amazon, eBay, and Google can attest. Rather than being centrally controlled, the development process often winds up looking like an ongoing, old-fashioned barn raising, with all the neighbors taking part, or perhaps a gold-rush fantasy in which the prospectors have quit competing and are helping each other to get rich. With so many smart people thronging cyberspace and discovering how to tailor it to their own needs, the Web's users (over a billion and counting) have made a quantum leap from occasional surfing to intense searching, from solitary reading to group activism, from introspection to collaboration. This is the deep significance of what many are referring to as Web 2.0.

Web 1.0, with its search engines and e-commerce, was an "I" phenomenon. Web 2.0 is an "us." If Web 1.0 was about what "I" could do, then Web 2.0, a term popularized by technology publisher Tim O'Reilly, is about what "we" can do, or what you think of what I've blogged or posted. People are running their own news blogs and podcasts, and launching common-interest networks using photosharing sites such as Yahoo's Flickr. Here's an astonishing fact: one out of three South Koreans—16 million people—has a personalized home page on a social networking site called Cyworld.com. At the similar U.S.-based MySpace.com, 67 million monthly visitors, as of 2007, spent countless hours a day sharing ideas, music, and photographs with like-minded friends. And an astonishing 52 percent of American young people surveyed by the Pew Foundation have created content for the Internet, a fact that provides ample proof of just how widespread the Web 2.0 phenomenon is.

Ross Mayfield, chief executive officer of Socialtext, a pioneer in online collaboration, sees the fifth-wave Web as no longer an imagined place but a literal doorway to countless services—from Craigslist classifieds to Meetup activism. On his own blog, Mayfield described the new scene: "They Google, Flickr, blog, contribute to Wikipedia, Socialtext it, Meetup, post, subscribe, feed, annotate, and above all, share. In other words, the Web is increasingly less about places and other nouns, but verbs." And by the time you read this, a whole new crop of such services will have emerged.

Openness is a direct outcome of network technology and the transparency that tends to come with it. The result is shifting responsibility and control—and not just in the technical specialty of software development, but in society itself. Where once experts voices were the only ones heard, now we all can have our say. As one digital sage put it recently, we are witnessing a dispersal of the "right to fork," geekspeak for the freedom to go our own way.

The transformation from a top-down to an open, user-created world is suggestive of the stark contrast between purely mechanical and biological systems. Mechanical systems—production lines, for instance—require top-down direction. They need blueprints and master builders, as well as directors, auditors, and coordinators. Biological systems—beehives, let's say—often exhibit what Kevin Kelly, *Wired* magazine founding editor, famously called "out-of-control behavior." They are systems without a center, without an overall director or coordinator, but that nevertheless exhibit complex adaptive and emergent behavior when confronted with something new or threatening. They represent a new, accelerated form of what I have taken to calling "social innovation." And this is the significance of the Internet, which, in short, is making it possible for people to interact and create in entirely new and collaborative ways. Digital technology thus enables what in time we will recognize as a digital nervous system for innovation.

Diversity of perspective has long been recognized as a spur to creativity. Participants may vary in terms of such basics as their gender, age, sociodemographics, and geography, not to mention their discipline base, level of expertise, and life experience. In a military context, different ranks and specialties enforce a kind of diversity; in a political environment, a mix of national or regional participants and parties will often do the trick. In a corporate setting, diversity is achieved by bringing together stakeholders who don't often have a chance to interact in the normal course of events—representatives of both the public and private sectors, customers and suppliers, think-tank gurus and academics.

Diversity also directly influences the power and richness of open innovation. The greater the variety, the wider the range of issues considered and the fundamentally more innovative the process. Diversity will also increase the likelihood that a process will deal meaningfully with the kind of wicked problems the world now faces. Including all stakeholders and all points of view is hard work, but it is the kind of democratizing of innovation that shows us the way toward wicked solutions.

Networks and network technology provide the means for integrating various perspectives and supporting consideration of the ideas that emerge from the mix. This is especially true when networks become porous, that is, when they admit others besides card-carrying members of the network—for example, alumni or customers, friends, interested parties, or even critics and competitors.

Diversity, however, is just the first step. Technology also enables transparency—in essence, a way for you to know and see what I know and see. This is critical to open innovation. Such transparency is wired directly into the workings of new forms of social software, such as bookmarking tools. These days, we can put a digital tag on anything we find interesting as we browse through the infinite pages of cyberspace and tuck it away for later use. Imagine that you are an expert on Czech hedge funds, Chinese missle defense, or Scandinavian trance music. If you open your collection of bookmarks to other people through a social bookmarking site like del.icio.us, they can "subscribe" to your knowledge base on these topics as represented by your digital tags. And any time you add something new to your list of tags, your subscribers will be notified in real time. Look for this feature to be embedded soon in the way search engines, and Web-surfing in general, operate.

If the initial stage of creativity is defined as interest, or anything that claims our attention, then the transparency that defines social bookmarking is a way of vastly augmenting a community's ability to be creative; it stokes and multiplies interest in new phenomena. And interest is also a fundamental precursor to spotting anomalies. It is the first step in forming a warning or horizon-scanning system and is directly related to Eric Raymond's open-source credo quoted at the beginning of this chapter, which holds that, "in a world of many eyeballs, all bugs are shallow." Here, "many eyeballs" refers both to quantity and quality, to the diversity of perspectives that can help us recognize and respond to anomalies that may arise.

Things get even more interesting when such expressions of interest are aggregated to show trends in the tags available for observation by a whole group, and when the tagging trends within the group itself become transparent. Wouldn't it be interesting to know, for example, that the interest in topic X came from researchers in a particular company's lab? Or perhaps from people at a corporate level well placed to fund a new initiative? A continuous monitoring of its employees' tagging habits enables an organization to know what it knows and to become aware of what it is interested in, as patterns of meaning-laden interactions begin to emerge. Such knowledge can inform decision making in entirely new ways.

Finally, innovation is driven not only by what we know we don't know (something we may research someday), but also by what we don't know we don't know (something that comes out of the proverbial left field). What is emergent is frequently our most important agenda item—and the most elusive. And such serendipitous generation of knowledge becomes possible through a combination of transparency, diversity, and the ability to connect to other people in ever more powerful ways. That combination is inherently woven into Internet search functions. We typically search online when we know little or nothing about something and would like to know more. The answers we get build our knowledge, taking us that much closer to a new idea or insight. But we realize additional and hidden value when our search engine surprises us: we may happen upon data we never dreamed existed, or link with someone or a group of someones who have a radically different perspective from our own, or become part of an emergent community opinion.

Such principles of open innovation are significant for their broad sweep. Their application is hardly confined to high-technology and software development. Open innovation is already under way in fields as diverse as politics, education, and health care, among others. They will be key to the task of taking America's national innovation capability in new directions.

TRANSFORMING THE MILITARY

Openness as an attitude, a way of maximizing innovation, is also being used to striking effect by the U.S. military and intelligence communities. Those in charge of keeping us safe know, for example, that combating the nontraditional, less clear-cut threats posed by terrorism requires that we harness the power of the nation's military, intelligence, and first responder capabilities as a whole.

The popular comic-book writer and novelist Warren Ellis has captured this point in *Global Frequency*, his series of graphic novels set in the near future. The Global Frequency of the title is a bottom-up, networked organization of 1,001 participants, mostly freelancers and part-timers—except for a leader and a communications special-ist—who take on problems that no one else wants or is able to deal with. With their portrayal of just-in-time team collaboration and what I call porous networks, the books are a harbinger of the kind of changes that our intelligence community will need to undergo over the coming decade.

When I first began working with military and intelligence profes-sionals in the 1990s, I discovered that more than a few were skepti-cal about the hierarchical, top-down mind-set that had guided their elders during the Cold War. They no longer trusted the old way, which dictated that leaders would be the repositories of all knowl-edge and that foot soldiers would simply be dispatched to execute orders from on high. Roles were being rejiggered. In Afghanistan after September 11, 2001, for example, the military and intelligence communities relied not only on conventional units but also on elite operatives on horseback who were equipped with cultural as well as military intelligence, which they used to track adversaries and call in precisely the right "support" at any given moment, whether it be money, information, or B-52 air strikes.

In 2002, I attended a national security conference in Washington entitled "Towards an Ecology of Warning." Its central premise was that safeguarding our nation today demands a warning system far beyond the scope of a handful of ivory tower experts. An open-source world in which millions of eyes, ears, and brains are paying attention provides important new capabilities to spot potential threats and solve real problems.

Certainly, intelligence has been a keystone of statecraft ever since nation-states came into being. The United States formed the Office of Strategic Services (OSS) during World War II in response to the need for an entrepreneurial intelligence capability that would bypass traditional organizational silos and empower entrepreneurs and in-novators. Led by the legendary Colonel Bill Donovan, the OSS re-ported directly to President Franklin D. Roosevelt, thus obeying one of the main principles of a skunk works, namely, short lines of com-munication to the seat of an organization's power.

In 1947, the OSS was dissolved and the United States created the Central Intelligence Agency to capture data that would be deemed useful in the Cold War era. There was a certain symmetry and stabil-ity in the massed armies and nuclear arms the two competing giants aimed at each other across various national boundaries—the Ivy League leaders of the "Company" engaged in a chess game with the "cardinals" of the Kremlin. The work of intelligence largely involved looking for slight inconsistencies in large amounts of usually stable data. (Today's geeks would call it "looking for bugs" or anomalies that suggest the need for a shift in perspective.) Perceiving large-scale trends was not as high a priority in the glacial dance of the su-perpowers. The threat was real, but our adversaries were bureaucratic, rule-bound, and relatively slow to change.

This model of intelligence was practiced in cathedral-like institutions, with the elite thinkers, conceptualizers, and ideologues gazing down from the top of the organization, much like the officials of a church hierarchy. People in the operational sphere were the foot soldiers—or, to continue the analogy, the laity—whose orders were based on tightly compartmentalized information distributed on a need-to-know basis.

Today, however, the main U.S. adversaries are not flag-carrying nation-states but loosely coupled networks that resemble nothing so much as a swarm of bees. They are fast, lean, and innovative, with a distressing lack of palpability. Most important, our adversaries are networked from the get-go, and they use publicly available Internet tools to stay in touch and coordinate action. When your local Internet café becomes your command center, MySpace your letter drop, and Google Earth your reconnaissance toolbox, then intelligence becomes a commodity that anyone can have. Welcome to intelligence by Kmart.

Meanwhile, our own national security apparatus is often hamstrung even in its ability to do something as mundane as use the public Internet or to provide effective Internet connections between various intelligence agencies, whose professionals are often marooned on the equivalent of digital islands.

That is changing. To analyze terrorist dangers abroad, intelligence professionals are learning to take the pulse of entire communities at ground level using an ever-increasing ability to scan oceans of communications traffic. It is the difference between listening at a single café and listening at a marketplace. As one officer explained to me, "This isn't about spotting big, obvious things like missiles in Cuba. It's about spotting the fanatic who has a brother who's a chemist who has a friend with a van who has a cousin who can forge a passport."

The influence of the grassroots, networked approach is visible in preparations for the battlefield as well. In the 1970s and 1980s, in response to our disheartening and divisive slog through Vietnam, new doctrines of warfare were developed to increase the agility and flexibility of our troops. The latest models of so-called network-centric warfare will rely upon communication networks that enable foot soldiers in a sector to instantly share with one another their descriptions of the terrain and their interactions with the enemy. Armed with this real-time, networked data, they can often outperform their opponents in the so-called OODA loop (the acronym is short for "observe, orient, decide, and act"), which was introduced by maverick Air Force colonel John Boyd as a tactical device for dogfighting fighter pilots, The self-synchronization that results enabled decisions and actions to be taken more independently, without using precious seconds or minutes to seek approval through the hierarchy. The OODA concept also has vast strategic application. One might say, for example, that Boeing got inside Airbus's OODA loop by waiting until the latter were committed to double-decker planes before responding by building more efficient, smaller airlines that go point-to-point, rather than relying on aviation hubs.

An increasing reliance on the grassroots can be found elsewhere in the military as the army and navy try to find ways to cut through bureaucracy. The traditional chain of command, from generals to lieutenants to privates, was necessary to ensure that units would continue to function in battle and communicate effectively when casualties potentially disrupted the hierarchy. But it tended to slow decision making and discourage risk taking. Today, efforts are under way to flatten the pyramid.

In its after-action reviews, for example, the army requires both officers and soldiers to discuss what went right and wrong with a particular action or program. Lessons learned are transmitted to other parts of the organization and codified for future reference. In addition, two army majors, Nate Allen and Tony Burgess, created CompanyCommand.com in 2000 to help captains, who typically command companies of one hundred to two hundred soldiers, share critical knowledge gained through real-life operational experience. The site, and a companion for lieutenants, PlatoonLeader.org, was launched without any official support. But in 2002, the army recognized the value of this bottom-up initiative and brought the sites into what it calls the Battle Command Knowledge System (BCKS) on the secure Army.mil domain.

Battle group chat is another mechanism for wide-open peer-to-peer communication. It began as a way for young sailors in battle groups at sea to enter discussions in secure chat spaces about anything from exchanging films for movie night to checking supply levels and working out other quality-of-life issues. Over time, it evolved into a much larger horizontal capability for coordination and communication among battle groups. Eventually, it ran afoul of tradition; people down below were making decisions that had been the prerogative of the higher-ups.

Despite such misgivings, though, battle group chat has been brought into the navy mainstream and serves today as a critical tool in coordinating complex operations—including major campaigns that can involve several hundred chat rooms. Such publish-and-subscribe, opt-in systems for creating fluidity and flexibility in combat are playing an ever larger role in today's military planning.

The kind of transparency and openness that is increasingly needed to keep us safe is also good for business as well. The laurels go to companies that have learned the lessons of "bottom up."

BUSINESS NEEDS "US," TOO

As far back as 1984, businessman Jan Carlzon pioneered the application of open principles in business when he took over as CEO of Scandinavian Airlines System. SAS was awash in red ink, and Carlzon pinpointed its core issue as a lack of customer focus. The novel concepts he introduced in his quest to heal the ailing airline have since become legendary.

To begin with, the new chief executive determined to turn the traditional business pyramid on its head. He made it his top priority to bring frontline workers into contact with customers, and to teach them how to sense, and promptly respond to, problems. SAS, Carlzon memorably remarked, was nothing more than 50 million moments of truth every year, a reference to the points of contact between service providers and customers. He even entitled his manifesto for the SAS turnaround *Moments of Truth.*

Armed with a firm belief that people on the front lines know best, Carlzon decreed that they be empowered to make decisions with a minimum of interference. His words and actions were prophetic, coming as they did at least a decade before the Internet was even a dot on the landscape of commerce. The eventual arrival of the Internet amplified the importance of Carlzon's ideas, because it expanded the organizational pyramid and resulting conversational space to infinite size while also further flattening it. With new digital linkups, the distance between players at the top and bottom shrank, while the number of participants in the conversation increased.

Years after Carlzon's breakthrough, Amazon.com's chief executive, Jeff Bezos, went one step further, shaking the foundations of business when he and his top team debated whether to invite outsiders to share the $7 billion online retailer's most valuable asset—a huge database containing a decade's worth of customer reviews, prices, sales rankings, inventories, and so forth. This was the treasure Amazon had spent more than $1 billion to create and protect from competitors, the secrets of its success that outside entrepreneurs and programmers would give anything to scavenge.

Traditionalists were aghast, but Bezos argued that opening up Amazon was precisely the way to capitalize on its knowledge. By allowing smart outsiders to sample the information like a giant hors d'oeuvre tray, he reasoned, Amazon would inspire many to build new Web sites that could lead to potentially profitable partnerships for Amazon. Instead of being squirreled away in a hidden cache, Amazon data would become a dynamic engine driving the company's expansion. Bezos called it the ultimate non-zero-sum business model.

Some of his colleagues still needed convincing. They feared the effects of handing out the keys to the kingdom too freely. Where would it all end? But the debate bored Bezos, and he soon dismissed the doubters. With typical gusto, according to *Fortune*, he flung open his arms like a flasher spreading a raincoat and wisecracked: "We're going to aggressively expose ourselves!"

His instinct was dead-on. More than two hundred thousand digital foragers have since responded to an open-data site called Amazon Web Services, which was started in 2002. About one-third have used the company's free software to create hundreds of new moneymaking Web sites and shopping interfaces that link Amazon's eight hundred thousand independent sellers and their customers. Many of the digital developers have become Bezos's most ambitious business partners overnight. What was an experiment four years ago is now "a core part" of Amazon's strategy, says its former chief technology officer, Al Vermeulen.

Amazon's breakthrough is contagious. In the year after Bezos declared open house for all, eBay invited software developers to shake and bake the company's 33 million weekly auction transactions. Some fifteen thousand developers have since registered to use those listings and other software features. Nearly half of eBay's listings are now uploaded to the innovative sites they've built, allowing other Web businesses to tap into eBay's transaction databases and to list eBay auctions. This also sharply boosts market access for eBay customers.

Many of these new spin-offs are examples of what are termed "mash-ups." My old mentor Frank Zappa created a technique he dubbed "xenochrony," taking a guitar solo from one song and putting it in an entirely different song. This kind of musical mash-up has a long tradition, but the newer version has recently been transforming the way we use the Internet.

Mash-ups in the digital domain are combinations of data from a variety of sources put together in a novel way. So Chicagocrime.org, for example, takes data from the Chicago Police Department and overlays it on Google Maps so you can see—either in horror or relief—where crime occurs. Mash-ups are made possible by clever software frameworks called APIs (Application Programming Interfaces), which allow another program to grab data from storehouses like Google Maps, eBay's auctions, Amazon.com's product database, or Flickr's vast trove of photographs. Web sites like ProgrammableWeb.com track new mash-ups, which are proliferating by the dozens each week.

Mash-ups are part of what is embedding Google on the Internet at every turn. The team that developed Google Maps published the API that allows others to connect their programs to Google's application, and, to date, some forty-three thousand developers have added something on top of Google Maps to create digital mash-ups that enable new sorts of applications. For example, a mash-up of Google Maps and classified real estate ads gives users a bird's-eye view of the locations of houses for sale in a given neighborhood. Ditto the locations of ATMs, emergency rooms, and restaurants. There's even a mash-up to help the transgendered find gender-neutral washrooms.

What's emerging as a result is a radically new kind of business organization. It looks nothing like a *Fortune* 500 corporation, ensconced in its glass high-rise soaring seventy-five floors to the CEO's lavish aerie somewhere in the ozone layer above a major metropolitan area. The new model is basically an effortlessly expandable software platform that can include an infinitely broad array of customers and constituents. Scores of other businesses can log on to the platform and use it for selling related products and services. In the process, the participants constantly expand their markets while making their own customers ever more accessible to other participants. In short, the pyramid can become almost completely flat and its bottom layer infinitely large. Call it the new souk, a kind of digital bazaar that especially appeals to computer-savvy merchants and shoppers alike.

What this platform does best is enable participants to share their vital data. Thanks to web services, with their new software standards such as XML (extensible markup language), Web sites can exchange data and other functions automatically. Using the API skeleton keys, an online business like Amazon allows its data to be meshed with those of smaller online partners to create something new, which can be accessed and manipulated to multiply the market reach of all participants. Joining forces magnifies business for all members.

According to eBay, its fifteen thousand registered developers have already produced more than one thousand new services, the most popular of which enable sellers to automate the once laborious process of displaying their wares on eBay or other sites. Going further, some developers like Marketworks and Vendio offer eBay sellers their own auction services, piggybacked onto the eBay site. They are said to boost the sellers' productivity by an estimated 50 percent. The same data linking allows sellers to create virtual stores on eBay and skip the high cost of leasing brick-and-mortar shops. These digital storefronts, filled with visual inventory and easy transaction links, make it feasible for a seller to create a national chain of outlets without owning a single physical store.

The virtual world created by Second Life, discussed in the previous chapter, is another compelling example of open innovation. The people and companies inside Second Life are creating virtual retail businesses, conducting language training, and collaborating on a broad front. "Residents," currently expanding at a rate of a million per month, are busy having all kinds of fun; as of March 2007, they were spending 15 million hours per month in the Second Life environment. A favored form of activity is generating content others can use, whether it's virtual houses and clothing, scripts for autohypnotic training, textures that allow you to pick just the right kind of sand for your virtual beach, or myriad other products and services. Had this work been done by paid professionals, Second Life would have had to hire thousands of full-time people, compared to the one hundred forty it had on its payroll at the time of this writing.

At its best, Second Life is an emergent, bottom-up community that uses virtual meeting spaces and other social technologies to build new forms of participatory democracy and virtual capitalism. By early 2007, the daily volume of commerce in Second Life was over $2 million, and Second Life now boasts real-life millionaires, suggesting that "opt-in" is indeed a business model.

The birthrate of these new fifth-wave, open businesses is brisk. Though many never reach the toddler stage, the winners typically have a gift for spotting anomalies, unserved needs, or gaps in the marketplace that, in turn, suggest niches of opportunity in today's bazaar of digital offerings.

The open innovation spirit has burned brightest at companies that perceive the potential wealth of moneymaking ideas jostling around in the previously unconsulted heads of their smart employees and customers, to say nothing of outsiders. To take one of many examples, the worldwide programmers working voluntarily on one hundred thousand open-source projects, notably Linux software, have sold a majority of U.S. companies on the value of their work, which is given away free—although a large number of companies are prospering by providing support and services for open-source software. In a recent survey, for example, 52 percent of U.S. businesses said they had replaced Microsoft's Windows server software with Linux. Perhaps the most enthusiastic switcher to date is

IBM, which remodeled much of its business around open-source software.

The potential extends well beyond technology-based businesses—openness is a harbinger of new cultural attitudes. Consider the broader implications. As we have seen, companies that follow an open, networked model flourish, many beyond their wildest dreams, because of the enormous power of an idea—obvious and yet long ignored—namely that there is strength in numbers. We've always known that when it concerns armies or retail chains, but we've had to learn that it's true for information and ideas as well. That's the real lesson of a Flickr or a Second Life. Openness and transparency inspire contributions from the many. Diversity ensures that a variety of frames of reference will be included. When an e-business or an army battalion or a corporation commits to openness, transparency, and diversity, it is tapping into the power of those numbers. It is saying, in effect: "Bring it on. We want all of the connections and interactions, all of the friction and anomalies, all of the data and ideas we can get from our members or troops or employees, because we know that out of that stew will emerge the creativity and innovation vital to our progress."

THE "WE" IN WEB

Glenn Reynolds, the proprietor of a five-year-old political blog called instapundit.com, which gets about two hundred thousand unique visitors a day, is convinced that online individuals will soon "control the means of production," allowing mere Webheads to unite in deflating autocracies of all sorts.

The jury is always out when it comes to actually knowing the future, and it's too early to buy Reynolds's prediction that the web will inevitably doom tyrants everywhere. The bad guys, after all, may use the same technology to repress people that the good guys are using to liberate them. But it does seem unarguable that floods of web-carried information borne by blogs, podcasts, MySpace pages, and RSS feeds have lately bypassed the story lines dictated in Washington, New York, and other centers of the so-called MSM, or mainstream media.

Fundamental shifts in power are under way. In the digital industry, the Microsoft empire is threatened by programmers using the open-source programming language Linux. In entertainment, Hollywood is losing ground to 100 million people sharing movies and music online via bootleg programs that cost pennies to use. Jay Rosen, one of the keenest observers of the shift as it's happening with the media, is fond of using this simple, yet telling phrase: "the people formerly known as the audience."

Companies are using the new ecology of active, bottom-up collaboration in many different ways. The smartest organizations now capitalize on the ideas contributed by online customers and partners. By using such channels to gauge customer opinion, companies can react to changing demand much faster than if they waited for approval from layers of managers. The next step is for businesses to outsource the design of better products and services, especially when the outsiders work faster and more reliably than in-house researchers. That's exactly what's happening as a variety of external service providers are forming their own R & D companies.

InnoCentive, for example, is a Boston-based network of eighty thousand independent "solvers" in 173 countries. They handle research problems online for thirty big companies, including Boeing, DuPont, and Procter & Gamble. One result: P&G now derives 35 percent of its new products from the InnoCentive brain trust. In fact, P&G, long famous for its insistence on "invented-here" products, has announced that it wants to source the majority of its innovations from outside its corporate walls.

Not surprisingly, the most significant open-network innovations come from knowledgeable users of products and services. For one thing, those passionate about high-performance devices (computers, sailboats, racing bikes, etc.) tend to keep tinkering with and souping up their cherished gizmos, creating real innovations they take pride in sharing with others. The only payment they expect is peer recognition. In this regard, the 3M Company reports that innovations by users of its products have been eight times more valuable to the company than those created by 3M itself. Office supply retailer Staples runs an annual "Invention Quest" competition for new products. Among the items that have emerged are a combination lock that uses letters rather than numbers and a spindle to organize CDs and DVDs.

In some ways, the most pivotal advance is the emergence of wiki software, named by its inventor, Oregon programmer Ward Cunningham, for the Wiki-Wiki ("fast, fast") shuttle buses at Honolulu Airport. Wikis are Web sites that allow anyone to post material and edit it in his or her own language without knowing the complex programming lingo required for posting material online. To add a contribution either to existing content or a blank page, the user simply hits the "edit this page" button and starts typing. Moreover, multiple writers can take turns contributing to the same evolving text.

The wiki software's remarkable features spawned the free online encyclopedia Wikipedia, which attracts 45 million visitors a month, many of them eager to contribute some chunk of expertise to what now weighs in at 1.8 million entries in English—dwarfing the Encyclopedia Britannica's mere 120,000 entries. The Wikipedia also has editions of various lengths in another 251 languages.

Wikipedia's explosive growth suggests how easily an open team can mobilize a swarm of contributors and overwhelm an old-fashioned proprietary product. On the other hand, a Wikipedia-style approach could be a godsend for troubled newspapers and other print media seeking online help. For example, the South Korean online paper *OhMyNews* has wiki-fied participatory journalism by inviting thirty-six thousand citizens to contribute some two hundred stories a day about whatever interests them. By now, *OhMyNews* is so popular that it attracts a million visitors a day and has out rated one of the country's three television networks.

That's just the beginning. Once considered a sort of nerdish novelty, wiki software has lately emerged as an important change agent with the potential to improve how people work, allowing faster collaboration at lower cost. The prototypical model for wikis at work is a big corporate project with far-flung teams separated by long distances. With wiki software, they can all focus visually on the same page at the same time, brainstorming, editing documents, revising blueprints, tracking progress, coordinating marketing, and so on. The cost is pennies compared with travel to meetings, making phone calls, videoconferencing, e-mailing, and the time spent on all of it.

Even the most stodgy companies are catching on. A January 2007 survey of two thousand eight hundred executives by McKinsey & Company revealed that one-third have either invested in or are shortly planning to invest in wikis. Until something better comes along, wiki programs will join other collaborative software in dramatically improving the odds for openness as the highway to a renewed national innovation capability.

The wisdom of crowds has long been a force to be reckoned with in the investment arena, albeit as a reverse indicator—that is, when everyone piles in, it's time for smart investors to bail out. But now what the crowd knows is fueling the rise of a whole new industry called prediction markets. Prediction markets are essentially web-based exchanges that trade contracts based on the anticipated likelihood of a future event—whether senators Hillary Clinton or Barack Obama will be the next Democratic presidential nominee, say, or whether Larry Summers, whose tenure at Harvard produced more than its share of controversy, would be ousted as president of the ultra-elite Ivy League institution. (Summers announced his resignation in February 2006, when the prediction markets were betting his days were numbered.)

Intrade.com and its sibling Tradesports.com are the best known of the handful of exchanges that take bets on events instead of companies. The two sites are run by Trade Exchange Network, a Dublin, Ireland—based company founded in 1999 by a group of bankers. As the Intrade site explains, members "speculate on events that directly affect your life, like politics, entertainment, financial indicators, weather, current events and legal affairs" (or, in the case of Tradesports, athletic events). Contracts are traded only on events that will have an unambiguous outcome: The failed Enron Corporation's former chairman, Kenneth Lay, and its CEO, Jeffrey Skilling, will or will not be found guilty of a majority of the charges filed against them; the Palestinian ruling group, Hamas, will or will not recognize the right of Israel to exist before the expiration date of the contract, and so forth.

Another trading venue, the Hollywood Stock Exchange, started as a game for film buffs that rapidly became an important research tool. It enables fans to buy and sell stocks in individual films or movie stars. Owned now by Cantor Fitzgerald, a specialist in equity and fixed-income capital markets, it is able to sell the data from the trading activity it enables to studios and financial institutions because of its predictive power.

While volume on these exchanges is small compared to the number of contracts traded every day on major bourses like those in New York and London, business is growing rapidly. Growth in trading volume at Intrade and Tradesports is put at 165 percent a year.

If what these exchanges do sounds like little more than gambling, their backers are quick to point out how their operations differ from the roulette wheels in Las Vegas and Atlantic City. For one thing, Intrade takes only a small commission, 4 cents per contract, on each transaction, whereas gambling casinos set rules that always give "the house" an advantage. For another, savvy investors can hedge their risk by taking opposite trades, just as they do in the stock market.

And speaking of hedging, the value of prediction markets may prove most useful to business as a way of gauging and offsetting risks, such as those that accompany the introduction of a new product or the probability of a natural disaster that could devastate an insurer. The pharmaceutical house Eli Lilly certainly sees the value. It invites groups of employees to join its prediction markets, buying or selling virtual stock in pharmaceutical industry forecasts. On occasion, they have even gotten a handle on the results of drug trials long before the data were published. And when the services division at Hewlett-Packard had trouble predicting its operating profit in the first month of a quarter, it set up a market made up of fifteen people in finance who did not take part in the "official" forecasting. They turned out to be 50 percent more accurate in their predictions than the previous ones by division managers.

SUCCESS BREEDS SOME DISCONTENT

Every silver lining has its cloud, and the open innovation phenomenon is no different. Its success threatens organizations that have long benefited from closed systems—proprietary information protected by copyrights, patents, and trademarks. Not surprisingly, many of these old-style companies resist the new open model.

The question for policy makers is whether such resistance becomes impermissible when it stifles the public benefit, especially innovation, that healthy competition is supposed to produce. That's a question best answered by federal regulators, Congress, and the Supreme Court. So far, their answers have seemingly lagged behind digital realities and, in any case, favored the forces of anticompetition over the benefits of openness.

In 1998, Disney's copyright for its enormously profitable character Mickey Mouse was about to run out and enter the public domain.
Just in time, Congress extended copyright protection to seventy
years after an author's death.

In 2002, a crusading law professor named Lawrence Lessig challenged the Mickey Mouse decision in the Supreme Court case of *El-
dred v. Ashcroft*. Lessig argued that most creative works were not unique
but derived from or influenced by previous works—as, indeed, were
Shakespeare's plays, to say nothing of Disney movies like *Snow White*,
a remake of one of Grimm's fairy tales. As Lessig told it, the copyright extension harmed the public interest by reducing access to huge
amounts of public domain works that could otherwise be used to
help create new works. This argument failed to sway the Supreme
Court majority, which duly upheld the life-plus-seventy-years copyright rule.

But Lessig, who teaches at Stanford Law School, has since invented an intriguing way to chip away at copyright reform while
helping young musicians and writers make the law work to their advantage. Under the Copyright Act of 1976, an original work is automatically protected from unlicensed usage as soon as it becomes
tangible. Distributing, copying, or performing it is then illegal for
anyone but the originator or someone he or she licenses. In the case
of an unknown artist or author, of course, the chance of any commercial interest in the work is likely to be near zero. But Lessig has
developed a new approach to intellectual property called Creative
Commons, which enables the originator to grant free-use permis-
sion in advance to any online user who likes the work and wants to
share it with others. The incentive consists of online links or licenses
embedded in the work. Downloading typically costs the user nothing, with modest fees kicking in only when the user wants permis-
sion to sell or perform the work for money.

Science-fiction writer, blogger, and cultural critic Cory Doctorow used Creative Commons to help turn his first novel into a commercial success. After Doctorow's *Down and Out in the Magic Kingdom* was published in standard fashion by Tor Books in 2003, the author posted a downloadable version on his own Web site in hopes of sparking some buzz and boosting sales of the hardcover version. But Doctorow had no intention of squandering his rights as the creator of the work. So he chose an "Attribution-Noncommercial-NoDerivs deed" from Creative Commons that allows downloaders "to copy, distribute, and perform" his work, but only if they attribute it "in the manner specified" by Doctorow. And downloaders may not use the work for commercial purposes, nor can they legally "alter, transform, or build upon" it.

What this kind of license amounts to is a clever marketing tool to promote original work and get it distributed free throughout the immense Internet audience. The exposure generates popularity, which in turn generates commercial demand and a potential payday for artists who might otherwise never get anywhere. In Doctorow's case, the online version of his book was downloaded hundreds of thousands of times, and the initial 8,500-copy print run of the hardcover version was sold out. The publicity Doctorow got from giving away his book may also have earned him lucrative speaking engagements, not to mention bigger advances for subsequent books.

Based in Silicon Valley, Creative Commons has, to date, enabled artists throughout the world to grant rights in whole or part to more than 1.5 million pieces of music, video, text, and digital art. You may have seen its logo, a double C inside a circle, a takeoff on the standard © copyright symbol.

Right now, though, all this potential seems to incense rather than interest established media companies that control mainline books, movies, and music. They want copyright strictly enforced in order to minimize their competition and maximize their profits. To them, runaway Internet file swapping is illegal, subversive, even immoral.

To Creative Commons users, on the other hand, it's a cheap ticket for a one-way flight from Nothing to Something and a potential conquest of their generation's artistic Mount Everest as well.

They're not the only beneficiaries. It turns out that millions of computer users, inspired to share content by Creative Commons and similar efforts, are moved to spend significant sums on the new digital tools and services needed to stay current in the sharing economy. That means big money for Apple, Adobe, EarthLink, and other companies that sell the hardware, software, and so on that file sharing requires. By big money, I mean billions and billions worldwide.

In other words, openness is yet again proving to be a change agent on behalf of what the economist Joseph Schumpeter famously called "creative destruction." For his part, Lessig likens the potential economic phenomenon sparked by a Creative Commons to that which followed a late-nineteenth-century court ruling making it legally permissible to take someone's picture without their acquiescence. Eastman Kodak had just introduced its first camera, and if the court had decided otherwise, the photography industry would most likely have been much smaller and a lot less lucrative.

Whether or not Congress should now wake up and reexamine intellectual property laws—not only copyright but also the country's inadequate patent practices—is a question that should be the subject of national debate. Aside from questions of fairness, the laws as they stand are impediments to openness and invention. They stand in the way of the United States' efforts to reignite its innovation engine.

I've described the growing new world of technology-enabled openness at some length not just because of its inherent interest, but also because it is at the root of an effective national innovation agenda. Technology capabilities of the type we have described will be essential in weaving together the fabric of a diverse stakeholder group—federal, state, local, private, academic, and more—in order to rejuvenate our capacity for transformative innovation.

The new technologies bring many potential benefits, and they can shape our search for new business models that support our emerging global role as innovation systems integrator. The process of linking ideas to funding, human capital, and customer groups can be immeasurably enriched and accelerated by the new technology toolbox. Technology also reshapes such traditional arenas as politics, news, environmental sensing, customer insight, and more in fundamental ways that generate new opportunities. Finally, technology also can provide a bridge for the United States' offerings to the world as an Innovation Nation.

Despite the appeal of the virtual, it cannot, by definition, stand on its own. How best to integrate the collaborative possibilities of virtual space with the infrastructure of a physical location is a topic barely addressed in our search for national innovation capabilities. But I will go further and assert that even in a world in which old limitations imposed by distance can be defied, many factors matter in building optimal supporting conditions for innovation. National innovation requires significant evolution in the platforms that support it at the local and regional level. The next chapter looks at how to bring many different ingredients together to create the necessary platform for innovation.

EIGHT

WELCOME TO THE FUTURE

The future is already here. It's just not evenly distributed.
—William Gibson, author, *Neuromancer*

Back in the 1960s, someone with a sense of humor found a name for a new kind of organization to support business start-ups. These fledgling, innovative companies were sort of helpless, right? Didn't know quite what they were doing? Didn't have the resources they needed to grow and survive? Just like newborns, right? So what should we call an outfit intended to take care of newbies? How does "incubator" sound?

At its most basic, an incubator may provide little more than convenient office space. More typically, it delivers support services, shared technology infrastructure, and expert advice as well as space. Although there have been private sector incubators like Garage.com and Idealab that act like augmented early-stage venture funds, most incubators are some form of private/public partnership designed to boost a region's economy or to strengthen the ability of a university to spin off viable companies from the fruits of academic research.

The classic incubator business model is built on simplicity and efficiency. As Atari founder Nolan Bushnell once told me, the beauty of an incubator, from an entrepreneur's perspective, is that you sign your name fifty times, someone gives you keys to the door, and you're in business. By assembling necessary ingredients on a "one-stop-shop" basis, the incubator lessens the "friction" of a start-up—finding the right lawyer, setting up the right accounting system, and more—so that entrepreneurs can focus on launching their businesses rather than tending to administrative hassles. From an incubator's perspective, economies of scale are achieved by spreading services across a portfolio of ventures.

The first incubator had an unlikely genesis. In 1959, heavy equipment manufacturer Massey Ferguson closed its factory in Batavia, New York. The loss of jobs and the looming presence of an empty 850,000-square-foot factory depressed the whole area. A local business family, the Mancusos, bought the empty shell and sought companies that would create urgently needed employment. The first tenant was a Connecticut chicken hatchery. As Batavia Industrial Center founder Joe Mancuso put it, "We went from incubating chickens to incubating businesses."

But the Batavia innovation was slow to catch on. The National Business Incubation Association estimates that by 1980 there were only twelve incubators in the United States. Today there are several thousand incubators, and at least as many in Europe and elsewhere in the world.

Not everyone loves the idea. Smart money has been known to refer to the typical, well-intentioned incubator as corporate welfare. After all, the argument goes, would you want to invest in a company that needed life support to get started? And it's true that when you look at the great start-up successes of the past few decades—Apple, Cisco, Google—none emerged from incubators. Incubators seem destined for singles and doubles, not home runs.

But the incubator does have an appeal for those of us unwilling to rely entirely on Adam Smith's invisible hand to sort the wheat from the chaff. The availability of some kind of support seems only reasonable—but the incubator does have its limits. It was a model for a time in which the ingredients fueling a start-up were not easy to assemble. Start-ups needed to increase the efficiency with which they used scarce resources to accelerate their time to market. Universities were looking for technology transfer opportunities as well as training grounds for their students. Local governments were looking to stimulate economic development. Think of the incubator as an early version of the helping hand.

But the kind of innovation required to develop a region or a country depends on achieving a scale of ambition and activity that goes beyond the capability of an incubator model. It is possible to incubate a life science start-up, not a life sciences industry. The critical mass of start-ups, infrastructure, financing, and expertise that must be mustered to spawn a portfolio of winners in such emerging areas as nanomolecular materials or clean technology is beyond incubator scale. Nor can incubators deliver the level of disruptive innovation that can cope with society's wicked problems. What's needed is version 2.0 of the helping hand.

Many have pondered how the ingredients for regional development can best be combined to create in the social and economic sphere what the scientists who developed the first atom bomb termed a "fiercely exothermic" reaction. This originally referred to reactions in which the energy returned was far greater than the combined energy of the inputs. Now we are seeing a search for extraordinary economic returns from a given set of social inputs.

The United States already boasts a number of regional centers of innovation excellence that go beyond the incubator model. New York State has its Finger Lakes Trading Cooperative initiative, bringing together eBay, Kodak, HP, and HSBC to support the development of local entrepreneurs who want to globalize their offerings.

Ohio has hired IBM's consulting arm to figure out how to bring in new industries to replace lost smokestack industry jobs. The pages of our leading newspapers (and this book) are replete with accounts of how cities like Atlanta see the key to future prosperity as attracting the demographically significant 25-to-34 professional crowd by being "cool."

Putting in bicycle pathways or subsidizing the club scene are interesting social Band-Aids, but the most meaningful dynamics lie a level deeper. In his seminal book, *The Competitive Advantage of Nations*, economist Michael Porter laid out the concept of clusters, geographic concentrations of interconnected companies and institutions in a particular field. Porter writes: the "enduring competitive advantages in a global economy lie increasingly in local things—knowledge, relationships, motivation—that distant rivals cannot match."

The classic illustration of clusters comes from the formal and informal webs of companies, artisans, and experts that provided sustainable advantage to the silk weavers around Italy's Lake Como. Efficiency soared when all contributors to the making of a product were clustered in physical proximity. Others have used the cluster framework to explain the success of such varied areas as California's Silicon Valley, England's concentration of Formula One racing teams, and Australia's surfing outfitters on Great Ocean Road.

My concern is stimulating innovation on a national scale, and Porter makes a powerful case for the role of clusters. Companies within a cluster can experiment at lower cost, enjoy easier access to leading-edge buyers, find motivation from peer competition, and have a stronger connection to evolving technology and market trends.

As a road map for igniting innovation at a national level, though, the cluster theory has several crucial shortcomings. Looking at economic development in terms of clusters concentrates on the assets a region already has, rather than those it might be able to develop. It is about what is, not what could be. Given that much of innovation is emergent, rather than predetermined, this already poses a significant conceptual issue.

Clusters also focus on the incumbent, established players in a given area—large companies, large markets, and large systems that generate the kind of data that can be measured. Consider, as an example, Spain's Basque region. It commissioned some expensive work from a Porter follower for ideas on what could revive the area around Bilbao. Concentrate on steel and shipbuilding was the advice after months of careful analytical work. Those two industries were traditional strengths of Bilbao, but their decline was also part of the problem. The Basques took a radically different path. No cluster analysis would ever suggest that the key to reviving Bilbao would be to commission architect Frank Gehry to design a new Guggenheim Museum.

If you had occasion to visit Bilbao before the Guggenheim opened in 1997, you would have found a decaying industrial city down on its luck. Now there are trendy bars, hotels, and boutiques, the equal of anything in Madrid or Barcelona. Bilbao attracts over 1 million cultural tourists a year, 80 percent of whom say they came for the Guggenheim. In 2001, the *Financial Times* reckoned the museum had produced over $500 million in economic activity in its first three years, and an additional $100 million in taxes. City planners around the world now talk about the "Bilbao effect."

Another shortcoming of traditional cluster analysis is that it generally focuses on a region's or a country's strengths in isolation. But in a globalized economy, and particularly in service sectors, a region's greatest strength may well lie in how effectively it knits itself into a global network of relationships. It may not matter that you lack a local support network if you effectively tie yourself into an equivalent global one. Cluster theory in its origins concentrated on manufacturing industries—things and people making things—but with an increasing proportion of the global economy, and particularly advanced economies, devoted to services and new kinds of experience-based industries, local concentration may be less important as the Internet shrinks distance and serves as an integrative medium for distributed resources.

Think about the growth of Internet-based outsourcing as a basic business process, whether in terms of reading X-rays, preparing tax returns, designing Web sites, or a thousand other functions. India has, of course, a wealth of companies in this area that serve clients around the world, but software can equally be written (and is) in Monterrey, Mexico, and Novosibirsk, Russia. Retaining good workers in software development—or call centers or investment research—in Bangalore is notoriously difficult: workers meet and socialize with rivals every day, and job transfers are easy and frequent. So it might pay for a company in Bangalore to concentrate its efforts outside the cluster. In Novosibirsk or other locations downstream from Bangalore in the value chain, there may well be less competition and more incentive to stay put.

The value of locating in physical proximity has changed as we move into the early years of the twenty-first century. Local counts, but so increasingly does global. Hollywood, for example, may still be the dream factory, but its continued success depends on a growing web of international alliances, particularly when it comes to global distribution and financing, not to mention the production of digital special effects. Venture capital is leaping out of its Silicon Valley/Boston cradle to go global as well. And myriad American small businesses must increasingly reach out to the world for both customers and suppliers.

Another reason for looking beyond classic cluster theory is that many of today's start-ups, especially in the expanding global landscape of e-commerce and the social Internet, have a different global footprint and cost structure than their predecessors of just a few short years ago. I call them weightless ventures; their gossamer scale and agility go hand in glove with an ability to exploit the advantages of globalization.

Jim Hornthal, a San Francisco venture capitalist, for example, is nurturing a new venture in his one-man incubator at the San Francisco Presidio. His designer is in Japan, his front-end coding team is in Bangalore, his back-end programmers are in Russia, and he has a team of contractors sprinkled around the world. Most of these professionals remain faceless to Jim; he has never met them in person. And Jim intends to make use of Amazon's EC2 platform—short for Elastic Compute Cloud—which provides infrastructure, support, and distribution capability, leveraging off Amazon's corporate assets. When a fellow venture capitalist asked how much the start-up was costing him, Jim said "Three." Oh, $3 million, came the reply. No, said Jim, $300,000.

As further example of this new class of weightless ventures, consider a data point from Matt Gardner, head of Bay Bio, an industry association for the exploding Bay Area biotech community. He describes a virtual biotech venture that took itself all the way through phase two clinical trials without a single employee. Everything from fine chemistry and preclinical work through clinical trials was accomplished through outsourcing vehicles, alliances, and contractors, all available on a worldwide basis.

Classic thinking about clusters insisted on the importance of representing in physical proximity every activity that contributes to creating value in a product. What we need today is new thinking that leads us to achieve a critical mass of talent rather than a critical mass of things. Such talent has the power of networking via Rolodex and the Internet to the rest of the world to launch weightless ventures with enormous impact. The principle of "fiercely exothermic" reactions is thus increasingly available to the suitably empowered individual and may occur anywhere, and in highly unpredictable ways.

Cluster thinking is also often associated with grand plans and a certain omniscience about what areas are going to pay off. But such omniscience is bound to fail, since innovation tends to come from the edges and corners, not from the directed core. It is often the maverick engaged in some form of bootleg activity, not the well-publicized star from central casting, who winds up making all the difference. Therefore, those who would design a strategy for next generation innovation would be well advised to create the conditions for what is new and valuable to emerge, not to write the script. For it is the richness and tolerance of the seed bed that is fundamental to innovation. Frans Johansson has described "the Medici effect," wherein a group of highly diverse perspectives can be brought together—whether physically or virtually—to generate unpredicted explosions of creativity.

We have traveled from incubator to cluster, and now we need to move beyond cluster. We are in urgent need of new concepts to explore how innovation works as an emergent, global, networked, social phenomenon. Enter what I am tempted to call the Nexus. The word, which harkens back to my early exposure to nexialism, has a remarkably useful set of connotations: connection, channel, network, arriving at a critical juncture. However, for the purpose of more colloquial usage, I will refer to this version 3.0 model of the helping hand as the Innovation Hub.

SAN DIEGO AS AN INNOVATION HUB

For an instructive example of how an Innovation Hub can be created, consider San Diego.

The question: just how did a navy town known for surfing, the rough and tumble of real estate development, and tourism evolve into a powerhouse for world-class research and life sciences and telecommunications—and all in a scant fifteen years?

The answer: it was a blend of intention and accident, public and private initiatives, large and small moves. It emerged from a mix of private philanthropy and public investment, academic research and gloves-off capitalism. Ultimately it was about creating trust and community.

Mary Walshok, vice chancellor of the University of California at San Diego (USDC), who has been a driving force behind the city's rise as an Innovation Hub, says:

> When I graduated from college and you wanted a good job it was in St. Louis; it was in Minneapolis; it was in Philadelphia, even Indianapolis. It sure wasn't in Raleigh-Durham. It sure wasn't in Austin, Texas . . . It sure wasn't in San Diego.
>
> What is it that made San Diego, a Navy town with flower-growers and tourism turn into a world-class life science center? [How did we create] 50,000 new high-paying jobs in life sciences and telecommunications to replace 27,000 defense manufacturing jobs that went away with the end of the Cold War?
>
> The second-tier cities that nobody cared about or paid attention to were unencumbered by big companies, big consultants and big models that were based on the old economy, the Michael Porter view of the world, which is that it's all about large global companies and integrated value chains. They didn't have those luxuries, and so what happened in these small towns, not because they were smart, but maybe because they were desperate, is they did things in very unconventional ways.

One of the unconventional ways in which the government of San Diego enabled their innovation boom was by offering free land. General Atomics got free land from the city while the Salk Institute paid a dollar for property in the Torrey Pines mesa. UCSD was built on the site of Camp Matthews, a marine corps training camp in World War II.

Another key factor was that the city began some fifty years ago to build a portfolio of young institutions staffed by academic talents unafraid to leave the East Coast establishment and pioneer something new. Leaving tenured positions behind, they sought to create new interdisciplinary departments with a focus on emerging fields. For example, the nation's first cognitive sciences department—integrating psychology, computer science, and neurophysiology—was established at UCSD.

The secret sauce was a hunger to create new knowledge spiced by a lack of legacy. UCSD, Scripps Research Institute, and Salk were all founded between 1955 and 1960, young organizations determined to break through old academic boundaries. The region hasn't abandoned this spirit of fostering interdisciplinary work. A prime example: In 2001, UCSD created the California Institute for Telecommunications and Information Technology (Calit2) to integrate, in Mary Walshok's words, "entrepreneurial science with entrepreneurial business" in order to overcome gaps in the innovation process from invention to commercial application. Specifically designed for initiatives that blended technical and business agendas, Calit2 is an example of a second wave of San Diego–based interdisciplinary centers intended to spur the process of innovation by supporting prototype development and collaboration with industry partners. And by placing both funding and manpower at the disposal of a cadre of transplanted talents, UCSD acted like an academic version of a venture capitalist, driven by the hope of realizing extraordinary returns, both intellectual and financial.

Galvanized by the need to justify itself within a state university system that already contained established players like UC Berkeley, UCSD embraced knowledge at the edges of disciplines. For example, its business school was able to differentiate itself by focusing on students with technical backgrounds; today 80 percent of its M.B.A. students are also graduates in physics, chemistry, and mathematics. Even its music program focused on computer-generated and avant-garde music, not the classics. The theme was a restless search for the next new thing, for innovative niches in which to become a market leader.

What are other core lessons from the San Diego experience for constructing other Innovation Hubs?

First, the strategy at leading institutions like UCSD was to become a magnet for talent. The biggest priority was to invest in talent and then give it the resources to create. That's the cheapest and best strategy for creating a world-class academic research center like UCSD. The targeted talent base must be broad in order to create an innovation microculture, embracing not only skills in science and technology but also cultural intelligence and languages, design, the arts, and a range of post-industrial services.

A second lesson from the San Diego experience is that leading edge companies and entrepreneurs are catalysts for an explosion of regional innovation. San Diego had entrepreneur Ivor Royston, for example, who founded the diagnostics firm Hybritech, and Irwin Jacobs, who founded Qualcomm, the telecommunications pioneer. We see the importance of specific pioneers in other U.S. Innovation Hubs as well. Silicon Valley had its Hewlett and Packard. Genentech's Herbert Boyer and Robert Swanson led the way in San Francisco's life sciences boom, Genzyme's Henri Termeer in Boston's.

The San Diego experience also confirms that technocratic top-down solutions don't work in the fast-moving world of emergent knowledge. To create the right environment, you need a critical mass of resources, talent, financing, and capabilities that supports discovery and serendipity. Mary Walshok notes that "Twenty-five years ago you wouldn't know that wireless was going to be a cluster, because the standards were all different and Irwin Jacobs looked like Sancho Panza in *Don Quixote*." The assumption is that within certain broad guidelines talented people can figure things out for themselves in an environment that encourages the new and unorthodox.

Another key lesson from San Diego is the importance of building bridges that link local activity with the world. Global Connect is a worldwide network of regional innovation initiatives started by UCSD in 1985. It is a kind of high-level marketspace that links opportunity holders and resource owners. The names of some of the program's partners tell the story—BioPartners Cologne, Korea Advanced Institute of Science and Technology, South East England Development Agency, and the U.S.-Russia Center for Entrepreneurship.

Such connections beget an expanded palette of social and community networks, connecting players regionally and globally to find needed resources on a worldwide basis. Entrepreneurs can now go global through such mechanisms, which connect them to potential partners, markets, or manufacturing in any other part of the world. Such brokering and facilitation mechanisms also link clumps of small and high-growth, science-based companies to their counterparts around the world.

At its heart, the San Diego story shows how talent, investment, and creativity flow to places whose culture encourages the pioneer spirit, the search for the open spaces, and the hunger to express itself as much by creating value in a place as through the ideas and ventures that are generated by it.

San Diego to me is a leading indicator of version 3.0 of the helping hand—the kind of strategic platform I call an Innovation Hub.

I use the word platform in the sense that the computing field uses it: to describe a system comprising hardware (the physical machinery) as well as the operating system (the overall processes that define the rules by which things are done) that in turn support a group of applications (specific programs like word processing or graphics). In a national innovation context, think of all the manifestations of physical infrastructure (buildings, equipment, labs), combined with a national operating system (finance, information flows, laws and regulation, intellectual property protection, alliance mechanisms), integrated with the world through technologies of digital communication, all of that leading up to specific initiatives (a nanomolecular materials program, for example, or a lab for experiments in education). In addition, the notion of platform has a great deal to do with what one might call ambience, everything from a research center's intellectual vibes to a region's nightlife and social appeal to young talent.

In sum, the right platform is fertile ground, a seedbed of incentives (financial, political, technical, even emotional and sensual) ensuring bumper crops of innovation. For Americans determined to reenergize their national innovation engine, "platform" encompasses a spectrum of conditions that can enable talent to address wicked problems and opportunities on a national scale.

A BHAG FOR AMERICA

My BHAG (big hairy audacious goal, in management guru Jim Collins's pungent lexicon) for our country is twenty Innovation Hubs, devoted to twenty wicked problems, initially funded with $20 billion. Wait a minute, you say, that's a lot of money. To most of us as individuals, of course, $20 billion is an unfathomable sum. But in the U.S. federal budget, it is barely a rounding error. Let's say we finance each hub with an initial tranche of $100 million. That would amount to 0.09 percent of the federal budget—that's 90 cents out of every $1,000 of federal spending. By comparison, defense spending counts for $189 of that $1,000. If we look only at discretionary spending— leaving out Social Security, Medicare, and other mandated programs—our initial investment would be 40 cents out of every $1,000, compared to defense, which would account for $520 out of every $1,000. As an additional benchmark, the cost of the war in Iraq as of this writing was $2 billion each week.

So clearly we can afford this if we re-jigger our priorities. The question is, do we have the will and the fortitude to do it, and do it well?

Because Innovation Nation must have a firm lien on the future, these twenty Innovation Hubs will each focus on a specific wicked problem. One might be devoted to digital media, another to clean technology, a third to agricultural biotechnology, a fourth to nano-molecular materials. Just being in these places should make you feel as though you're living five to ten years into the future. They will explore not only over-the-horizon science and technology but also how they will be used, what our lives will be like, and what social, political, and process innovations will change the way we live and work.

Just another bureaucracy, some critics may grumble. Not so. These hubs would be set up as exemplars of entrepreneurship on a large scale. They would be launched with rigor, like the best venture-backed start-ups, with investment inserted in stages from seed round to mezzanine. The purpose of pegging the level of investment at $1 billion per hub is to signal serious intent and to create critical mass. The hubs would be run by the nation's best entrepreneurial leaders, drawn to the challenge of making this vision work, and motivated by incentives more customary in the private sector, such as founders' equity and performance-related bonuses. There would be disciplined oversight, to be sure, but relative freedom from entangling bureaucracy. The hubs would instead be motivated by a venture capital mind-set, entering into each initiative with the expectation that it will be a home run—but aware that the portfolio may well include some failures. There would be ample opportunity for a triple bottom line of economic, social, and environmental value.

Perhaps most important, each hub would be linked to a region, and would be a catalyst for that region's economic development. Despite our tendency to view the United States through a national lens, our country is actually a fabric of regions that over time have developed specific portfolios of economic activity defined by their rich history and legacy. These are also the regions, from San Jose to the Finger Lakes of New York, that have been experiencing the disruption of globalization and accelerating technological innovation. So part of the purpose of inaugurating these Innovation Hubs is to extend the dynamism—obvious in places like Boston, Austin, and Silicon Valley, which are supported by a thriving venture capital industry—to a national level. The design of these Innovation Hubs would capitalize on distinctive attributes as well as unrealized capabilities of regions. What could one imagine building on top of the credit-card and telemarketing expertise of the Omaha area, the light aircraft specialty of Wichita, the office furniture expertise of West Michigan, or the health care knowledge concentrated in the Nashville area? The intention is to regenerate and reinvigorate communities and regional economies, and to realize a social as well as economic return on investment.

The hubs would also enable new integrated approaches to education, linking K–12 education to mentoring programs, college and graduate school scholarships, and workforce retraining, not to mention the funding of research initiatives that could be integrated with a regional education strategy and provide resources to locate useful global partnerships. National and local funding would enable scholarship support for students in regionally strategic fields—such as agricultural biotech in Iowa, energy in Montana, and aerospace in California.

Each of these Innovation Hubs would be financed with a blend of private, local, state, and federal funds but sponsored and designed primarily by local stakeholders. They could rise from the ground up under the guidance of acclaimed architects, like Frank Gehry, and noted design authorities, such as Paula Antonelli and David Rockwell or rising young stars chosen via competition. The environments would have the flavor of cultural hot spots blending the performing arts, entertainment, and culture with science and technology, much like Singapore's One North development. Such a range of creative voices would make them not just training grounds in next-generation innovation but the United States' cultural and social skunk works. They also would serve as bridge-builders between creative industries and the business mainstream, following models pioneered by such organizations as the Learning Lab in Denmark and Arts & Business in the United Kingdom. Above all, they would be mechanisms for linking federal, regional, and urban development strategies.

These hubs would help to grow regionally relevant capabilities by channeling investment in human and intellectual capital while building new forms of social relationships that lead to collaboration and a culture of shared risk-taking and innovation. Experience shows this to be the real "secret sauce" behind such innovation phenomena as the Silicon Valley "habitat" and the San Diego biotech explosion.

The hubs would also feature low-cost living and working arrangements designed to accommodate young, demographically diverse, up-and-coming creators. Each facility would be an experiment in design customized in terms of local and regional historical influences and embodying leading-edge technology.

Is the creation of twenty Innovation Hubs really doable? How can such an ambitious, costly enterprise be accomplished? Is government-sponsored management of innovation really the American way? Don't we believe it's best to rely on the competition of the free market? I offer in evidence two of the country's greatest achievements: the Manhattan Project and the Apollo program. Both were government run, and both were organized to take advantage of the flexibility, creativity, and competition that we normally associate with the private sector.

In less than four years (1941 to 1945), the Manhattan Project grew to an empire-sized 150,000 employees—larger than the car industry of the day—all to produce enough fissile material for a handful of bombs. From virtually nothing in 1957, when Russia's Sputnik spacecraft shocked Americans, the U.S. space program grew to consume 5 percent of the federal budget by 1964. Less than twelve years after Sputnik, the United States landed a man on the moon.

The two projects offer a set of powerful lessons about how Innovation Hubs should be "run."

- A compelling narrative—clear and well-defined—inspires heroic performance. Those who worked on the Manhattan Project believed that their efforts would shorten the war and save American lives. As the old Kansas saying goes, you have a lot more motivation if you're running for your life than if you're running for your dinner. And with the Apollo program, our national pride and perceived national security interests were at stake in our race to the moon.

- Managing a portfolio of innovation initiatives is more effective than focusing entirely on one grand plan. A grand plan is the enemy of the serendipity and improvisation that are at the heart of the innovation process. Since you don't know what will work, it's vital to keep experimenting and trying different things. And this requires flexibility in such areas as funding, setting management agendas, and leadership style.

  Confronted with many different ways to create chain reactions, the Manhattan Project team decided to try them all at once and see which one worked fastest. In the end, all were needed. A key example of this approach was the implosion system that wound up being the trigger for the plutonium chain reaction. It was entirely the work of a small team that program manager Robert Oppenheimer allowed to tinker on their own in a remote nook of the project. Suddenly they had a Eureka insight that turned the whole lab in a new direction. Had they insisted on dogged pursuit of a preconceived plan with the usual compartmentalization and standard processes, this crucial step might never have occurred.

Project Apollo followed a more linear path, but it remained relatively nimble. When Apollo was created, mission heads planned on a direct ascent to the moon—using an immensely powerful booster rocket named Nova, the spacecraft would travel directly to the moon, land, and then return as a unit. A few dissidents came up with the idea of a lunar orbit rendezvous, in which the program would be a kit of parts: booster rocket, main spacecraft, and detachable lunar lander. If the Apollo leadership had struck this seemingly crazy idea off the list in 1961, it is unlikely Neil Armstrong would have stepped onto the Sea of Tranquility in 1969.

- Free access to resources optimizes productivity. The Manhattan Project platform represented an extreme example of that privilege. Here's what Richard Rhodes, author of *The Making of the Atomic Bomb*, told me on the subject: "They had a way of cutting through all the bureaucratic crap. If they needed copper for the bullets to save American lives on Iwo Jima and they needed copper for the electro-magnetic separation systems at Oak Ridge, the copper went to Oak Ridge." Never has there been a more graphic example of government resolve regarding a large-scale, unproven project. The Apollo Mission, too, had ample resources with which to push forward boldly as the recipient of some $135 billion (in 2006 U.S. dollars) in government funding.

- Free flow of ideas optimizes intellectual productivity. I believe that innovation emerges from free interaction among a community of likeminded peers. That the Manhattan Project was able to maintain that quality of interaction in spite of the constraints of wartime secrecy was a prime example of the kind of successful balancing act that a national innovation platform requires in terms of what we have previously referenced as "guarded openness."

"To the extent that you kept things secret, you couldn't make it happen," Rhodes told me. "To the extent that you allowed people to talk to each other, they made progress. But since it was the biggest secret of the war, that was the really interesting problem for the bureaucratic side, the security side." Meanwhile, the scientists were constantly interacting with the engineers—"they were all learning as they went along."

So in a sense three freedoms characterized these great projects: the freedom to pursue multiple paths to success, the freedom to access resources, and the freedom to exchange information. As we begin the work of designing the next generation platforms— the Innovation Hubs—that support our national innovation agenda, we need to keep all three freedoms in mind.

MEET THE CHAMPIONS

There is one additional lesson that both the Manhattan Project and the Apollo program teach us. The Innovation Hubs will require a special breed of leader.

Robert Oppenheimer, leader of the Manhattan Project, was a man of enormous gifts and complexities, a master of Sanskrit as well as nuclear physics. Project Apollo's Wernher von Braun, a onetime German rocket maker, became a well-known icon of the United States' NASA. In both cases, however, two other men played major roles, particularly in building and maintaining the project platforms, while receiving little of the credit—General Leslie Groves for the Manhattan Project and James Webb for Apollo.

The Manhattan Project's Groves was a true heavyweight champion. He was trained in engineering, and he had a striking track record. His construction of a national network of military bases, plus the colossal Pentagon building, in the U.S. preparations leading up to World War II actually dwarfed the subsequent Manhattan Project in physical scale. Along with his in-depth knowledge of many different disciplines, he had considerable expertise available to him in the huge Rolodex of government and private sector people he could tap. He had a tremendous cache of social capital, and did not hesitate to use it.

While his style could be considered abrasive, his emotional intelligence was highly developed. He was an excellent handler of talent, picking and managing the high-strung Oppenheimer, for example, and bringing out his latent leadership qualities. As Richard Rhodes told me, Oppenheimer had never previously directed anything: "He was a theoretical physicist who famously would break instruments just by walking through the lab." But Groves perceived Oppenheimer's very deep need to please and his astute psychological sense of other people. And perhaps Groves picked up something else about Oppenheimer. "He was an actor," Rhodes said, "and during the war, he pretended to be the world's best lab director." That Groves would pick and support Oppenheimer fits well with the sometimes voiced notion that the leader's job includes "making useful exceptions."

Groves also knew that his job was about defining and overseeing a portfolio of possibilities, not creating a master plan and driving it to completion. He understood the importance of improvisation, and the need to create conditions within which new ideas could emerge, as was the case with the previously mentioned implosion trigger system.

So it was Groves's task to take hold of the lab bench stuff, the geniuses, and the facilities scattered around the country, and mold them into a huge industry, and make it all work the first time. He had to integrate the vagueness of ideas, the theoretical rigor of physics, and the brute force of manufacturing and logistics in order to squeeze out results. He saw to the scientists at Los Alamos working on the bomb design (Oppenheimer's bailiwick), the team at the University of Chicago's Metallurgic Laboratory figuring out how to manufacture the fissile material, and the massive industrial complexes in Oak Ridge, Tennessee, and Hanford, Washington.

Groves's gift was the ability to set up the conditions for serendipity and for the right things to emerge, creating the maximum degree of freedom within tight deadlines and structure. "There's no way to overestimate the value of highly intelligent, extremely talented, creative people working in an organization and able to move back and forth to different places," Rhodes said. If Archibald Wheeler and Enrico Fermi hadn't been at Hanford when the Hanford pile started poisoning itself, he added, there could have been a disaster. As it was, they worked out the problem within twelve hours.

Groves mastered these vast challenges and managed to knit the pieces together, endlessly shuttling back and forth by train to maintain the motivation of the program's key people while supporting their refusal to play by bureaucratic rules. The people from Los Alamos would get on the train, and he would talk to them. They'd get off, the train would roll east, and the people from Chicago would get on. Along the way, he'd pick up others, ad hoc, as he needed them. One wonders what he would have been able to do with the Internet.

While Groves was a master of detail, Jim Webb, the father of NASA, had a different heavyweight style: he left the details of the space program to people he appointed and trusted. His great skill was navigating through the many interests in Washington to ensure that NASA's budget kept growing and that its mission was protected. He also juggled the salivating pack of contractors eager to get their share of NASA's largesse.

One example: In the early days of NASA, he had to pick a location for the new manned space center. Northern Virginia seemed the logical choice, since it was already home to Langley space center, where the relevant administrators, scientists, and engineers were based. But as Webb told the director of Langley at the time, "What the hell has Harry Byrd ever done for you or for NASA?" Byrd was the senior senator from Virginia. Webb moved the center to Houston, the homeland of Vice President Lyndon B. Johnson. It was also in the district of the House Appropriations Committee chairman, who agreed to a crucial budget deal with President Kennedy in return for hosting the space center. And somehow Webb managed to keep Harry Byrd happy as well. Only a heavyweight could have managed that maneuver.

Who are some other heavyweight examples? I think of national leaders such as founding prime minister Lee Kuan Yew and Sheikh Mohammed bin Rashid Al Maktoum, who have put their indelible stamp on the innovation capabilities of Singapore and Dubai, respectively. In the world of business, I think of Ivor Royston and Howard Birndorf, fathers of San Diego's biotech industry. In 1978 they founded Hybritech, which pioneered the use of monoclonal antibodies for diagnosing disease. This was at a time when there was next to no high-tech action there, but they had faith in San Diego, and so did their venture capital partner, Brook Byers, of Kleiner, Perkins. Eventually the company was acquired by Eli Lilly, but its alumni went on to establish a number of other successful biotech companies in San Diego. Years later, Byers described the two founders as "role models of responsible risk taking, good technology transfer business practices, and good corporate partnering structures."

Kelly Johnson, the legendary founder of the Lockheed Skunk Works, is the archetypal heavyweight champion. He knew from age twelve that he wanted to be an aeronautical engineer, a dream fueled by reading Tom Swift novels. Initially turned down for a job by Lockheed because of insufficient experience, Johnson rose to be chief designer there in his thirties and spent forty-two years with the company. Such legendary flying machines as the P-38, the F-80 (concept to initial prototype in 143 days), and the U-2 (eight months) took shape under his wing. Perhaps one of the most revealing anecdotes about his willingness to improvise came from the earliest days of the Skunk Works. When he had trouble finding the right place to house his program, he decided that a circus tent could do the trick and bought one.

Johnson operated the Skunk Works according to a set of principles that might well warrant study by the heavyweight champions who will lead our future national innovation initiatives. Here are some of the principles along with my annotations:

- *"The Skunk Works program manager must be given practically complete control of the program in all aspects—while still reporting to a senior manager."* Johnson saw that heavyweight champions must have control in order to integrate the operation, save time, and maintain momentum. They must have the clout that comes from support at the top, balanced with accountability.

- *"The number of people having any connection with the project must be severely restricted."* Use 10 to 25 percent of the number in a so-called normal system, making sure they're good at what they do. This creates some of the leanness associated with a start-up that imparts a feeling of the necessary Spartan spirit. Challenges and constraints can spark a culture of insurgency and serve as a spur to innovation.

- *"The drawing and release system should be very simple, and reports kept to a minimum."* In other words, administration friction and red tape should be fought whenever possible.

- *"Both the client and the vendor should have strong project offices on site, but they should be small enough to ease the integration of client and vendor viewpoints."* Close integration between client needs and the company's operations is essential, especially since so much of innovation comes from customers. Walls between stakeholders reduce the fluidity and transparency necessary for the right level of collaboration.

- *"Strive for trust."* I couldn't agree more. Without trust, there can be no risk-taking, no exploration, no deep collaboration—in short, no innovation.

The achievements of heavyweights like Leslie Groves, Jim Webb, and Kelly Johnson set a high bar for the men and women who will manage national innovation initiatives. I use the word heavyweights in a bow to the phrase "heavyweight project managers," coined by my former colleague Kim B. Clark, until recently dean of the Harvard Business School. He was talking about "product champions" within the corporate bureaucracy, but the idea is the same: someone who makes a bridge between stakeholders who may be unaccustomed to collaborating, motivates the right kind of action at the right time, insulates talent from the adverse effects of noble failure, and maintains the momentum of a complex initiative. The business heavyweight runs interference for an idea through his or her corporation's naysayers and bureaucracy. The champions we are talking about for our national innovation agenda face a far greater set of hurdles: bureaucratic silos, lack of imagination, parochial interests, standard operating procedures, and mind-set differences.

Accordingly, the heavyweight champion must be a translator and diplomat, able to spark collaboration across diverse and even conflicting communities and cultures. George Leonard, author of *Mastery: The Keys to Success and Long-Term Fulfillment*, once remarked to me that the most important attribute of a teacher is the ability to create a positive atmosphere in which a student's belief in his or her eventual progression to mastery is a given. Heavyweight champions are aware of this as they inspire individuals and teams to believe that great feats can be accomplished and that the rigors and uncertainties of the journey will be worth it.

A large part of what I am describing is the skill of an excellent facilitator. Facilitators make it possible for their team or organization to achieve their goals faster, more effectively, and with greater satisfaction than the norm. They shape the agenda, aligning the group's mission with its process and vice versa.

There is not, however, any single style that characterizes the heavyweight champion. Some may come into battle on a white horse, others showing a far more introverted modus operandi. A rare few may fit into the neat boxes beloved of most headhunters, with credentials from the best schools and gradually ascending corporate résumé, but the fact is that the skill set of heavyweight champions can't be captured from books. At best it's gained via on-the-job training and apprenticeships to develop the deep smarts required. What the heavyweights share are the attributes of curiosity, risk taking, and comfort with ambiguity. They show a high level of personal flexibility, maintaining order when it is needed, permitting disorder when it has a constructive intent.

To put it succinctly, the heavyweight champion must possess a particular kind of emotional intelligence—the ability to see, assess, and manage emotions, one's own and those of others, in the interest of creating what is new and valuable.

Jan Carlzon, former CEO of Scandinavian Airlines, once remarked that "all business is show business," and heavyweight champions also need to have a bit of the showman about them. They must not only be able to hear the call, but also to formulate a compelling story and communicate it to others. Ideas must be staged and marketed if the desired changes in behavior and mind-set have a chance of being realized. Heavyweights create the tempo—they define a sense of urgency—and they orchestrate the campaign. When to double-time, when to rest—in that sense, they are like a band leader, always trying to get the best performance out of an individual, a team, or an organization.

When a company or a country is dedicated to breakthrough innovation, the managers of that process must be the heavyweight champions of the imagination. They must design the conditions that maintain a flow of new ideas and design and protect what is new and unproven from being overwhelmed by conventional mindsets, the demand for short-term performance, or business-as-usual metrics. Wherever possible, they must lead with a loose rein to allow talent to express its inclinations. They must let new ideas emerge and give them sufficient breathing room to develop. Asked to name the most important attribute of a band leader, jazz legend Miles Davis replied with typical brevity: "Don't say too much." In other words, don't overstructure, don't overcontrol.

The great heavyweight champions of innovation know how to "presence," to use a term popularized by Peter Senge and his colleagues. It refers to the awareness of possibilities and the ability to manifest them in concrete form. As champions of disruptive innovation, heavyweights make possibilities tangible through the narratives they create and share with the organization, the prototypes and experiments they commission, the unusual and symbolically important hires they make, and the evangelizing they constantly engage in.

Finally, heavyweight champions are heavyweight because they have the clout to drive an idea through the bureaucracy, the established interests, the silos, the ricebowls, the naysayers, and the standard operating procedures. They possess power, and they exercise it.

I have no doubt that the United States possesses the heavyweight champions to lead us toward today's versions of the Manhattan Project and the Apollo Program. One major question remains: Could we pull it off today?

IN SEARCH OF THE
BUREAUCRATIC IMAGINATION

In the post-9/11 era, a diagram appeared in several newspapers showing the relationships among the U.S. agencies responsible for national security. It was a depressing visual that more or less resembled the entrails of a gigantic transistor radio run amok. There wasn't a mahogany table in Washington big enough for all the stakeholders to sit at, let alone have a productive conversation about what needed to be done.

Isn't this a perfect example of why the federal government should stay well away from any national effort to stimulate innovation? Isn't my proposal for the government to take the initiative in creating twenty Innovation Hubs much too "top-down" in approach, especially considering all that I've said about how important bottom-up collaboration and skunk works style operations are in giving birth to innovation?

When I talk about government's role in enabling a U.S. innovation renaissance, I often encounter a deep strain of skepticism. For decades, many of us have scoffed at government as intrusive, counterproductive, incompetent, even corrupt, views humorously summed up by the late Will Rogers: "There is good news from Washington today. Congress is deadlocked and can't act."

As the case of our Byzantine national security apparatus makes clear, there is good reason to be skeptical. But the right government initiatives can make extraordinary new opportunities come to life. Witness the following three examples of successful federally initiated and run programs that managed to work their way around stultifying bureaucracy to produce stellar innovation results.

The Marshall Plan, from its first vague proposal by Secretary of State George C. Marshall in 1947, was a brilliant combination of the visionary and the pragmatic. Marshall argued that the United States had a responsibility to help rebuild Europe; that the plight of the war's survivors was appalling and couldn't be ignored. He also argued that by giving aid to Europe, the United States would achieve a number of strategic goals: we would enhance U.S. prestige and diplomatic power; we would deter Europeans from electing Communist-leaning governments, fending off any revival of German expansionism; and we would create markets for U.S. exports, thereby stimulating our own economy. In short, we would do good and do well.

All told, the European Recovery Plan, as it was officially called, provided $12.5 billion in U.S. grants and loans to Europe in its three years of operation. Europeans used the funds largely to buy U.S. agricultural products and capital goods. But the help didn't stop there. Director Paul Hoffman and his ambassador to Europe, W. Averell Harriman, assisted by a staff of just 630 Americans and eight hundred Europeans, supervised projects that were to change Europe forever and foster a long-term vision of European unity. Roads, railroads, and canals were rebuilt, and mines and refineries modernized. European businessmen were sent to the United States to study U.S. production techniques. The plan's staffers made economic surveys of the European infrastructure, provided logistical help with aid shipments, gave advice on monetary and fiscal policy, and set up export controls to deny strategic goods to the growing Soviet bloc.

The Marshall Plan's accomplishments were huge and lasting. In its three years of operation, European production of goods and services rose by 32 percent; by 1951, industrial production in the sixteen target nations was 40 percent higher than it had been before the war in 1938. And in the next twenty-five years, Europe experienced the highest economic growth in its history. The plan demonstrated that massive government expenditures in foreign aid could be, in fact, a good investment—and that generating peace and prosperity abroad would promote even more prosperity at home.

In its idealism as well as its pragmatism, in its grand sweep and its attention to detail, and in its modest staffing as much as its great goals, the Marshall Plan is an exemplary model of federal government initiative.

Now consider the case of Sematech. This is the name of a semiconductor manufacturing technology consortium founded in 1987 to respond to the United States' steady decline in a crucial, strategic industry. Japanese companies, in particular, had seized market leadership, and U.S. manufacturers were finding it difficult to maintain vital supply chains as their market heft diminished. They came to the conclusion that their problems were so severe that no company acting alone could save the U.S. industry. The federal government came together with fourteen U.S. semiconductor manufacturers to pool resources and share risks in solving common manufacturing problems. Government involvement was spurred largely by the Department of Defense, which decided that foreign control of critical computing resources threatened the country's military and economic security.

With pooled resources through Sematech, industry R & D increased and U.S. companies were able to win back market share. It was successful enough that by 1994, Sematech's board voted to seek an end to federal funding, reckoning that the industry had returned to health and strength.

Ironically, Sematech's DNA extends back to the nineteenth century, with a federal initiative that enabled a similarly strategic, integrated, and smart approach to agriculture. The United States became preeminent not only in agriculture but also in higher education because of its rich endowment of land and because of a well-integrated federal approach to intelligent use of that resource. In Abraham Lincoln's administration, at the height of the Civil War, the Morrill Act of 1862 gave the states federal land to raise capital and establish colleges that would teach agriculture, science, and military tactics. Our great system of state universities was the result. In 1887, the

Hatch Act used the same mechanism to enable states to create experimental agricultural stations.

Now, fast forward to the present era and California's success with its Institutes for Science and Innovation. At the turn of the millennium, California was riding high. The world was transfixed by the dot-com boom, with the San Francisco Bay Area as its epicenter. Some even described the Bay Area as a modern equivalent of Florence during the Renaissance. Fortunately, California's political leaders were also taking a sober look at the state's future.

In his 2000–2001 budget, then Governor Gray Davis proposed the creation of up to four California Institutes for Science and Innovation. The idea was to "ensure that California maintains and expands its role at the leading edge of technological innovation in the twenty-first century" and to "give rise to world-class centers for strategic innovation that combine excellence in cutting-edge research with collaboration and training for our next generation of scientists and technological leaders." The subjects chosen were explicitly cross-disciplinary: biomedicine and bioengineering, nanosystems, telecommunications, and information technology.

The price tag wasn't high for a state that would rank as one of the world's ten largest economies if considered as an independent entity. California guaranteed $100 million over four years to each of the four institutes. There was no diktat from on high about the design of the institutes: Proposals would be screened and selected by a gubernatorial panel and the institutes administered by the University of California. Each institute had to find private sector matching funds of at least twice the level of state support and had to be hosted by at least two UC campuses.

Today we find the California Institute for Quantitative Biological Research (QB3), the California Nanosystems Institute, the California Institute for Telecommunications and Information Technology (Calit2), and the Center for Information Technology Research in the Interest of Society (CITRIS). Hundreds of companies have supported the institutes with funding well above the state's minimum expectations. And the research already emerging covers an exciting range of topics: At CITRIS alone, for example, projects include the design of energy-efficient smart buildings, developing a cure for malaria, next-generation technologies for memory and computation, new computer visualization environments for computer gaming that could be applied to distance learning, and technology-driven collaborative work environments.

Take QB3 as an example. This consortium of three University of California campuses with approximately 150 distinguished faculty affiliates is addressing a massive new wave of innovation: the "application of the quantitative sciences—mathematics, physics, chemistry, and engineering—to biomedical research." One of the activities under its umbrella is the UC San Francisco Center for BioEntrepreneurship, specifically designed to "develop the next generation of entrepreneurs and leaders in the life sciences industry." In the terminology of Forrester Research's Navi Radjou, they are developing not only inventors, but also brokers and transformers as well.

Meanwhile, CITRIS aims to help the "application pull" of major social needs meet the "technology push" typical of researchers who are following their creative inclinations. Among the areas in which it sponsors research are energy conservation, transport efficiency, advanced diagnosis and treatment of disease through the use of information technology, and expanding business growth through richer personalized information services.

Each of these three examples—the Marshall Plan, Sematch, and the California Institutes—was strategic, integrated, and smart. Choices were made regarding long-term capability, new ways were found to integrate the interests and perspectives of different stakeholders, and approaches to augmenting the quality of intellectual and human capital led to the continuous generation of new know-what and know-how. They also demonstrate that government has a vital role to play as a catalyst for large-scale innovation. Government should not seek to dictate, micromanaging every aspect of an agenda, but rather to serve as steward by convening and facilitating. Government can also spur innovation by funding invention, pursuing smart education policies including workforce retraining, creating and enforcing the right protections for intellectual property, focusing attention on flagging sectors of our economy such as manufacturing, enabling connections and alliances by supporting networking, and fostering key elements of infrastructure such as broadband.

Previous models of national innovation such as the Marshall Plan were crafted in an industrial era during which best practices involved centralization, economies of scale, and mass production. A contemporary innovation initiative of comparable scope must draw from the cutting-edge business models of today—practicing strategic foresight, aggregating specialized expertise and knowledge, setting technical and business standards that promote collaboration, and serving as a hub for alliances. Setting up an all-seeing, all-knowing government agency as the end-all and be-all solution is the last thing in the world I am recommending.

There is an analogy for how the federal government should operate—not to be overstretched—which comes from Hollywood, certainly no stranger to innovation-based business models. Through this lens, the federal government functions like a movie studio, state and local government like a production company under the studio's umbrella, and specific film projects are operational activities staffed with particular talent and technical experts. Think Viacom, which owns Paramount Pictures, which provides a home for DreamWorks, which is coproducing the next *Indiana Jones* film with Steven Spielberg directing.

In the Hollywood ecosystem, the studio has specific functions: to set standards of quality, pick talent and nurture projects, mobilize specific forms of in-house business expertise (how to negotiate with the unions comes to mind), and sell the product through its well-defined channels of distribution. Oh yes, the studio also acts as the bank. Meanwhile, it is up to the production company to manage its local portfolio of projects, and up to each creative team to maximize the impact of a particular film by, as they say in Hollywood, "putting every dollar on the screen."

Crafting the role of government in the national innovation agenda, and setting up organizational structures to ensure the optimal blend of top-down and bottom-up input, will surely not be easy. Especially tricky will be working out the collaboration among federal, state, and local governments, which are given to turf battles about control, prerogatives, and funding. And the complexities of stewardship will be further complicated by other stakeholders who will insist on a voice in the process: nonprofits, experts, entrepreneurs, professional groups, companies, academics, think tanks, and leaders in society.

Moreover, today's government is infinitely more complex than that of the 1940s. General Groves managed the entire Manhattan Project with just four staff members, fewer than now serve the average CEO of a small company. Certainly it helped that a clear mandate came directly from the president of the United States. Given the hopes riding on his leadership, he was arguably, if briefly, more "heavyweight" than the president himself. For his part, Apollo's James Webb at one point personally controlled the $6 billion or so; in 1966 dollars, it must be remembered, that represented some 5 percent of all federal spending. Groves and Webb succeeded because they were free to use vast resources and their own judgment in mobilizing the talent and tools needed to accomplish missions hugely important to the United States.

Today, getting large-scale things done is incalculably harder than it was forty years ago. In the current political climate, consensus is the exception rather than the rule and even the challenge of hiring the finest experts for a vital mission is usually politicized. Meanwhile, a culture of careerism has invaded public service. Far too many of our public servants calibrate their careers in terms of three-year tours, mastering the "slow roll" of saying "yes, sir" and then moving on to a higher-paying, private sector job.

Equally depressing is today's paucity of creativity, highlighted when the 9/11 Commission cited a "failure of imagination" as a key reason for our vulnerability.

Given these pitfalls, do I really believe that government can tackle the huge complexities of Innovation Nation? Do we have the nerve? My answer is yes. We have no alternative but to try. We'll need to get the right combination of ideas and people working and build the political and societal will to make it happen. But we must face the future and move forward. The chapter just ahead suggests how we can go about doing so. Welcome to the national innovation agenda.

NINE

A NATIONAL INNOVATION AGENDA

There is a profound difference between getting it and getting it done.

—Eric Best, futurist

In the last chapter, I recommended twenty Innovation Hubs as a centerpiece for our national agenda. Regional hubs such as the San Diego area, for example, or the California Institutes for Science and Innovation, show us how to practice innovation in a smart, integrated, and strategic way. But to achieve a national innovation transformation, our optics have to step up a level.

I am proposing in this chapter a three-pronged agenda—a National Innovation Advisor, a National Innovation Council, and an Office of Innovation Assessment—to equip the federal government with the capabilities it needs to turn the vision of a national innovation agenda into a reality. Beyond that, I suggest additional initiatives that need to be taken by the public and private sectors to enable America to be Innovation Nation.

I recognize that any institutional change at the federal level—to say nothing of the state and local levels—requires enormous political commitment, but the importance of reinvigorating our innovation drive demands bold steps. I also recognize that—in today's politicized climate—any proposed bold steps are likely to encounter resistance made up of a blend of thoughtful debate, ideological posturing, and questions of feasibility along the lines of "You can't do that!" One of my own success metrics is the level of that very resistance to new thinking. My purpose here is to frame the logic of what is needed, which in turn can serve as a lightning rod around which the exacting discussion of "how" can unfold.

NATIONAL INNOVATION ADVISOR

Like the National Security Advisor and the National Economic Advisor, the National Innovation Advisor would report to the president of the United States. This should be an activist position, to be located in the West Wing and armed with the clout to marshal cooperation from cabinet-level players. The last thing we need is another bureaucracy to be housed in a new building on the Washington Mall with a huge staff. As much as possible, the National Innovation Advisor would stand apart from the turf wars of various agencies and thus be able to advance the kind of strategic, integrated, and smart agendas that require alignment among them.

To fill the job, we need someone in the mold of a heavyweight champion like Leslie Groves or Kelly Johnson. This person might have roots in science and technology, but his or her title should focus on innovation. He should be able to see innovation in a broader context—commercialization as well as invention, application as well as discovery, social as well as scientific advances. She should have the full support of the president, who in turn should have a deep understanding of the United States' innovation challenge. In fact, I believe this must be a criterion for selecting a president in 2008 and in future election years.

The example of Robert Rubin may be instructive in this regard.

In 1947, in the aftermath of World War II, President Harry Truman created the National Security Council to provide institutional stability and authority for policy making in areas that crossed the boundaries between the military and the State Department. When Bill Clinton was elected president in 1992, he created an analogous organization, the National Economic Council, and made Rubin its first director. The NEC became the powerful focal point for the coordination of domestic and international economic policy. If turf wars broke out between the Treasury and state, it was Rubin who knocked heads together and made sure decisions were consistent with the president's goals and agenda. With direct access to the president, and with the knowledge and skills honed during his years heading premier investment bank Goldman Sachs, Rubin was said to have extraordinary clout. He might be an interesting model for the National Innovation Advisor.

There are signs that the need for high-level strategic and integrative thinking about innovation is being addressed in other countries. Brazil, for example, has recently created a cabinet-level position called the "special secretariat for long-term action" with a mandate to define a long-term strategy for Brazilian government and society. Roberto Mangabeira Unger, a Harvard Law School professor, was named to fill the post.

NATIONAL INNOVATION COUNCIL

The National Innovation Council would be convened and led by the National Innovation Advisor. Its select membership would include CEOs, scientists and technologists, cultural leaders, media mavens, policy experts, financiers, and more. There would be representation from the private and nonprofit sectors, and a blend of ages, professions, ethnicities, and genders. Members would be expected to serve for an extended period and to place the national interest above political partisanship. The Council of Economic Advisers at its best might perhaps serve as a model.

In the parlance of John Kotter, change-management guru, this would be a "guiding coalition," setting direction and overseeing the innovation transformation process for our country. Its responsibilities would include adjudicating competing priorities, making useful exceptions, and orchestrating funding from multiple sources. Existing organizations, like the Office of Science and Technology Policy, would operate under the council's umbrella. As the steward of the national innovation vision, the council would select and apply a well-chosen set of metrics to assess the country's progress. It would also be responsible for embedding the innovation agenda within government so it can weather changes in political leadership or intellectual fashion. To be effective, the council would need to be compact in size, well facilitated, and adequately resourced. Think special forces, not soldiers on parade.

One of the council's most important tasks would be to initiate and preside over an ongoing national conversation involving academics, students, entrepreneurs, professional service providers, community leaders, and concerned citizens from all over the country. That conversation—technology enabled as appropriate, but face-to-face as much as possible—would, among other things, create a continuous flow of information about such matters as demographic shifts, applications of emerging technology, regional distribution of innovation resources, educational performance, best practices in supporting new ventures, and new financing mechanisms. Wherever possible, these information flows would be available to all, using state-of-the-art design and information graphics as well as online repositories to clarify significant trends and capture groundbreaking ideas.

The council would be responsible for staying abreast of global best practices as well as new technological and social developments that could affect the success of our national innovation agenda. It would also convene communities of interest in such areas as workforce retraining, technology infrastructure, and cultural investment. In sum, the council would serve the functions described in a *Harvard Business Review* article by HBS faculty member Robert Kaplan and David Norton, CEO of Balanced Scorecard Collaborative, as an "office of strategy management," creating and executing strategy, benchmarking results, creating accountability, communicating for alignment, and enabling continuous improvement. The agenda arising from the council would also shape the agenda for the twenty Innovation Hubs I have proposed. They would emerge from work done on strategy and priorities as part of an effort to develop an overall innovation road map, designed not as a grand plan but as an ongoing conversation among a broad array of stakeholders.

Most important, the council would have the ability to fund innovation and to use its influence to coordinate the innovation funding efforts of other agencies to ensure that the overall result is strategic, integrated, and smart. Robert Atkinson has suggested that the United States examine the model of Tekes, the Finnish national funding agency for technology and innovation. Tekes has a $500 million budget and a staff of three hundred people. Recall that Finland is a country of only 5 million people with an economy one-sixtieth the size of the United States and the scale of the Finnish effort becomes truly significant. Tekes's mission statement is eloquent: to "build up a platform for future choices." Tekes funds projects that can originate from a company, a research institute, or a university and takes an active role in facilitating cooperation among communities as well as between domain experts and potential international partners.

OFFICE OF INNOVATION ASSESSMENT

The third vital step we should take at the federal level is to create an updated and vastly expanded version of the Office of Technology Assessment (OTA), which was established in 1972. Its purpose was to provide Congress with "objective and authoritative analysis of complex scientific and technology issues," and it became a model for injecting scientific and technological knowledge into the process of governance that was widely copied around the world. Yet in 1995, Congress axed OTA as part of a wave of budget reductions. The grand savings: $22 million a year.

What I am proposing is broader—call it the Office of Innovation Assessment, as a congressional, not executive, agency. The job of keeping up with the latest discoveries and inventions, as well as with larger trends in technology and science, has never been more vital. We must develop a more concerted, coordinated national program for identifying and more deeply understanding technologies that stand astride large new streams of opportunity like gatekeepers, and removing bottlenecks to their realization.

The domain of this office should not only encompass science and technology. It must be integrative—equally immersed in the kind of social "coolhunting" that yields insights about how technology will be used, in relation to a view of what the lives of our citizens may be like in the future, and the kind of social, political, and process innovations that will change the way we live and work. As an example, a computer is about technology, but a $100 computer of the type being developed by the nonprofit OLPC (One Laptop Per Child) foundation is an economic innovation because of its cost, as well as a social innovation because of how it can be deployed to transform local education and commerce in developing countries.

To be able to take such a mental journey into the future involves a facility at grappling with the unknown. Specific approaches such as technology road maps, immersive collaboration, prediction markets, ongoing scenario planning, and forecasting can provide a more accurate sense of emerging agendas around the world that in turn can provide at least a rough map suggestive of future possibilities to guide action and investment.

At its heart, the Office of Innovation Assessment would have a knowledge management mandate—to keep us current about developments at home and abroad, to be aware of opportunities to generate new knowledge, and to provide knowledge to those who need it, from members of Congress to the small business owner.

The end product would include a constantly evolving, easily searched, global repository of important new scientific and societal knowledge that also serves to integrate knowledge contained in separate databases of our public and private institutions. The objective would be to avoid the "we don't know what we know" syndrome. Even in Silicon Valley, archetype of the innovation-driven community, knowledge management can be a daunting task. One leading figure lamented to me recently about the challenge of making information flow in that storied community: "If Silicon Valley only knew what Silicon Valley knew, we would be in much better shape." The same notion, writ large, could be said about the United States.

I know this to be a big problem. Much of my work with government and corporations is simply making sure that team A knows what team B knows: I am often cast in the role of the honeybee, whose influence comes from the simple authorization to fly from flower to flower.

Galvanized by the government's resources and ability to generate data, but fueled by private-sector zeal and technologies, the Office of Innovation Assessment would ensure that the right knowledge is available to guide the work of U.S. decisionmakers. Call it the keeper of a national innovation dashboard.

The steps we take to ramp up our abilities to identify the most important emerging technologies should also include an upgraded version of the National Critical Technologies (NCT) process, which served us well for so many years. The Defense Appropriations Act of 1990 mandated the establishment of an NCT Panel to report every two years on its assessment of critical technologies and the country's standing in them. The legislation recognized that some technologies are so fundamental to national security or so highly enabling of economic growth that the capability to produce these technologies had to be retained or developed in the United States. But the NCT is now moribund.

A revived and improved NCT would serve as a guide to national investment decisions as well as a road map for so-called dual use technologies, those that can serve both emerging civilian uses as well as crucial defense functions.

•   •   •

These three ingredients—leadership in the form of a National Innovation Advisor, a guiding coalition in the form of a National Innovation Council, and a knowledge management platform in the form of the Office of Innovation Assessment—would provide for a healthy and productive interplay between executive and legislative branches of government, a balance between Washington insiders and a broad array of national community interests, and the introduction of an entrepreneurial model into a government inured to bureaucracy.

Other initiatives must also be put into place as part of a complete picture of national innovation renewal. I firmly believe, for example, that our government needs to create parallel structures within the current bureaucracy—specifically, a public sector skunk works or network of skunk works dedicated to the practice of innovation.

As I have discovered in my work with government clients, on any given large-scale project, the built-in momentum and legacy culture of the system is usually too powerful to change in any reasonable time frame. What is needed is a culture of insurgency.

In working on the Pentagon's aircraft-carrier program, for example, it quickly became clear to me that much of the work had its own, very-difficult-to-change momentum and culture. Clearly, transforming the mainstream organization was out of the question, absent a huge resource base to support an army of change-management consultants. The right answer was to set up a parallel organization that was empowered to see things differently, act differently, ask irreverent questions, and experiment. The result was an increase in morale, alignment around objectives and strategy, and the elimination of unstated differences in mind-set that had posed intractable obstacles to progress.

Parallel organizations are actually nothing new to the military. So-called red teams are sometimes organized to play the part of the adversary, so that the mainstream can learn how to "make war on itself," in the pungent words of one army colleague. During the Cold War, there was an actual aggressor squadron that wore the clothing and used the symbols of our potential enemies. The idea was to avoid groupthink and, instead, grow knowledge and understanding of the adversary through an officially sanctioned counterculture that encouraged new ideas and capitalized on the emergent and "in between" knowledge it generated—knowledge in between disciplines, bodies of knowledge, geographies, organizational silos, generations, ethnicities, and ranks. What would a red team for public sector innovation look like, one wonders?

All this is meant to lead us as a nation to the benefits of being able to reconcile diverse stakeholders and points of view. To get there, we must become aware of the enormous value of a national commons. Commons originally referred to common land, which could be used by the "commoners" for a variety of purposes. In Oxford, England, for example, citizens of the city could graze their horses in Port Meadow—and they are still doing so after hundreds of years. But commons has come to mean any resource that a community recognizes as being accessible to other members of that community. My emphasis on openness and transparency in developing and propagating a national innovation strategy rests on belief in the importance of a national commons for innovation that embraces all the stakeholders.

THE LARGER INNOVATION AGENDA

In order to enhance our society's potential for innovation and get the biggest bang we can out of the creation of twenty Innovation Hubs and the federal initiatives mentioned above, we must work on a number of other key fronts, many of which I have discussed in the course of this book. My list contains a bouquet of ideas, not meant to be exhaustive, but rather to recognize additional facets of our national innovation strategy.

We need to take out the national checkbook and spend what it takes to fix the U.S. education system. That means paying teachers better, creating incentive compensation systems, better measuring and rewarding the performance of schools, establishing national standards for teaching science and math, finding new ways to enhance the stature of teachers in society, and even convincing retirees and others with technical skills to come into the teaching force as part-time mentors, for example.

In order to elevate the current sagging prestige of the teaching profession, we might modify a Japanese idea. Since 1950, that nation has honored "bearers of important intangible cultural assets" as "national living treasures." A potter, a painter, or a designer can enjoy the kind of social status that allows them to pass their knowledge on to others and do their best work free of distractions. We need to create a living treasure status for our best teachers, providing them with additional resources, financial support, and the ability to influence change, as well as the intangible rewards of public admiration.

We might also take a page from our own playbook, circa 1958. That's when Congress passed the National Defense Education Act, which provided an intelligent stimulus to education in science, math, modern languages, area studies, geography, and technical education, among other fields. The act gave universities the financial encouragement to provide low-interest loans to students studying for degrees in the specified areas and to pay for fellowships for graduate students and research facilities. It also provided federal support for the improvement of elementary and secondary education.

We also need to look at new concepts of investing in what I call career arcs. What if the Department of Education in collaboration with the National Science Foundation and other agencies sought to identify kids with budding talent in specific areas of science and technology as early as age fourteen and provide them with special mentoring, internship, and apprentice programs? What if this program were also available to young designers, social scientists, and entrepreneurial brokers? Perhaps these young talents could be given the status of National Innovation Fellows and have access to new forms of grant support and other types of career development opportunities.

There are some early examples of such career arc planning. Purdue's highly rated engineering school has created a department of engineering education, part of whose remit is to develop innovative programs to groom new generations of engineers—with activities starting as early as preschool. You could imagine UCSD doing something similar for bioengineering or the University of Oregon for environmental engineering. Again, different places will have different competitive capabilities and opportunities. But such creative incentive programs could build a huge talent pool that would be integrated with national strategic goals, including the human capital requirements of the Innovation Hubs. One imagines a focus on certain areas: cultural intelligence, energy and environmental sciences, media/Internet, nanotechnology, proteomics. You might have your list; this is mine.

Specialized approaches to education enrichment, including those emanating from the private and nonprofit sectors, should not be overlooked. For example, Wendell Butler's dream of a nonprofit devoted to space science has blossomed over more than two decades into the Young Astronaut Council, the largest aerospace organization in the world, with multimedia education programs that have been used by more than 2 million students and educators worldwide. Meanwhile, the National Foundation for Teaching Entrepreneurship, started by investment banker Steve Mariotti in 1987, has reached over 150,000 young people from lower income communities and trained more than 4,100 certified entrepreneurship educators.

We need more passionate, novel programs like these that excite students about fields that are so important for our future. One of the key elements in the best of these programs is mentoring. High school children enrolled in an NFTE program on entrepreneurship, for example, might be mentored by an M.B.A. student from a local business school or a retiree who had run a small business.

The workforce we need to do the work of innovation in the future will also require skills as facilitators of the collaborative process. I envision the establishment of facilitation as a core skill for government with a corps of well-trained facilitation professionals who would enable government decision makers to think better and differently. They would be the vanguard of a national campaign to impart the benefit of facilitation and collaboration methods to public and private organizations throughout the country.

We not only have to cultivate our home-grown talent better, but we also need to stimulate the flow of talent into our country. That means handing out more H1B visas and making it easier for qualified foreign students to get green cards. Government and the private sector should also join in a program to make the United States more friendly and sticky to talent from around the world with fellowships as well as other incentives and opportunities. The involvement of the private sector must be enlisted in an integrated effort to coordinate outreach to young talent worldwide about what the United States has to offer.

We must also learn to nurture our cultural intelligence, so necessary for accomplishing our national innovation goals. To coin a phrase, "it's the diversity, stupid." How can we hope to convert others to our way of democracy if our knowledge of other cultures is lacking?

Paradoxically, we have the resources for cultural intelligence in abundance. Consider Silicon Valley, which might be considered a poster child for diversity. When the *San Jose Mercury News* analyzed 2005 census figures, they found that Santa Clara County had the largest population of Hindi speakers in the country, the second-largest number of Vietnamese speakers, the third-largest population of Farsi speakers, and the fifth-largest number of Chinese speakers. What an extraordinary resource. But there is no strategy for capitalizing on our diversity or cultivating the improvement of our cultural intelligence at a national level. Chicago, with one of the world's largest Thai-speaking populations, should be forging strong links with that Southeast Asian tiger economy. My own Bay Area could do far more to bolster its ties to India and China, two of the principal sources of our population's diversity.

Remember the success of the National Defense Education Act of 1958, passed in the aftermath of Sputnik? It boosted spending on science and engineering, of course, but it also expanded languages and area studies. The federal government can again help improve our cultural intelligence by funding scholarships and incentives in these areas.

Technology is a major entry in the innovation agenda, and the communication and collaboration intrinsic to Web 2.0 represent an area of our national comparative advantage that should not be overlooked. While the private sector continues its march toward ever-superior networks, social software, user interface design, and prediction markets, the government should be helping to support and shape the invention process in these areas to encourage transparency and participation through its role in establishing standards, providing seed financing, and acting as a source of demand. Academia and nongovernmental organizations (NGOs) also have a role to play. A national expert panel—commissioned by the National Innovation Council around practical, actionable outcomes that may result from adoption of new technologies—can have an important role in shaping this agenda.

One simple example of a potentially relevant technology is Snippets, the email-based internal tool used by Google's talented employees to publish on a weekly basis updates to Google community at large on what they are doing. Snippets are multimedia, searchable, and convenient. They go a long way, with relatively simple methods, to creating a shared brain in which each person in the Google community can know what every other person knows and then act on it. Something like Snippets could be a boon to our national community of innovation stakeholders.

The Internet is essential to the connection and knowledge sharing that underlie our national innovation capabilities. The availability of broadband must be accelerated. There is no reason why the United States should be fifteenth worldwide for penetration in such a strategic area. There is also no reason why U.S. broadband should be generally slower than broadband elsewhere. And there is no convincing reason why the Internet should not remain neutral and free of corporate preferences and agendas.

We need to make a greater and more coordinated investment in artistic disciplines: fine art, design, and performing arts. They are foundational for culture and environments that support innovation. In Singapore, for example, anyone who donates a piece of art for public consumption receives a 200 percent tax credit. Singaporean policy makers view the arts as providing an important common language and frame of reference for all creative disciplines. As Pierre Levy, a noted professor and world-class thinker on collective intelligence and knowledge-based societies, has pointed out, artwork is a "cultural attractor drawing together and creating common ground between diverse communities; we might describe it as a cultural activator, setting in motion their decipherment, speculation and elaboration."

Our government must also review its role as an important source of innovation demand. The Pentagon should be given a larger mandate to view its colossal R & D budget as an integral part of the overall fabric of national innovation. Our government seemed to understand that idea back in 1958, when DARPA was established in the wake of the launching of Sputnik. The agency's mission was couched in these words: "to assure that the U.S. maintains a lead in applying state-of-the-art technology for military capabilities and to prevent technological surprise from her adversaries." Of late, though, DARPA has favored applied research over the basic research that is so essential to a renewal of our innovation chops. In computer science, for example, DARPA has scaled back the basic research it did through leading university departments. Tightening the funding screws doesn't just mean chopping bad programs. "When funding gets tight, both researchers and funders become increasingly risk averse," according to William Wulf, president of the National Academy of Engineering.

But DARPA's current list of projects still has enticing elements: self-forming networks, chip-scale atomic clocks, real-time language translation, biological prosthetics, quantum information science, low-cost titanium, and alternative energy. The Pentagon needs to reaffirm and support DARPA's commitment to basic research as part of the national innovation agenda. By doing so, it would also build a much-needed bridge between our national security community and a private sector whose innovation clock speed is racing ahead of the Pentagon's. Also needed: new funding criteria that encourage higher risk, longer time horizon, and more cross-disciplinary projects.

It isn't just the Defense Department, of course, that can play a role. The Small Business Innovation Research Program (SBIR), which makes grants from eleven federal departments—including the Pentagon, the Department of Energy, and NASA—has made important contributions to invention in the United States, providing grants of up to $850,000 for early-stage R & D. Apple, Chiron, Compaq, Federal Express, and Intel are some of the companies that have received support. But the SBIR program should not operate in a vacuum; it needs a strategic context that points out salient agendas and focuses the potential for social as well as financial returns. Given its success to date and the necessity of boosting American innovation, I believe the SBIR program should be dramatically expanded in line with new strategic directions established by the National Innovation Advisor and the National Innovation Council.

In regenerating our national innovation capability, we need not only more discovery, but also more implementable intellectual property. That leads to the need to provide more resources for an overloaded patent review system. Matt Gardner of the biotech industry association Bay Bio points out that the U.S. Patent and Trademark Office has a five-year backlog in the biotechnology industry, while the FDA's review times have gone from twelve months to roughly double that. These delays can translate directly into loss of competitive position for U.S. companies.

A greater investment is required for virtually every item on the innovation agenda, private as well as public. To have venture capital more broadly disseminated as a catalyst for regional innovation capability, for example, I propose that we put together tax and matching-fund programs to encourage the development of venture capital funds around the country. The heavy concentration of venture capital in Silicon Valley, Boston, and New York means there are a host of regional innovations and innovators outside of these prime locations that do not receive the same level of support and attention. We should also bolster the many existing local networks of angel investors through such means as information-sharing networks and tax policy. They have an important role to play in financing earlier-stage projects requiring less capital, more hands-on involvement, and the assumption of potentially more risk than those that might interest mainstream venture capital firms.

A new wave of philanthropy has begun to stimulate innovation in a wide variety of fields and deserves scrutiny and support. Among the standouts: the Omidyar Network, the Google Foundation, the Bill and Melinda Gates Foundation, the Skoll Foundation, and the Broad Foundation. Typical of the new spirit is Skoll, founded on the fortune Jeff Skoll made with eBay. The foundation behaves like a venture capitalist, seeking social entrepreneurs who have already made a difference locally and need capital to move to the next level. "Our hope is to find real inflection points in their work where we can partner with them to make them more successful," Jeff Skoll explained.

One new approach is called advance market commitment (AMC): foundations or nations promise to provide a market to entice pharmaceutical companies to produce medications to be sold at affordable prices in poor countries. The Bill and Melinda Gates Foundation, for instance, has joined with several countries—including Italy, Russia, and the United Kingdom—in backing an AMC to develop a pneumococcal vaccine suitable in price and effectiveness for the developing world. It's an important agenda; pneumococcal diseases like pneumonia and meningitis kill up to a million children a year.

Many of the foundations are exploring new incentives, a practice that has a long tradition. In 1714, for example, the British Parliament came up with an innovative way to spur innovation: it offered a vast reward to anyone who could come up with a way to calculate longitude. As detailed in Dava Sobel's best-selling *Longitude*, the clockmaker John Harrison solved the problem and eventually won the prize.

Something more like the longitude prize has been adopted by the X Prize Foundation—a cash award. The Ansari family, which had founded and then sold (for $750 million) Telecom Technologies, became title sponsors of a $10 million award to be given to the first nongovernment group to launch a reusable manned spacecraft into space. SpaceShipOne claimed the prize on October 4, 2004, the forty-seventh anniversary of Sputnik.

More recently, entrepreneur Richard Branson and former vice-president Al Gore announced a $25 million prize for the person who finds the best way of removing carbon dioxide from the atmosphere. Any method that will remove at least 1 billion tons of carbon per year from the atmosphere is eligible for the prize.

And the list of civilian incentive givers goes on. Perhaps such legacy organizations as the Nobel Foundation might get involved, establishing thematic as opposed to discipline-based awards. And our government might consider joining the crowd by offering prizes for new discoveries in selected fields, or by supporting the creation of such prizes through fiscal policies.

Important as they are to the innovation agenda, dollars can only go so far. People have to be inspired and organized to achieve our goal. To that purpose, I propose a National Service Corps, which would mobilize talent to teach in schools, mentor children, provide stewardship at the local community level, and offer needed guidance for would-be entrepreneurs. As a parallel organization, a Global Service Corps could be established to build on the DNA of the Peace Corps and create bridges of service to the developing world while showcasing a renewed American ethos of innovation. One place to look for volunteers: the millions of baby boomers, retired or throttling back, who still possess the skills, knowledge, and experience to make the world a better place. They of all people do not want to be a generation that leaves America, and the world, worse off than they found it. And they still have time to do something about it.

We have a long way to go before we can begin to realize the innovation agenda I set out in these pages. But some small beginnings can be glimpsed, some understanding that a new kind of dynamic is in the air. In that spirit, I'd like to share with you an experience I had in the spring of 2007 at the Quadrus Conference Center on Silicon Valley's storied Sand Hill Road.

I am part of a team that organized a meeting to look at the next wave of emerging innovation patterns in the valley. The attendees include Wayne Johnson, who heads university relations for HP; Stan Williams, founding director of HP's quantum science research group; Marissa Mayer and Shailesh Rao, of Google; Paul Saffo, of Stanford; Navi Radjou, of Forrester Research, whose work on innovation networks I have cited above; Matt Gardner, who heads Bay Bio, and Reg Kelly, who runs QB3, one of the California Institutes. There are a half dozen CEOs from companies with cool names like Nano-Stellar, Perlegen Sciences, Renovis, and Gigabeam that cover such fields as nanomolecular materials and cancer genetics as well as a smattering of traditional service organizations like McKinsey and Hill & Knowlton. Other stakeholders include BASIC, the Bay Area Science and Innovation Consortium, and the California Space Authority, sponsors of the event, and academic colleagues from UCLA, UC Davis, and Stanford.

All in all, it is a potlatch, information-age style. Participants network easily, exchanging business cards and anecdotes, and in many cases rekindling old relationships. And it is a globally connected group as well. Shailesh Rao is going to New Dehli in two months to run Google India. Stan Williams is going to China in a month to visit nanotechnology institutions. Reg Kelly and David Cox have just returned from China, where they have been meeting with academic institutions in the molecular genetics area. And Paul Saffo and I have just returned from speaking in Singapore at a conference on risk assessment and horizon scanning.

Interesting themes emerge in the discussion: cooperative bridges between young and mature companies; techniques to improve knowledge sharing throughout the community; proposals for a more effective interface between Silicon Valley and the endless stream of foreign visitors intent on hunting down the valley's innovation recipe.

Far from being allergic to government, the group actively discusses ways in which government can play an important role. One important issue emerges quickly: there is no science and technology "czar" within the California state government to lend a high-tech perspective to government deliberations and to advocate for a more enlightened science and technology policy. The attendees inventory their Rolodexes, devise a strategy for approaching the governor, and move on.

The genesis of this gathering is worth noting. The California Space Authority got the money from a WIRED (Workforce Innovation in Regional Economic Development) grant, part of a $195 million program sponsored by the Department of Labor to "focus on the critical role of talent development in attracting economic development and new high-growth, high-skill job opportunities for these regions." BASIC (Bay Area Science and Innovation Consortium), an NGO, did the work and named an organizing committee from the community. The participant list and agenda emerged out of a series of discussions among the organizers, who also worked on the agenda and the invitee list.

No one directed the process, but the whole affair sizzled with the spirit of a Silicon Valley start-up—the same kind of networking, enthusiasm, openness to new ideas, trust, and desire to build something valuable.

Within the mix of public and private, the NGOs were able to contribute and enrich the overall collaboration. They provided funding, information, and logistics advice. The agendas of federal, state, and local officials, such as investigating the future workforce or defining the California "innovation corridor," coexisted comfortably with the agendas of private sector participants, such as finding new partnerships and sources of funding and exploring social responsibility issues.

This gathering offers a glimpse of what the future of our country's approach to innovation might look like on the ground. Our national agenda should not be a grand project along the lines of the old top-down five-year plans, but rather a free-flowing, unencumbered dance among the private and public sectors, among academics and NGOs, entrepreneurs and individual citizens. It is neither the bureaucratic top-down of a government agency, nor the invisible hand of the private sector. What we need is a blend of the two that finds the sweet spot between the invisible hand and the controlling hand— in short, the helping hand.

To realize that goal, we as a nation still have some soul-searching to do. The next chapter explores the vision and values needed to realize our dream of Innovation Nation. It also addresses how our renewed national ambitions reconcile with a globe rapidly evolving toward what I call Innovation World.

TEN

WHAT'S GOOD FOR THE WORLD IS GOOD FOR AMERICA

The world is my country, all mankind are my brethren, and to do good is my religion.
—Thomas Paine, pamphleteer and revolutionary

When corporate and government leaders want to work with me, one of the first things I ask them is, "If innovation is the answer, what is the question?" That's a deceptively simple inquiry, but one that gets to the heart of a fundamental question we in the United States must strive to answer at this critical juncture in world history: What, in fact, do we as a nation want from innovation? What collective purpose will it serve? Where can it take us?

On a personal level, innovation might be the means to finding fulfilling work and achieving wealth. In business, it could be the key to successfully navigating a treacherous competitive environment and coming out ahead. At a national level, it might well be the vehicle for fulfilling a society's dreams for itself. But for innovation to bring about such a transformation, it has to spring from and help us accomplish a set of big ideas—ideas that encompass a vision of what we value and how we want things to be.

Swedish consultant Bo Ekman frames the question in a slightly different way. The tall, elegant, and self-assured Ekman fits the central-casting image of a trusted adviser, plus he's a good listener with a knack for spotting and articulating the core insight in any discussion. He also has a bit of a roguish reputation in Swedish business circles. In 1999, he published an editorial in *Expressen*, a leading Swedish newspaper, under the headline: "What's the Use of Sweden?" He said to me, "People think we Swedes are nice people; we do high-quality work. But, really, what is the use of Sweden?"

In a sense, this is akin to the corporate question, "What are we in business for?" If, for example, you were to ask Disney what its purpose is, senior leadership would not respond: "We're in the theme park business." Nor would the first thing out of their mouths be: "We want to deliver X return on shareholder equity." No, the purpose of Disney is stated in fifteen words: "We create happiness by providing the finest in entertainment to people of all ages, everywhere." Happiness—that's Disney's underlying reason for being in business.

Simply striving to maintain wealth or a standard of living is, in our increasingly complex, globalized world, a recipe for stagnation. A more ambitious, compelling sense of mission and purpose is required to fuel the engine of innovation on the scale that, I argue, is critical.

When it comes to nations, great waves of innovation often correspond to what we may think of as a heroic period. An outpouring of innovative energy comes as a response to some massive challenge, usually external, that requires clarity and boldness of purpose. Myriad people suddenly share an overarching goal that promises ample reward for the hardships of reaching it. And as they strive to fulfill that vision, they transform both themselves and their country.

In varying degrees, a galvanizing sense of purpose energized the peak eras of ancient China, Greece, and Rome, as well as the rise of the British Empire. In the United States, a bold vision drove our entry into World War II and subsequently provided the blueprint for rebuilding Europe. So, too, our energetic and sometimes audacious pursuit of Cold War–influenced agendas—the Apollo space program, for example.

Some say that the United States' national sense of self is rooted in the revolutionary drama of 1776, in the notion of the country as a land of liberty that enables the pursuit of happiness, by which Thomas Jefferson meant what philosophers have called the "good life." But, as I see it, what shaped us even more was the expansion of our frontier and the dreams it nurtured of a manifest destiny, the belief that the United States was fated to become a leading world power. That is probably the overriding national purpose that has shaped the U.S. narrative up until now.

In the real estate deal of all time, Jefferson's Louisiana Purchase, the United States paid $15 million, or less than 3 cents an acre, for 828,000 square miles of primeval expanse stretching from Canada to Mexico and westward from the Mississippi River to the Pacific Ocean. Soon, the young republic added California, Florida, Texas, and Oregon, where in 1846 a territorial compromise with British Canada forestalled what could have been our third war with Britain in fifty years.

The Oregon crisis inspired a journalist, John L. O'Sullivan, to sum up the new mood of Americans as a select people. Nothing must interfere, he wrote in an 1845 editorial, with the "fulfillment of our manifest destiny to overspread the continent allotted by Providence for the free development of our yearly multiplying millions." It was this same sense of a predetermined path to greatness that drove our push into outer space and, I would argue, our exploration of the inner reaches of cyberspace and the human genome.

Today, though, the United States' sense of mission seems blurred. In the wake of 9/11, we rallied—at least in spirit—but our energies have since been dissipated by a flawed strategic vision. Now we seem to be at a loss to conjure up and express a concept of leadership that fits into an increasingly complex world narrative. What we need now is a renewed and evolved sense of national purpose. Our historical belief in manifest destiny must be reconsidered in light of a rapidly evolving, ever more globalized context. In short, we need a new understanding of where and how we fit into this landscape. The conventional zero-sum objective of "I win, you lose; the United States as number one" no longer automatically fits the role we must play on the world stage.

Were we to embrace the goal of becoming an Innovation Nation, it would certainly put us at a far remove from any regressive and willful desire to exert hegemonic power over the world. It would, instead, express an appreciation of our evolving role as a nation whose still mighty innovation engine could help bring about what I call Innovation World. That is, a world in which a highly interconnected and integrated global society is suffused with myriad hotbeds of innovation, empowered individuals, and open infrastructures dedicated to the betterment of mankind.

Obviously, many would continue to see the world through the narrow lens of comparative advantage and operate based on that constricted vision. Robert Atkinson, writing in *The Past and Future of America's Economy*, catalogs practices from around the world that amount to innovation-driven mercantilism—tariff relief, for instance, that is granted to bring high-tech manufacturing to one's home country or other rewards doled out for establishing laboratories there. And today the practitioners of theft, the baldest form of mercantilism, can escape the penalties for pirating intellectual property such as software, while also enjoying the economic returns gleaned from selling pirated DVDs, handbags, and shoes.

We must play by a different set of rules. It used to be said that what was good for the United States was good for the world. Now we must reverse that logic and affirm that what is good for the world is good for the United States. Our future prosperity and our standing in the world will emerge from a display of wisdom and a reoriented long-term perspective that moves us to take the lead in addressing global wicked problems. In sum, globalization seen through the lens of innovation can frame a new ethos for us.

We must press ourselves to become the first fully realized Innovation Nation in part so that we can assume the role of global enabler, one to which we are uniquely suited. No other country can tap into so many different sources of expertise. No other country has the mental freedom, the financial and creative resources, and the ability to organize those resources to achieve the critical mass needed to accomplish great deeds.

But our preeminence may not last forever. The sobering fact is that whether we lead the charge or not, the rest of global society will continue its rapid evolution toward Innovation World. Our opportunity for stewardship and influence will be diminished and, in the worst case, lost altogether should the United States move to disengage or to adopt a new form of isolation. Certainly, the day will come when many countries will be at least as impressive in their innovation capacities as we are.

Consider the following words taken from a recent policy paper:

A culture of innovation breeds innovative endeavors, while innovative endeavors in turn spur the culture of innovation. . . . We shall encourage the innovative spirit of daring to be first and daring to take risks. We shall tolerate failure, conquer shallowness, and provide a stage for various innovative ideas and activities to display their individual attractions, so that the sparks of creation can converge, spread, and give off their radiant light.

Is this inspirational message from Silicon Valley? The Thames River Valley? Singapore? No. Those enlightened and enlightening words come from the People's Republic of China.

Or consider this example of a country hard at work building a national network of biotechnology laboratories to advance agricultural production, drug manufacturing, and clean technology. The country's efforts to break the genetic code of the avian flu virus H4N1 have been described as "critical" by no less an authority than Ernst & Young in its *Beyond Borders* annual review of global biotechnology. Only a few years ago, China or a part of Eastern Europe might have come to mind, but, perhaps surprisingly, this is Vietnam that is stepping up to the innovation plate to participate in a globally strategic industry.

And then there is Ethiopia. One of the world's poorest countries and rated 104th in an INSEAD study ranking the world's innovators, Ethiopia is putting in a 4,000-kilometer fiber-optic network that will bring all its 74 million citizens to within a few kilometers of a broadband point of presence by 2007. It will also deploy $100 million of its limited resources to buy computers for schools and government offices. One might imagine that an Ethiopian Steve Jobs or Bill Gates is logging on to the web for the first time at this very moment.

These are just a few markers that point to a changing global landscape. Investment bank Goldman Sachs observes that the combined economic productivity of BRICS (Brazil, Russia, India, and China) may surpass that of the United States, Japan, the United Kingdom, Germany, France, and Italy by 2039. It further notes that China is on course to become the world's largest economy, outpacing the United States by 2041. It will have more Internet users than the United States by the end of this decade. And it is no longer a great surprise to hear a tech leader like Jack Ma, founder and CEO of Alibaba, China's homegrown version of eBay, say that, "today, Silicon Valley is in China."

Globalization is, on the whole, to be embraced, if only for what *New York Times* columnist Thomas Friedman calls the "The Golden Arches Theory of Conflict Prevention." No two countries with a

McDonald's, Friedman says, have ever gone to war with each other. In other words, the stronger our economic links, the less contentious our relations will be with other countries. I would add a related argument that I'll call the "Silicon Valley Effect," which holds that countries bound together by common cause, countless links of collegiality, and distributed innovation capability are also less likely to fight each other.

Just as U.S. military schools train officers from other countries, so too are the foreign alumni of Silicon Valley going back home not to launch winner-take-all strategies against us, but to find self-interested ways of collaborating in an endless evolution of global business models. John Ruggie, head of the Center for Business and Government at Harvard's Kennedy School of Government, has observed that "life in a world of sustainable globalization is a permanent negotiation." To which one could add, it is also a permanent opportunity for creative arbitrage.

Arbitrage usually refers to taking advantage of differing prices for something financial: you buy a bond in London, say, and sell it for a little more in New York. But by creative arbitrage I mean taking advantage of cultural, market, and technological differences. Formidable advantage comes to those who can bridge cultures and social systems because of their heritage, experience as repatriates, or as exemplars of what UC Berkeley's AnnaLee Saxenian calls "brain circulation." We are talking about people whose career paths and chosen projects span multiple geographies; a new class of commuter between Silicon Valley and Beijing is one example. The arbitrageurs can then use such factors as differences in market and technology development, cost structure, and regulatory environment as a business model, bringing products, processes, and know-how from where they are abundant to where they are scarce, thereby earning profits.

Whether or not one is a fan of globalization, the next act in the global drama will unfold with the force of inevitability. Back in the early 1960s, the renowned economist Robert L. Heilbroner wrote a book entitled *The Great Ascent—The Struggle for Economic Development in Our Time*, in which he declared that through the process of economic development, the "social, political, and economic institutions of the future [were] being shaped for the great majority of mankind. On the outcome of this enormous act will depend the character of the civilization of the world for many generations to come." Now, at the dawn of the twenty-first century, the concept of a great ascent is being refashioned in terms of the drive for innovation on a global scale. As never before, global society is eager for unorthodox ideas, new sources of value, and strategic innovation capabilities.

As I've indicated, emerging centers of innovation are challenging the United States' position as the world's preeminent innovator; our role is shifting from one of absolute exporter to importer of innovation as well. That the innovative output of the rest of the world is becoming increasingly important is confirmed by many sources, not least the U.S. intelligence community. When we were in toe-to-toe competition with the Soviet Union, our intelligence services had the primary task of preventing national secrets from being stolen by others. Now, increasingly, the work of intelligence involves the gathering of knowledge and information about technological innovations occuring outside our borders. The proverbial canary in the coal mine will be the emergence of technologies that we don't understand. We're said to be tracking a few right now.

The flow of innovative products, services, and processes emanating from outside the United States is like a climate change that reroutes streams of commerce and creates new currents, thus causing massive shifts in the flow of innovation. Now you can see the flow of inventive ideas coursing between China and Africa, for example, or between Singapore and the Persian Gulf. We might regard these circulatory changes as evidence of the democratization of innovation on a global basis.

What we are also seeing is the emergence of an international culture of commerce and technical exchange that increasingly rewards a
combination of imagination and pragmatism, long accepted as a cultural hallmark of the United States. In its values, attitudes, appetite
for risk taking, and willingness to cross lines, this culture provides
evidence that the U.S. idea—at least as it applies to innovation—is
now the global idea.

In addition, and as noted previously, multinational corporations
are also important accelerants of innovation on a global scale. They
operate with increasing independence from their country of origin,
driven by an abiding concern for saving costs and being able to draw
on the widest possible pool of talent. They are shipping manufacturing, design, and especially R & D abroad at a ferocious pace. In a
survey of 186 companies conducted by consulting firm Booz Allen
Hamilton in 2006, 75 percent of new R & D sites planned by global
corporations were slated for China and India, and the overall share
of R & D sites outside a company's home market increased from 45
percent in 1975 to 66 percent in 2004. This breakneck pace of globalization prompted Craig Barrett, chairman of Intel, to remark to
me that his company may not even qualify as American anymore.

The innovation offshoring phenomenon (taking your assets to
another country as opposed to the outsourcing that involves hiring a
company abroad) is a major driver of globalization, especially as the
motivation shifts from saving costs to leveraging the imaginations of
increasingly capable overseas workers. And the vectors of offshoring
flow tell their own story: India is now offshoring to countries in
Latin America and elsewhere, some of which, like Canada, have high
standards of living. For example, in 2006, India's Aditya Birla Group
acquired the Canadian outsourcing management company Minacs
Worldwide in order to cut telecom costs and reduce language and
cultural barriers as part of its effort to reach the American market.
The viral spread of innovation capability and culture also extends to

individuals; consider the Chinese or Indian Intel (or Cisco, Apple, IBM) employee who may one day leave for greater opportunity elsewhere, taking both their technical knowledge and, more important, their understanding of the entrepreneurial process with them.

For the United States, the overarching message in all of these globalization developments is that the historical hub-and-spokes, U.S.-centric model of innovation—a configuration so central to our prosperity in the last half of the twentieth century—is giving way to a more distributed, multicentric model. The sea change gives urgency to our own evolution into Innovation Nation so that we can offer our services—within an expanded strategic framework—as innovation systems integrator, financier, broker, and educator. Otherwise, we risk being left in the dust by a fast-evolving Innovation World.

But why does the United States have to pick up its pace of innovation, you might ask, if so much is now going on elsewhere? Why not be what economists call a "free rider," spotting innovations that emerge overseas and capitalizing commercially on them? On the face of it, being a free rider might sound pretty good, but business history shows that disproportionate rewards accrue to the originators of truly new concepts, and that both resources and imitators are attracted by the originators' breakthroughs. Hence the enormous success of Silicon Valley and its resident geniuses. And though conventional wisdom discounts distance in a global economy, as I've pointed out before, economic geographers still find that, for all the ballyhoo about the "death of distance," location still matters greatly and local innovation hubs play a critical role.

Of course, Innovation World will not evolve overnight. Its emergence will be a long and challenging process as nations struggle to shed outmoded mind-sets, focus their energies and resources on innovation, and interact with one another in new and increasingly complex ways that require fresh depth of discussion, collaboration, and knowledge sharing. And of all the profound changes required, the most difficult may be cultural.

THE CULTURE CHALLENGE

It is morning in Dubai. I awake in my room at the sleek Jumeirah Emirates Towers and take the newspaper-service dangler off my doorknob. I may still be groggy, but I think I see not one or two newspapers on offer, but one hundred and seventeen! On closer examination, I see that the papers are culled from 51 countries. Six newspapers are from Finland, including my favorite, *Kainuun Sanomat*, and two each come from Brazil, New Zealand, and Nepal, where I am delighted to see that *Gorkhapatra* is available.

A few months later, I am happily ensconced at the Shangri-La Hotel in Singapore and reading a similar dangler. Not to be outdone, the Singaporean service—referred to as an International Newspapers Catalogue—contains 358 newspapers from 62 countries, including a whopping 28 from Russia alone. Here, I am excited to see publications written in the Slovak, Macedonian, and Papiamento languages.

I later discover that the company behind these offerings, Newspapers Direct, is based in Canada, where it was founded by an expatriate Pole with U.S. and European venture capital. Talk about crossing cultures.

To become a leader that accelerates the pace of innovation in this fast-globalizing world will require an evolved cultural intelligence, including a sensitivity to other peoples and languages and an openness and desire to connect to the world as a whole.

Every country has its version of a cultural challenge to overcome. For the United States, it is our distressing lack of language skills and cultural knowledge. On September 11, 2001, we had a mere handful of Pashto speakers in our government, putting us at a distinct disadvantage among the Pashtun people of Afghanistan, where we would soon be at war. And in December 2006, the bipartisan Iraq Study Group reported that out of the one thousand staff members in the U.S. embassy in Baghdad, only thirty-three spoke Arabic and only six were fluent.

Despite their success in multiple markets, Asians are not immune to cultural challenges, either. Take China, for instance. It will have an increasingly difficult balancing act in reconciling a centralized, largely opaque political process with the desire for transparency among an expanding subculture of high-tech entrepreneurs, artists, and mavericks. And despite all of its commercial success, Japan continues to be burdened by a hierarchical culture that resists openness and imposes strong pressures to conform. "The high nail must be hammered down" is a still pertinent saying, not a quaint historical footnote, that describes a way of life in Japan even amid the proliferation of *shin jin ryu*, or "new human beings," who can be seen walking the streets of Harajuku or Shibuya in all their high-fashion splendor on any given day. Perhaps as a result, at least in part, talented engineers have become what the *New York Times* recently called one of Japan's hottest exports.

To observe a successful model of the interconnection, networking, and integration that must evolve around the world, look at Europe. According to the World Economic Forum's *Global Competitiveness Report,* that continent contains seven of the world's ten most competitive nations—Switzerland, Finland, Sweden, Denmark, Germany, the Netherlands, and Great Britain. So much for the image of EU bureaucrats in Brussels squabbling endlessly over how to define a banana.

In fact, the top five countries in the index are all extremely cosmopolitan; most of their citizens speak several languages and also understand cultural differences. Switzerland, for instance, the centuries-old neutral meeting ground for the rest of Europe, is an amalgam of France, Germany, and Italy but with its own international culture. Cultural and political diversity has made it the home of many international agencies. In Denmark, another top competitor, foreign language ability is taken for granted, as any visitor there can attest. The Danes' ability to empathize with people of different cultures and build bridges of understanding has made them successful as diplomats, peacekeepers, and international businesspeople. It helps them design products that appeal to people around the world, from those little multicolored Lego blocks to high-end Bang & Olufsen electronics.

Singapore, number five on the list and Asia's top competitor, is unlike most of its neighbors. The island city-state is the offspring of three different cultures—Chinese, Indian, and Malaysian—shaped also by a considerable amount of Anglo-Saxon foster parenting under the British Empire. In fact, the official language of government is Malaysian, but the real national language is English, and the unofficial emotional language is Chinese. In Singapore, Anglos, Indians, Malaysians, and Chinese all live together in a vibrant community whose unique flavor of diversity and tolerance is derived from its rich cultural mix.

This blending creates vital cultural intelligence that is important not just because it builds bridges of empathy, but also because it stimulates creativity. Forming connections and understanding across diverse cultures can lead to fruitful new ideas. Scott Page, a professor of complex systems at the University of Michigan, persuasively makes the case in his recent book, *The Difference—How the Power of Diversity Creates Better Groups, Firms, Schools, and Societies,* that multiple viewpoints are more important than individual brainpower when it comes to solving big problems.

Certainly, the networks through which innovation evolves will thrive and its systems will become integrated not by dint of any grand plan, but rather as a result of the millions of choices that will be made by individuals, companies, and governments. That's because innovation begins with collective intelligence, the interactive sparking of many minds. It doesn't spring forth fully formed; it is learned bit by bit from a series of conversations, false starts, and errors.

But if government isn't the dominant player, it will shape the global game board, as we have noted before in discussing national agendas. It can enable innovation, set the rules to channel it, and provide the leadership without which innovation cannot achieve its true potential. The question for the world, then, just as for the United States, is where are the world leaders to galvanize us to action? And which institutions can best support this journey?

Our increasingly interconnected global society will need to consider what large-scale initiatives to invest in. Pursuing future streams of opportunity in, say, pharmaceuticals or nanotechnology, will involve efforts not even remotely covered by the odd $10 million or even $100 million sprinkled in the right places. Billions of dollars over many years will be needed. The staggering magnitude of investment required is one of the most compelling arguments for global coordination of effort in some meaningful form.

We may worry that such coordination is simply too difficult to manage or an invitation to a new form of super-bureaucracy. But, in some areas of scientific research, cooperation on a large scale has already been achieved. European governments banded together to fund the Extremely Large Telescope project in Chile and the Large Hadron Collider particle accelerator at Geneva's CERN, the world's largest particle physics laboratory. This collaboration is perhaps another sign that the profusion of European countries at the upper end of various competitiveness indices is not an accident.

I would argue that the same variety of large-scale cooperation can be applied to the notion of innovation stewardship. What's more, the challenges presented to global civil society by climate change, poverty, disease, security threats, educational breakdown, and the

lack of clean water demand that the countries of the world come together to collaborate.

Some may doubt whether countries can really step up to collaborative stewardship of innovation on a global scale. But once again,
consider Singapore, which I have often cited in these pages as a kind
of Innovation Nation in the making. Further evidence of that evolving status came in 2006, when the government announced
World●Singapore, an initiative to explore how Singapore might ex-
port elements of its public sector and infrastructure advances as a
product/service offering to the rest of the world. Specific examples
might include Singapore's education curriculum designs, airport
construction know-how, and technical standards for e-government.
In launching the program, Peter Ho, permanent secretary of Singapore's Ministry of Foreign Affairs and also the head of its Civil
Service, even said that World●Singapore could lead the world to innovate inside Singapore, or, alternatively, that Singapore might innovate for the whole world.

Singapore, it seems, is ready to leverage its innovation expertise
by exporting it as a public-sector service to the world. I believe the
United States should follow suit as our innovation capability evolves
on a global scale. If the United States does set its sights on tackling
the wicked problems facing the world, it will be crucial that we not
do so unilaterally—an admonition that is as true for global security
as it is for life sciences research. Terrorism expert Thomas Quiggan
reminds us in his book *Seeing the Invisible* that "threats to national security are not controllable at the national level. The state must learn
to operate in the complex and uncertain international environment."

In generating and shepherding the international cooperation
needed to get to Innovation Nation, however, the United States
must demonstrate a renewed engagement with, as well as respect for,
international processes—ineffective though they may sometimes

seem. Just as America was the driving force behind the post–World War II institutions that did so much to increase world prosperity and bring about a certain level of political stability, we ought to set our sights on embracing that kind of leadership role once again. Doing so would renew our standing in the world while also securing our own national prosperity.

But before the United States can resume that role, we have to reignite our own commitment to innovation, which, in turn, requires us to reevaluate for ourselves what the ancient Greeks referred to as *ethikos*, which means a "theory of living." As we grapple with the momentous challenges of reevaluating our role in the world and reenvisioning our desired future, we must also search deep within ourselves and our society to evaluate the ethos we now live by.

AN ETHOS FOR INNOVATION

Our ethos, or theory of living, is the set of beliefs and attitudes that guide our behavior. For our purposes, let's think of it as the theory of living that impels us toward the uncertain shores of successful innovation or prevents us from ever reaching them. Having smart policies will mean little if a national ethos is not in place to breathe life into their implementation.

I believe that our culture has become too focused on near-term goals and personal gain, and that it has lost its zeal for national excellence and its love for acquiring the skills that will be so crucial to our future in innovation. The values of the young are probably the best mirror of the greater culture's values, and in our country they often seem at odds with the requirements of the innovation journey. In this corner is a hedge fund partnership or a slot on *American Idol*. Over here is a doctorate in quantitative biology or a slot in a national service corps. Which one has more appeal?

As Dean Kamen, inventor of the wearable insulin pump, the iBOT wheelchair, and the Segway personal transporter, told me:

For a whole generation or more, the great American lie has left kids thinking that what they need to excel at to be rich and famous and have status is to excel at bouncing a ball or being in Hollywood, or being up on stage or at the NFL. The role models by which kids in this country see "success" of every kind, by every metric, is the world of sports and entertainment. In fact, I doubt most kids could tell you the name of a single living scientist, engineer, or Nobel laureate in biology or chemistry or physics or medicine. Yet, every one of them could literally tell you the names of more people in the NBA and NFL and Hollywood than they could tell you the names of people that they are friends with.

How did we get here? Kamen's insights are worth repeating in full:

We got here very innocently. Parents did what they always try to do—give their kids a better, easier life than they had. But somehow in the translation to "better," the "easier" got a capital "e" and it left out things like work and competence. We lived for a while in privileged circumstances . . . the kids had plenty of leisure time and then sports and entertainment became experiences we could really savor. But the unintentional consequence was to shift the values of a generation. The rest of the world was picking up values of hard work, creativity—the rest of the world was trying to follow our example at the same time that we weren't keeping our eye on it. Now we are in a very vulnerable position that has left us with a generation growing up in which a substantial number of people just don't have the education, resources, or culture to work hard at things that matter.

To renew our innovation capabilities, we will need to aim higher. Innovation expert and author Dorothy Leonard emphasizes the crucial role in innovation of what she calls "deep smarts," and what we might think of as mastery versus gaining only the skills we need to achieve tactical, incremental success. Deep smarts are essential to thinking and acting for the long term and to being able to look under the surface and make wise choices. One longs for deep smarts at the highest levels of national and corporate governance. But our experience often seems to suggest that something other than mastery is at work—to our detriment.

How does mastery come about? Consider for a moment the perhaps unlikely example of sushi making. The aspiring sushi chef, someone who wants to become a master and not merely the person who spends his days putting slices of fish on sushi plates, must undergo rigorous training. For the first year or so, it is said, the apprentice sweeps the floor. In the second year, he participates in buying fish at the market. Only after a considerable period has passed is he even allowed to pick up the knife.

The concept of apprenticeship is not unique to sushi and Japan, of course. It's an ancient system of training new craftsmen in many fields that has been practiced in many countries. Still today, the William Morris talent and literary agency makes its would-be agents work in the mailroom; taking the mail to everyone's office is both humbling and, it is said, a good way to help the would-be mogul "learn the business." At Annapolis, freshmen—known as plebes—face numerous tests, including a fifteen-hour endurance race and a climb up a greased monument on campus. First-year hires at strategy consulting firms crunch numbers. And even Donald Trump, as millions of viewers of the television show *The Apprentice* know, makes the distinction between beginners and masters.

The lesson to be taken from the sushi master's path is that apprenticeship must follow a certain tempo. Important learning takes time, and most of it is a tacit, hard-to-verbally-express knowledge in the fingertips, not the textbook, that is gleaned from observing the behavior, sometimes quirky, of master practitioners.

Mastery in any field does not come easily. As with learning to play a musical instrument, the skills cannot be obtained overnight and can never be faked on demand. Rather, they take years of rigorous practice. Therein lies the problem for a "quick-fix" culture like ours. George Leonard, when asked what the essential ingredient of mastery was, said, "Love the plateau." He was referring to the importance of patient, disciplined practice. It is a love that is an end in itself. The plateau refers to the experience all disciplined practitioners have— whether athletes or musicians or innovators—of finding that one's rate of progress sometimes flattens out despite one's best continuing efforts. Thus, loving the plateau means finding satisfaction in practice without the need for immediate feedback and reward. As the old saying goes, the master is one who knows and knows that he knows. No external validation is required.

In the same spirit, David Bell, the young French inventor of parkour—the extreme sport of running, jumping, vaulting over, and moving between and around buildings—says: "I'm still learning. I'm not sure of anything yet. I'm just trying to be as complete as I can. What I do is not really something that can be explained. It can just be practiced." Or as the Nike ad says, "Just do it."

The implications of these insights about mastery are numerous. First, we need to see our work on innovation as involving disciplined practice, not the quest for short-term wins. This is an obvious problem in our instant-gratification, quarterly-earnings-based culture in which corporate managers (and politicians) are evaluated and rewarded based on their success at maintaining a continuous upward trend that produces immediate results. At times, it seems like the question "What have you done for me lately?" approaches the status of a business model. If resource allocation, decision-making processes, and career-path planning all obey a short-term logic, while the important challenges facing both organizations and society are mostly long term, isn't the disconnect obvious?

At its heart, mastery is about the ability to incorporate apparently paradoxical elements into a single unified perspective. Its achievement requires an aptitude for seeing both sides of a coin. John Heider, in his masterful rewriting of the Tao Te Ching (*The Tao of Leadership: Lao Tzu's Tao Te Ching Adapted for a New Age*), states that the wise leader learns to see things backward, inside out, and upside down. While this admonition is the sine qua non of creative thinking—the discipline of lateral thinking pioneered by psychologist Edward de Bono rests on this principle, for example—it is also a necessary skill for acquiring the kind of wisdom we will need to cultivate Innovation Nation.

Richard Saul Wurman, a prominent designer and information architect, once said something that really struck me: We are moving from an era of either/or to and/also. Think about how the pendulum has swung in management theory, from an emphasis on differentiation and specialization to one of integration. The shift requires a balance between top down and bottom up, between planning and emergence, between open and closed, between federal and local, between large companies and start-ups. Mastery is about saying "and/also," which is, in fact, the only way that wicked problems can ever by addressed—through the inclusion of all points of view, as previously mentioned, under a common roof.

Even the innovator's dilemma may, at its heart, be revealed through this lens as a bit of a false dichotomy. We need both what new business development offers us—innovation, risk taking, and market acceptance—as well as what the mainstream requires in the form of control, predictability, efficiency, and margin. The trick is balancing the two agendas on an ongoing basis. Keeping the balance depends on having the right integrative mechanisms in place: common standards, shared understandings, knowledge-management protocols, and alignment around big ideas and a far-reaching vision.

The danger lies in allowing the integrative mechanisms to become a straitjacket or to dictate another kind of orthodoxy. One could argue that the U.S. system works because of its ability to balance contradictions in the spirit of "and/also." The Founding Fathers built a dynamism into our system of government that was meant to weaken the forces that tended toward centralization, and they provided myriad checks and balances to maintain a constant tension between the forces of standardization and diversity, and between federal and state, local and regional. No level of government can be allowed to dominate in such a system. Instead, we must encourage a kind of constant negotiation, one that only grows increasingly complex when other voices—public, academic, think tank—are included in the mix.

Every country must search for its own version of balance. Countries like Singapore, which were built around cultural notions of hierarchy and respect for authority, might have to engineer a different kind of experimental ethos. Singapore already understands that; it even invented something called the Phoenix Award, which actually celebrated entrepreneurs who had triumphed over some significant business setback and turned around their enterprise.

Mastery also requires singular approaches to its cultivation. Simply put, it doesn't come out of books—although the idea of mastery can be described in them. There is a reason why mastery was once cultivated in guilds, where recognized masters could guide apprentices through rigorous training. The deep smarts of innovation mastery will be instilled best not by textbooks or academic knowledge, but by direct transmission through the kind of mentoring programs that bring apprentices into contact with experts. Dorothy Leonard uses the term "guided experiences" for the various methods—guided practice, guided observation, guided problem solving, and guided experimentation—by which deep smarts can be cultivated. This is why I stressed earlier that well-developed, well-placed mentoring programs should be an important part of our national innovation drive.

LITTLE VENTURED, LITTLE GAINED

Have you had occasion to look at a stepladder lately?

The commonplace and intuitively usable contraption is now festooned with warning labels:

Do not overreach.
Do not stand above this step.
Set all four feet on a firm, level surface.
Lock spreaders before climbing.
Keep steps dry and clean.
Keep body centered between both siderails.
Duty rating: 225 lbs.
Danger! Metal conducts electricity! Use extreme care near any
    electrical current.
Danger: Do not stand at or above this level.
You can lose your balance.
Danger: Do not stand or sit.
Do not climb back section.
Ladders are dangerous.
Misuse may result in injury or death.

Then come the twenty numbered warnings, in small type, many repeating the same cautions listed above. Among my personal favorites are:

3. You should never use a ladder if you are not in good physical condition.
5. Do not use a ladder in front of unlocked doors.
7. Never place anything under or attach anything to a ladder to gain height or to adjust for uneven surfaces.
12. Use extreme caution getting on and off the ladder.
19. Windy conditions require extra caution.

In other words, anyone who uses a ladder the way normal human beings have always used ladders is as good as dead. This, of course, is caution carried to the point of absurdity, but I believe the ladder and its labels carry a deeper and more disturbing message for us all. American society is in danger of embracing risk aversion as an organizing principle, of being more concerned with avoiding failure than achieving greatness. Baseball players refer to this problem as the mid-career from mindset shift "hit the ball" to "don't miss." It's the same feeling we may have when watching the latest space shuttle launch. The news seems to focus on the bad thing that didn't happen, on the successful landing or the absence of a dreadful explosion, rather than on the explorer's ethos that inspired the launch in the first place.

But commerce has always teemed with risk. A new product is a walking land mine. What if it doesn't work right? What if the manufacturing process is flawed? Do you have enough working capital to cover emergencies? Will the foreman quit? What if the plant burns down? Will the customers like the thing? What if they order but don't pay?

We're fortunate that the United States still has plenty of risk takers, but it's hardly a truly national phenomenon in terms of the distribution of venture capital funding of companies in the United States. In 2006, Silicon Valley and the Boston area accounted for almost exactly half of that funding. Add the next four highest-funded regions—New York City, Los Angeles, Austin, and San Diego—and you account for 72 percent of funding. Little wonder the venture development firm Y Combinator insists that the companies it funds locate in either Silicon Valley or Boston. As it explains, "Frankly, we would not be doing start-ups a favor by encouraging them to locate in places other than Silicon Valley and Boston. . . . It's not a bug that founders often have to move to accept funding from us. It's a test of commitment and (since they're moving to start-up hubs) improves their chances of success." One wonders, therefore, what's going on in the rest of the country.

When I asked Mary Walshok of the University of California San Diego to name the most important ingredient in that city's entrepreneurial boom, she immediately pointed to a culture of shared risk. It is this kind of culture that enabled visionary entrepreneurial scientists to join with early venture capitalists, who themselves resembled nothing so much as patrons of the arts in their appreciation of the value of talent and their willingness to tolerate the uncertainty inherent in the development of new ideas. It is this kind of culture that built major U.S. industries. Recall that Henry Ford launched his motor company into a commercial environment that already had some fifty car companies competing for market share. Thomas Edison famously failed over and over again to make a lightbulb work. History, in fact, is filled with accounts of entrepreneurs who quit their jobs, mortgaged their houses, moved their families, and borrowed from friends and family in a valiant quest to make their dream come true.

The ethos from which these breakthroughs emerged reserved its highest accolades for risk takers whose ventures shared two specific attributes: the ability to disrupt the status quo and to make long-term improvements in the quality of life. Most of us can spot near-term objectives and opportunities, but the long-term picture tends to remain fuzzy no matter how good the optics. For instance, where will wireless content go next? What will be the killer application for Internet-delivered movies? What health and wellness innovation will capture the most attention from the aging baby-boomer generation?

Of course, it is easier to operate in the short term. We have the analytics, the standard operating procedures, and the consultants to tell us how to do it. But the safety of the short term is an illusion. The hot winds of disruption swirl all around us, whether they be in the form of new competitors, business models, technologies, consumer preferences, or geopolitical factors.

Economist W. Brian Arthur, a professor at the Santa Fe Institute

and a leading authority on technology-driven growth, compares the marketplace of innovative ideas to a casino. Over here, you have wireless communications; over there, search technology. If you want to ante up, each game will set you back a billion or two. Do you want to play? And if you do, are you sure you're ready to accept loss and even failure, which is, in fact, an unavoidable part of the go-for-broke, long-term innovation process?

For this reason, it might seem as though the best way to encourage long-term risk taking would be to provide some form of government safety net, a guarantee to help entrepreneurs pick themselves up and try again. But that would be discordant with a true risk-taking ethos. Instead, what our society must do is work to instill awareness that the inevitable counterpart of stunning success is sobering failure, and that the most successful of us have often forged the way to success through a number of failures.

Howard Gardner, dean of American educators, recounts an anecdote from his travels in China some twenty years ago. It is worth retelling verbatim:

> My wife and I were visiting Nanjing with our 18-month-old son. . . . Each day we allowed Benjamin to insert the key into the key slot at the registration desk of the Jinling Hotel. He had fun trying, whether or not he succeeded. But I began to notice that older Chinese people we happened to pass by would help my son place the key in the slot and would look at us disapprovingly, as if to chide us: "Don't you uncultivated parents know how to raise your child? Instead of allowing him to flail around and perhaps become frustrated, you should show him the proper way of doing things."

In this anecdote lies a key to understanding the success of Silicon Valley. There, learning comes with the appetite for taking a responsible level of risk and sometimes failing. The key qualifier is "responsible." I am not talking about repeated mistakes or failures that come from carelessness or a lack of intent; rather, I am referring to a noble failure—one that results from a good idea that just doesn't work. In Silicon Valley, such a failure is celebrated. If you take a fall after trying hard, you are most often encouraged to get up and try again. Failure does not cast you out of the network. In fact, the knowledge you've gained via failure tends to be applauded and encouraged.

Contrast the Silicon Valley ethos with the state of affairs in Europe or Japan, for example, where business failure is usually still an indelible black mark in future dealings with a bank, in raising money, or in finding partners. Indeed, the appetite for experimentation and risk is what will carry an idea forward in the Valley and allow it to keep reinventing itself and find the "emergent patterns" of innovation. We must work to spread this ethos throughout our society.

MAKING CHANGE

The pioneering Austrian economist Joseph Schumpeter famously spoke of "creative destruction" as the underlying engine for entrepreneurship. I think the same sort of demolition sets in motion the change process necessary for innovation. A would-be innovator has to get rid of something in order to make room for something new to emerge. In fact, I often point out that a chief destruction officer can be more important to a company than a chief innovation officer.

There is no better (and quirkier) example of creative destruction than the way in which Tiger Woods rebuilt his golf swing. Woods, who went professional in 1996, had utterly transformed the golfing world and record books by 2002. He had won eight major championships, including the so-called Tiger Slam, when he held all four major titles at once. But Woods determined that he could be better still. He decided to completely rebuild his swing—something usually done only by golfers who are struggling. To the horror of many, Woods won no major championships in 2003 and 2004. Was that early promise false? Hardly. In both 2005 and 2006, he picked up two of the four major championships.

It could be said that Woods' creed is "I improve, therefore I am." As he explained in an interview: "People thought it was asinine for me to change my swing after I won the Masters by twelve shots. . . . Why would you want to change that? Well, I thought I could become better." He was also candid about the risks involved. "I've always taken risks to try to become a better golfer, and that's one of the things that has gotten me this far."

And Woods had a long-term perspective, because he was looking for fundamental change. "I knew I wasn't in the greatest position in my swing at the Masters," Woods said. "But my timing was great, so I got away with it. And I made almost every putt. You can have a wonderful week like that even when your swing isn't sound. But can you still contend in tournaments with that swing when your timing isn't good? Will it hold up over a long period of time? The answer to those questions, with the swing I had, was no. And I wanted to change that."

Clearly, what was important to Woods was not seeing an endpoint, but rather a process of continuous improvement. His swing coach, Hank Haney, remarked, "He's looking for getting better. That's what he looks for every day."

Crucial for Woods in accomplishing his goal was a willingness to change, an acceptance of the discomfort of moving away from what was familiar. He had an openness to new possibilities, and the humility to go back to the beginning.

Relative to the family of nations, the United States is an old country. By comparison, the People's Republic of China, although culturally old, operates under a form of government born in 1949. India achieved its independence only in 1947. Even some of "old" Europe is new: both Germany and Italy, after all, were unified in 1871, nearly one hundred years after the creation of the United States. As an incumbent, therefore, the United States must learn to adopt a "beginner's mind" that looks beyond our current "installed base" of competencies and considers what we need to create anew.

If we are to renew our commitment to being the world's leading innovator, we must teach three foundational values—the will to mastery, the spirit of risk taking, and the embrace of continuous change—supplemented by a crucial fourth value that rejects the idea of global competition as a zero-sum game. In other words, we must fully embrace the profoundly transformative notion that what is good for the world is good for the United States. This does not in any way suggest that we ought to squelch our competitive spirit or appetite for doing well, far from it. But we must understand—and teach our children—that we can best compete in the fast-globalizing world by being collaborative and by facilitating the enhancement of life outside of our borders as well as inside them. Rather than seeking to dominate the world economy, we must seek to lead it as a visionary and progressive problem solver.

WHAT'S THE STORY?

The first step on the road to resurrecting our national commitment to innovation is to emulate Sweden's Bo Ekman by asking: What is the use of America? In what way can we mature the American idea? Unless and until we come up with a compelling answer, our nation won't be able to shift back into high gear.

My proposed answer is that America accept the mantle of accelerant for global innovation by steering the world toward addressing the formidable range of wicked problems we face. Inspiring an entire society to mobilize around such a grand vision will be no mean feat, but it has been done before.

Imagine sitting at home by your radio in March of 1933, and hearing the calm, reassuring voice of your new president, Franklin Delano Roosevelt, speaking to you directly about the banking crisis and the country's ability to recover. Over the next eleven years, through depression and war, FDR would give another twenty-nine of his "fireside chats," speaking in vivid, easily understood language (over 80 percent of FDR's words were among the one thousand most commonly used words in English). Here is what Roosevelt had to say about his revolutionary program: "I have no expectations of making a hit every time I come to bat. What I seek is the highest possible batting average, not only for myself, but for the team."

Roosevelt clearly understood a national leader's power to raise the consciousness of a citizenry through effective storytelling. Howard Gardner has remarked that the only way to change minds, whether it be individual attitudes or a whole society's collective prejudice, is to tell a transformational story in diverse ways, through what he calls redescription, in order to drive it home.

As the preceding chapters have shown, the United States is in need of a new national narrative. Against all evidence, we continue to behave as if we will always be number one in innovation and in everything else. That's akin to the myth that Silicon Valley can never be mortally wounded by competitors, to say nothing of its recurrent cycles of boom and bust. For the digital faithful, the unsupported belief that the "Valley will always come back" has almost become a mantra. Once the idea and practices of Silicon Valley achieve global acceptance, the notion of the Valley's immortality will carry no more weight than the myth that the United States will always be top dog, no matter what we do or say.

Other dangerous U.S. myths arise from misguided and unworkable propositions for mending our ways. We think, for instance, that education can be reformed merely by piling on extra homework, or that we can speed innovation by devoting more of our resources to devising and developing new commercial products. Such remedies may be incrementally useful, but they don't address the need for fundamental reform of the innovation process or of education itself.

Myths like these must be dispelled. In their place, we need a new national narrative around innovation. Just as FDR provided the country its healing narrative during the Depression, or Winston Churchill talked Britain through its wartime struggles, today's leaders will need to articulate a new story around innovation. They must make a simple and easily understood yet vivid case for the goal of becoming the world's first Innovation Nation, persuasively laying out the motivation behind it and the plan for reaching it. I have attempted in this book to provide some food for thought in crafting that narrative.

The stewards of our national innovation agenda must ask what, specifically, is our desired future state. What is the purpose of the United States? What do we stand for in the twenty-first century? Who do we choose to be and what agendas do we choose to engage in? What ideals do we choose to embrace? Which parts of our national narrative do we need to leave behind and which parts should we affirm, invent anew, or refresh? And how do we articulate this narrative in many ways to shift mindsets and build alignment?

Our understanding can be deepened by considering best- and worst-case scenarios. These should be fleshed out for the public as I have sketched the story of Jim Polk in preceding chapters. The specific global challenges and wicked problems we face must be explained clearly and forcefully. They inevitably endanger us as much as they imperil our neighbors, and the U.S. public can surely be rallied to take on those problems with the same energy and conviction, the same ingenuity and resilience, that we brought to the great challenges we faced in the twentieth century.

There is fertile ground to work with. Presenting innovation as a generational challenge to preserve our leadership role in the world seems certain to resonate with our citizens and to instill a sense of urgency.

Some analysts of the world order have argued that the last century may have been the "American Century," but that the twenty-first century is a brave new world. I agree that the United States is unlikely to dominate world economics and geopolitics in this century as we did in the latter half of the last century. I also assert, however, that the United States can and should rise to the occasion of leading global society forward in this fast-evolving new world. It is within our power to earn anew the status of "indispensable nation" by using our mastery of innovation as a force for good in the world.

EPILOGUE

There is no avant garde. There are only those who are a little late.

—Edgard Varèse, composer

The sheer, vertical walls of El Capitan loom large over California's Yosemite Valley. The mountain rises 3,400 feet from the valley floor, roughly equivalent to six Washington Monuments or two and a half World Trade Centers. It is thought to be the single largest piece of granite on earth. Its majestic bulk is unmistakable. Touching it, in the words of one climber, is "as if you've put your hands on the side of a planet."

And the existence of such commanding height is matched only by the all-too-human itch to conquer it.

In 1958, legendary rock climber Warren J. Harding succeeded in scaling El Capitan. The ascent took more than six weeks and was described as a siege approach—waves of ropes secured in stone by iron pitons, massed teams, a methodical hand-over-hand climb.

Though the initial achievement was not to be diminished, subsequent years brought a spate of new firsts: the first climb in "free style" without inset ropes; the first use of cam anchors; the first woman to reach the top. And with successive climbs, the time required to scale the heights began to shrink.

Fast-forward to 2002. In that year, American Hans Florine and Japanese Yuji Hirayama climbed El Capitan not in weeks or even days, but in an astonishing two hours and forty-eight minutes. The reason for the pair's blistering speed? Improved equipment, improved climbing methods, and, most of all, improved attitude. Each succeeding new accomplishment shaped their sense that the seemingly impossible could, in fact, be achieved, that they could dance at the edge of risk and prudence without stopping until they had scaled the mountain face in record time.

What is striking is that the search for ever greater speed and the improvements in equipment and technique that enable it are continuing unabated in the climbing world. Performance today is aided by nanotechnology-enhanced climbing attire, new kinds of adhesive soles for climbing shoes, and more refined concepts of operations and tactics. And as the climbers' performance becomes more sophisticated, so do their goals. Above all, though, what underpins the continuous push to stretch the outer limits is the constantly changing sense of what is possible.

The story of El Capitan and those who have conquered it is a perfect metaphor, I believe, for the global race toward the innovation high ground, a contest in which each country, not just the United States, has an opportunity to fulfill its own vision of Innovation Nation. It is the story of how massed teams and top-down methodologies have given way to lean entrepreneurial partnerships and improvisation in the field; how heavy equipment has become light; how an appetite for risk taking has led to innovation; and how technology has enabled dramatic performance improvements.

Most important, the story speaks of talented performers who are open to dramatic possibilities and redefining one's perceived parameters. Countries all around the world these days are harking to the siren song of conquering new peaks, of stretching the outer limits of human progress, of giving full expression to the human spirit.

What will a world of Innovative Nations be like? It all depends on how innovation is used. If China pursues innovative ways to master information technology to pursue network-centric warfare in order to defeat the U.S. Navy in some future conflict, then China's innovative capabilities will threaten global stability. As inventor Dean Kamen has aptly remarked, any tool can also be used as a weapon. Conversely, if China chooses to invest in clean technologies so as to ease her entry into the ranks of developed nations, then the world will reap a huge dividend in the form of reduced air and water pollution, carbon-based emissions, and environmental degradation.

Soon, though, we won't even speak of innovation in terms of a single nation, whether it be China, the United States, Denmark, or any other country on any continent. Our interest and concern will shift to the spaces between the nodes and away from the nodes themselves. We will have more and more opportunities to look at the world through the same kind of conceptual lenses that we have historically used for considering a single country.

A strong United States will certainly be central to global progress and to the advent of Innovation World. Perhaps we will become the Silicon Valley equivalent on the world stage. No nation is perfect, of course, and the United States is no exception. But we do have an unmatched record of altruism and of translating humanistic values into social action. The United States' scale, wealth, and history of influence will, I believe, continue to make it the "indispensable nation" in a world of innovators, but it will no longer own the keys to innovation exclusively. It may be the dominant player at times, a coparticipant in some opportunity spaces, and only a follower in others. And a *pax Americana* springing from innovation preeminence will no longer be possible; unmoored from traditional geographical, political, and social boundaries, innovation will increasingly spring from global open sources.

And that's as it should be, because what we need in a world of wicked problems that challenge all citizens of the earth is a global innovation system for all of us, one that has the potential to benefit each individual. And to gather all of the relevant players and elements of each global challenge under one roof, as legitimate work on wicked problems requires us to do, our analyses must go beyond national borders.

That brings us to the question of where the commons for reflecting all stakeholder interests will be located. Will it be a newly resurgent United Nations, a new set of institutions as yet unknown, or a new social space united by the power of a new set of technology but without a traditional center? Will it be a coalition of the willing that harnesses the wisdom of crowds and their bottom-up power to come to grips with an emerging agenda of major problems? Will technology and platforms mature in ways that allow them to replace centralized institutions? Right now, the answers are only beginning to take shape in the minds of a few visionaries. Only time will reveal the answers.

In any event, the phenomenon of innovation on a global scale will proceed along a path that will become increasingly familiar as country after country makes the journey. For example, talent and capital will continue to flow to hot spots, locations where the work of innovation can occur. Genius will still benchmark itself based on a world-class scale of peers. It will then, as now, take note of the availability of enabling technology and the temper of the work and living environment, comparing them to today's innovative hot spots like Silicon Valley, Bangalore, Helsinki, and Singapore.

What is most important, however, is that the next big ideas can now truly come from anywhere. Talent is not confined to any culture or geography. No one has a monopoly on ideas. And that will make the world a more thrilling place to inhabit, one in which the catalytic nature of diversity and the power of innovation on a planetary basis may well unleash the full potential of human beings to better themselves and to create a world well worth living in. All of which is a very good thing, because there are still many El Capitans left to climb.

NOTES ON SOURCES

The journey of writing this book took me over a vast literature, some of it in academic and public-sector source material, some in the popular literature, and not an inconsiderable amount online. Toward the end of this process, my office resembled the reading room of a small library, which is not surprising given the "wickedness" surrounding the question of what we should do about our national innovation posture.

The notes in this section are intended not to be a full scholarly apparatus, but rather a guide to some of the more interesting sources, as well as a way to illuminate some of the complexities underlying the discussions in the book. The Innovation Nation Web site, www.innovationation.org, has a more conventional bibliography as well as full URLs for the Web sites mentioned in these notes.

INTRODUCTION

Page 1   five-year plan: Comprehensive information on China's eleventh five-year plan can be found at english.gov.cn/special/115y_index.htm.

Page 2   national innovation strategies: For examples of some of the more interesting national innovation strategies, see *Innovative Sweden*, published by the Ministry of Industry, Employment and Communications, October 2004; *Shaping Australia's Future Innovation*, an October 1999 report from the Department of Industry, Science and Resources, which was prepared for the country's First Innovation Summit, held in Canberra in 2000; and *Achieving Excellence: Investing in People, Knowledge and Opportunity*, from the Canadian government, available at www.innovationstrategy.gc.ca.

Page 2   Beijing will have the world's largest nanotechnology research: Stan Williams, head of H P's quantum science research group in Palo Alto, is my source for China's nanotechnology research capability. Mark Bunger of Lux Research is my source for different national approaches to nanotechnology research.

Page 3   Hungary: *Beyond Borders: Ernst & Young's Global Biotechnology Report 2007* is largely about the established centers of biotech research and corporations. But it also contains brief essays on a fascinating array of new biotech hotspots, such as Hungary.

Page 4   Pew Global Attitudes Project: The Pew Global Attitudes Project, www.pewglobal.org, provides an invaluable gauge of global opinion on a range of issues.

Page 5   Council on Competitiveness: The two most valuable of the various reports on U.S. innovation and competitiveness—particularly in terms of background data—are the Council on Competitiveness's *Competitiveness Index: Where America Stands*, issued in March 2007, and the National Academy of Sciences' *Rising Above the Gathering Storm: Energizing and Employing America for a Brighter Future*, issued in 2005. Both are available online. The council's report can be found at www.compete.org and the NAS report at www.nap.edu.

Page 8   arbitrageur: I first expanded on my notion of arbitrage in "The Worldwide Web of Chinese Business," *Harvard Business Review*, March-April 1993.

Page 13   I'm reminded of the debate: For some insight into the changing world of mountaineering, see Reinhold Messner's *The Challenge* (Oxford University Press, 1977) and the idiosyncratic *Mount Analogue: A Novel of Symbolically Authentic Non-Euclidean Adventures in Mountaineering*, by René Daumal (City Lights Books, 1959).

CHAPTER 1. BRINGING INNOVATION TO INNOVATION

Page 18   Economist Muhammad Yunus: There is a large literature on microlending, but Muhammad Yunus' firsthand account, *Banker to the Poor: Micro-Lending and the Battle Against World Poverty* (Public Affairs, 2003), provides a good overview as well as details of his inspiring story. The Young Foundation report, *Social Innovation: What It Is, Why It Matters, and How It Can Be Accelerated*, by Geoff Mulgan, offers the best overview of the subject. The report is available online at www.youngfoundation.org.uk/publications.

Page 22   Clayton M. Christensen: *Knowledge and the Wealth of Nations*, by David Warsh (W. W. Norton, 2006), provides a brilliant survey of how economists—from Adam Smith to Robert Solow to Paul Romer—have wrestled with the contribution of innovation to economic growth. Clayton M. Christensen's book *The Innovator's Dilemma: When New Technologies Cause Great Firms to Fail* (Harvard Business School Press, 1997) introduces his concept of disruptive innovation. He extends his analysis in both *The Innovator's Solution: Creating and Sustaining Successful Growth* (Harvard Business School Press, 2003) and *Seeing What's Next: Using the Theories of Innovation to Predict Industry Change* (Harvard Business School Press, 2004).

Page 24   The term "wicked problem": Some of the more interesting books on global "wicked problems" are Jean-François Rischard's *High Noon: 20 Global Problems, 20 Years to Solve Them* (Basic Books, 2002); Bjørn Lomborg's *Global Crises, Global Solutions: Priorities for a World of Scarcity* (Cambridge University Press, 2004); and Lester Brown's *Plan B 2.0: Rescuing a Planet Under Stress and a Civilization in Trouble* (W. W. Norton, 2006).

CHAPTER 2. SILENT SPUTNIK

Page 30   "silent Sputnik": I am indebted to Professor Rita Colwell of Johns Hopkins University for the term "silent Sputnik." *Sputnik: The Shock of the Century* (Walker & Co., 2007), by Paul Dickson, provides a good, popular history of Sputnik and its consequences.

Page 32   Shanghai Jiao Tong University: The main international survey
           of universities is conducted by Shanghai Jiao Tong University.
           The results are available at ed.sjtu.edu.cn/ranking.htm. The
           National Science Foundation does an annual survey of doctor-
           ates in science and engineering, www.nsf.gov/statistics/srvy-
           doctorates. The NSF is also the principal source for data on
           research and development spending, www.nsf.gov/statistics/
           showpub.cfm?TopID=8. Quarterly data on venture capital
           funding in the United States can be found at the Pricewater-
           houseCoopers Money Tree, www.pwcmoneytree.com.

Page 32   numbers of students being trained: There are many sources
           useful for tracking higher education and science. The National
           Science Foundation's Survey of Earned Doctorates has been
           mentioned above. Its statistical breakdowns by subject, citizen-
           ship, gender, and many other factors are valuable. Isihighlycited.
           com is a free database of the most-cited researchers in science.
           Vivek Wadhwa at Duke University has conducted valuable re-
           search comparing availability and skill of engineers in the
           United States, China, and India. A good summary can be found
           in his article "Where the Engineers Are," in *Issues in Science and
           Technology*'s Spring 2007 issue.

Page 34   The Program for International Student Assessment: Interna-
           tional comparison of educational achievement is a highly con-
           tentious field. If you Google either of the main studies, the
           Program for International Student Assessment (PISA) or
           Trends in International Mathematics and Science Study
           (TIMSS), you'll find as many polemics for and against as plain
           reports of the findings. The Organization for Economic Coop-
           eration and Development (OECD), which runs PISA, has vol-
           umes of data and background on the methodology at www.pisa.
           oecd.org. The National Center for Educational Statistics, part
           of the federal Department of Education, is the best portal to
           access TIMSS: nces.ed.gov/timss/.

Page 35   According to the National Math & Science Initiative: The National Math & Science Initiative, www.nationalmathandscience. org, was launched in March 2007. Data on age-appropriate books were pointed out to me by Thomas Kalil, special assistant to the chancellor for science and technology, University of California, Berkeley. They come from C. Smith, R. Constantino, and S. Krashen, "Difference in Print Environment for Children in Beverly Hills, Compton and Watts," *Emergency Librarian* 24 no. 4, (1997), 8–9.

Page 35   trade group of Indian outsourcing companies: Nasscom's figure on the migration of thirty thousand Indian-born professionals is cited in "Indians Find They Can Go Home Again," *New York Times*, December 26, 2005. Data on Hsinchu Industrial Park are from a presentation by Irving Ho, chairman, EIC Corporation, to US-Japan Technology Management Center, School of Engineering, Stanford University, October 1999.

Page 37   A global study of R & D tax credits: Robert Atkinson, who runs the Information Technology and Innovation Foundation, has done extensive work on R & D tax policies and U.S. high-tech trade. His article "Deep Competitiveness" in the Winter 2007 *Issues in Science and Technology* provides a clear summary. The federal Bureau of Economic Analysis, www.bea.gov, tracks U.S. R & D spending. Eurostat does the same for the member states of the European Union, ec.europa.eu/eurostat/.

Page 39   venture capital's move overseas: Accountancy group Ernst & Young publishes an annual survey of venture capital, the *Global Venture Capital Insights Report*. Quarterly figures on U.S. venture capital investment and fundraising can be found at the PricewaterhouseCoopers MoneyTree, www.pwcmoneytree.com.

Detailed breakdowns of U.S. trade figures are available through the Bureau of Economic Analysis, www.bea.gov/international/index.htm. The Census Bureau also provides trade figures, with a more user-friendly presentation of the data, at www.census.gov/foreign-trade/www.

Page 41   The American Society of Civil Engineers: The American Society of Civil Engineers' infrastructure report card is available at www.asce.org/reportcard/2005/index.cfm.

Page 44   noted futurist Pierre Wack: Pierre Wack wrote about his approach to scenarios in two *Harvard Business Review* articles: "Scenarios: Unchartered Waters Ahead," *HBR*, September/October 1985, and "Scenarios: Shooting the Rapids," *HBR*, November/December 1985. The standard introduction to scenarios is *The Art of the Long View: Paths to Strategic Insight for You and Your Company* (Currency, 1991), by Peter Schwartz, the cofounder and chairman of Global Business Network.

CHAPTER 3. THE NEW GEOGRAPHY OF INNOVATION

Page 55   Singapore is an island nation: Some sense of the extraordinary variety of Singapore's innovation initiatives can be gained through the Biopolis Web site, www.a-star.edu.sg/astar/biopolis/index.do; One North's Web site, www.one-north.sg; and the Web site of the National Research Foundation, www.nrf.gov.sg/.

page 56   A monograph on Biopolis: The JTC Corporation's useful monograph is called *Biopolis, Design for Life!*, JTC Corporation, Singapore, 2006.

Page 60   world leader in wind power: Denmark's pioneering energy program is described with some wonderful anecdotes in "How Denmark Paved the Way to Energy Independence," *Wall Street Journal*, April 16, 2007.

Page 61   My brief visit: Information in English about the Danish Innovation Council and links to its reports can be found at www.innovationsraadet.dk/indhold.asp?id=205.

Page 62   flexibility and security: A helpful summary of flexicurity can be found at A Fistful of Euros, fistfulofeuros.net/?p=2468. Nordicmodel, aplefebvre.wordpress.com, is an interesting Web log covering all aspects of the Nordic economic and social model.

Page 63   The school my friend runs: Kaospilots and its novel approach to management education is described in *Kaospilot A–Z*, by Uffe Elbaek (Kaos Communication, 2006). The school's Web site is at www.kaospilot.dk.

Page 69   As a recent report by The Asia Society: The Asia Society's report, "Math and Science Education in a Global Age: What the U.S. Can Learn from China," published in May 2006, is available at www.internationaled.org/mathsciencereport.htm.

Page 75   U.S. helicopter industry: The slide of the U.S. helicopter industry is an instructive case study of how the United States has ceded the innovation high ground in some critical areas. The Department of Defense study, *The Vertical Lift Industrial Base: Outlook 2004–2014*, can be found at the Web site of the Pentagon's industrial policy site, www.acq.osd.mil/ip/.

CHAPTER 4. MAKING TALENT

Page 84   Finland spends 6.4 percent: Useful background on education in Finland can be found at the Finnish Ministry of Foreign Affairs information site, www.finland.fi/Education_Research/. The most comprehensive set of comparative data on education systems is generated by the OECD, www.oecd.org/education/. A simpler tool for comparing countries in terms of education, and in many other areas, is Nation Master, www.nationmaster.com, which aggregates data from many sources including the OECD. The graphically brilliant Gapminder, www.gapminder.org, enables comparisons of a small set of data across time.

Page 86   The country with a brand identity: Comprehensive information on Singapore's education system can be found through the Singapore Ministry of Education, www.moe.gov.sg.

Page 89   educational excellence: Ireland: A good summary of Ireland's educational leap forward is in "The Luck of the Irish," *Fortune*, October 25, 1999.

Page 90   And according to *Tapping: Tapping America's Potential*, www.tap2015.
             org, has as its goal doubling the number of science, engineering,
             technology, and math graduates in the United States with bach-
             elor's degrees by 2015.

Page 91   Consultants at McKinsey: McKinsey & Company's three-part
             study on offshoring and the global labor market is available
             through the McKinsey Global Institute, www.mckinsey.com/
             mgi/. Even though the McKinsey figures on the impact of off-
             shoring may seem startling, some observers believe they under-
             state the problem. Princeton economist Alan Blinder, a former
             vice chairman of the Federal Reserve, has been particularly out-
             spoken. His working paper, "How Many U.S. Jobs Might be
             Offshorable?" is available through Princeton's Center for Eco-
             nomic Policy Studies, www.princeton.edu/~ceps/.

Page 91   Harvard professor and education authority Howard Gardner:
             Howard Gardner's recent *Five Minds for the Future* discusses the
             importance of ethics in education (Harvard Business School
             Press, 2007). He also explored this territory in *Good Work: When
             Excellence and Ethics Meet*, coauthored with Mihaly Csikszentmi-
             halyi and William Damon (Basic Books, 2002).

Page 93   Eager young veterans: Two recent books chronicle the extraor-
             dinary impact of the G.I. Bill. Susan Mettler's *Soldiers to Citizens:
             The G.I. Bill and the Making of the Greatest Generation* (Oxford Uni-
             versity Press, 2005) is an academic work based on surveys of
             nearly 1,500 beneficiaries of the bill. Edward Humes's *Over Here:
             How the G.I. Bill Transformed the American Dream* (Harcourt, 2006)
             is a more journalistic account.

Page 97   Since 2000, the Bill and Melinda Gates: A critical evaluation of
             the efforts of the Bill and Melinda Gates Foundation in high
             schools was "Bill Gates Gets Schooled," *Business Week*, June 26,
             2006. The foundation's own information and analyses of its ef-
             forts can be found at www.gatesfoundation.org/UnitedStates/
             Education.

Page 105   And these integrative approaches: Howard Gardner's *The Disciplined Mind: What All Students Should Understand* (Simon & Schuster, 1999) eloquently describes the education that, in Gardner's words, "every child deserves." John Seely Brown's description of new models of learning environments was originally presented to the Forum for the Future of Higher Education's Aspen Symposium in 2005. It can be read at his Web site, www.johnseely brown.com.

Page 110   FIRST: Details of FIRST and information on the latest challenges set for its young competitors can be found at www.us first.org.

CHAPTER 5. SEDUCING TALENT

Page 114   *Flight of the Creative Class*: Richard Florida's two books, *The Rise of the Creative Class* (Basic Books, 2003) and *The Flight of the Creative Class* (Collins, 2005), contain a wealth of information and analysis on what I term "seducing talent." In addition to examining the conditions that best attract the "creative class," Florida for a while compiled a Creative Class Index that ranked cities based on their attractiveness. When he last published the results, San Francisco was number one and Austin number two.

Page 115   A study by scholars: The work of Vivek Wadhwa, Gary Gereffi, and their colleagues at Duke University's engineering school has already been cited. In addition to Wadhwa's "Where the Engineers Are," see the major report, *Framing the Engineering Outsourcing Debate*, available for download at memp.pratt.duke.edu/ outsourcing/.

Page 116   Globalization and the easy movement: AnnaLee Saxenian, *The New Argonauts: Regional Advantage in a Global Economy* (Harvard University Press, 2006), looks at the phenomenon of globalized, commuting entrepreneurs who gravitate recurrently to necessary resources and knowledge centers rather than maintaining loyalty to any particular home base.

CHAPTER 6. THE IMPORTANCE OF PLACE

Page 132   Jazz clubs, in contrast: My earlier book, *Jamming: The Art and Discipline of Business Creativity* (Harper Business, 1996), expands on the metaphor of jazz as an open system for innovation.

Page 134   In 1595, the Italian Jesuit: *The Memory Palace of Matteo Ricci* (Viking, 1984), by Yale sinologist Jonathan Spence, is a delight of historical writing. The memory palace is part of the story, but the real focus of Spence's work is the experience of the sixteenth-century Catholic missionary in China.

Page 134   imagination can soar: Stewart Brand's *How Buildings Learn: What Happens After They're Built* (Penguin, 1994) provides numerous examples of how the best buildings adapt over time to their users. Inflexible structures both stifle users and prove inadequate to support the inevitable changes in any organization over time. Brand himself builds on the work of Christopher Alexander, notably *A Pattern Language* (Oxford University Press, 1977) and *A Timeless Way of Building* (Oxford University Press, 1979).

Page 136   the original Skunk Works: The background of the original Skunk Works can be found in *Kelly: More Than My Share of It All*, the autobiography of its founder, Clarence "Kelly" Johnson (Smithsonian Institution Press, 1985). It is rife with colorful anecdotes and Johnson's particular brand of wisdom.

Page 136   A skunk works is an elegant: Charles O'Reilly and Michael Tushman, "The Ambidextrous Organization," *Harvard Business Review*, April 2004.

Page 138   hearing aids: I wrote up the Oticon story as a Harvard Business School case study: Oticon (A) # 395144, published May 2 1995. It is available through HBS Press Online, http://harvardbusinessonline.hbsp.harvard.edu/b02/en/cases/cases_home.jhtml.

Page 144   "see what you mean": I believe firmly in the importance of facilitation, but the literature on the subject is pallid at best. My own *Facilitation Manifesto* (Kao & Company, 2007) provides a brief introduction, but the best understanding of the power of facilitation may come through studying great movie directors and their talent for coaxing diverse talent to perform cooperatively and beyond their expectations.

CHAPTER 7. THE "US" IN USA

Page 154   The literal meaning of open source: There have been numerous books explaining the open-source phenomenon. *The Success of Open Source* (Harvard University Press, 2005), by Berkeley political scientist Steven Weber, and Yochai Benkler's *The Wealth of Networks: How Social Production Transforms Markets and Freedom* (Yale University Press, 2006) are rigorous, academic examinations of the political economy of the networked world. Eric Raymond's essays are collected in *The Cathedral and the Bazaar: Musings on Linux and Open Source by an Accidental Revolutionary* (O'Reilly Media, 2001). The Demos pamphlet, *Wide Open: Open Source Methods and Their Future Potential*, by Geoff Mulgan, Tom Steinberg, and Omar Salem, offers some interesting speculations on how open-source ideas could be adopted in many different fields.

Page 159   "out-of-control behavior": Kevin Kelly's *Out of Control: The New Biology of Machines, Social Systems and the Economic World* (Perseus Books, 1995) is an excellent overview of emergent behavior.

Page 162   The popular comic-book: Warren Ellis is my favorite graphic novelist by a mile. His series *Global Frequency* is a visionary look at the future of networked intelligence. His other work provides eye-opening and bent views of the future of journalism, celebrity, space exploration.

Page 165   dogfighting fighter pilots: Robert Coram's *Boyd: The Fighter Pilot Who Changed the Art of War* (Little Brown & Co., 2002) discusses the OODA loop and John Boyd's many other innovations and eccentricities.

Page 172   Glenn Reynolds: Glenn Reynolds's *An Army of Davids: How Markets and Technologies Empower Ordinary People to Beat Big Media, Big Government, and Other Goliaths* (Thomas Nelson, 2007) is a euphoric work about the power of user-created new media. A more measured stance can be found in my colleague Lance Knobel's "Nullius in Verba: Navigating Through the New Media Democracy," in *Barons to Bloggers* (Melbourne University Press, 2005).

Page 174   The wiki software's: *Wikinomics: How Mass Collaboration Changes Everything* (Portfolio, 2006), by Donald Tapscott, does a good job of explaining Wikipedia and other "crowdsourcing" ideas. James Surowiecki's *The Wisdom of Crowds* (Doubleday, 2004) covers just why mass collaboration can be so successful, and is particularly good on prediction markets.

Page 178   But Lessig has developed: Lawrence Lessig writes passionately on his blog, www.lessig.org/blog. His *Free Culture: The Nature and Future of Creativity* (Penguin, 2005) explains the ideas behind both his legal battles and the creation of Creative Commons.

CHAPTER 8. WELCOME TO THE FUTURE

Page 184   The National Business Incubation Association: The National Business Incubation Association, www.nbia.org, maintains data on incubators in the United States.

Page 186   In his seminal book: Michael Porter's *The Competitive Advantage of Nations* (Free Press, 1990) not only established the standard vocabulary for discussions on regional economies, but also sparked an entire industry of consulting firms advising cities, regions, and nations. Porter himself helped found Monitor Group, one of the leading companies in the field. *The Competitive Advantage of Nations* was preceded by Porter's *Competitive Strategy* (Free Press, 1980) and *Competitive Advantage* (Free Press, 1985), which were standard-setting books on corporate strategy.

Page 190   Frans Johansson: Frans Johansson's *The Medici Effect: What Elephants and Epidemics Can Teach Us About Innovation* (Harvard Business School Press, 2006) argues that innovation occurs when diverse groups and resources combine to "ignite an explosion of ideas."

Page 191   Mary Walshok: Much of my material on San Diego comes from numerous conversational jam sessions as well as more formal interviews with Mary Walshok, associate vice chancellor, Public Programs, University of California, San Diego.

Page 195   But in the U.S. federal budget: The Center for Economic and Policy Research provides an online budget calculator that enables users to place specific spending or tax numbers in the context of the overall federal budget: www.cepr.net/calculators/bc/cbc.html.

Page 200   Here's what Richard Rhodes: The definitive history of the Manhattan Project—and an essential text for anyone interested in understanding the dynamics of large-scale innovation—is *The Making of the Atomic Bomb* by Richard Rhodes (Simon & Schuster, 1986). Rhodes also generously devoted a morning to an interview with me in which I was able to delve more deeply into the lessons the Manhattan Project holds for an effective national innovation agenda.

Apollo, to my mind, still lacks its Richard Rhodes. The best general history is *Apollo: The Race to the Moon*, by Charles Murray and Catherine Bly Cox (Simon & Schuster, 1989). *The Man Who Ran the Moon: James E. Webb, NASA, and the Secret History of Project Apollo*, by Piers Bizony (Thunder's Mouth Press, 2006), uncovers additional material and is particularly valuable on the subject of James Webb.

Page 205   Johnson operated the Skunk Works: In addition to *Kelly: More Than My Share of It All*, is Clarence "Kelly" Johnson's autobiography (previously cited), a more thorough account of the later history of the Lockheed Skunk Works can be found in *Skunk Works: A Personal Memoir of My Years at Lockheed*, by Ben Rich and Leo Janos (Little Brown & Co., 1994). Lockheed Martin maintains a helpful Skunk Works site, www.lockheedmartin.com/skunkworks, which includes Johnson's fourteen rules (and where fans can buy official Skunk Works merchandise). The Skunk Works is also covered as one of the case studies in *Organizing Genius: The Secrets of Creative Collaboration*, by Warren Bennis and Patricia Ward Biederman (Perseus Books, 1998).

Page 206   George Leonard, author of *Mastery: Mastery: The Keys to Success and Long-Term Fulfillment*, by George Leonard (Penguin, 1992), grew largely out of Leonard's own experience as an aikido master. But his theory of mastery holds important lessons for any pursuit, whether it is improving your tennis game or your national innovation capabilities. Leonard was also kind enough to spend part of a day speaking with me about mastery and effective teaching.

Page 208   Senge and his colleagues: For more on the topic of presencing, one may wish to consult the source: *Presence: An Exploration of Profound Change in People, Organizations, and Society*, by Peter Senge, C. Otto Scharmer, Joseph Jaworski, and Betty Sue Flowers (Currency Books, 2006).

Page 209   The Marshall Plan: There are surprisingly few popular accounts of the pioneering Marshall Plan. Useful scholarly essays on the plan and its effects can be found in *The Marshall Plan: Fifty Years After*, edited by Martin A. Schain (Palgrave Macmillan, 2001). Allen Dulles, later famous as a director of the Central Intelligence Agency, wrote about the plan when its passage was still in doubt in 1947. Dulles's work *The Marshall Plan* was uncovered by an academic researcher forty years after Dulles wrote it, and was subsequently published (Berg Publishers, 1993).

CHAPTER 9. A NATIONAL INNOVATION AGENDA

Page 219   Rubin its first director: Robert Rubin's own perspective on the National Economic Council and many other issues can be found in his modest, readable memoir, written with Jacob

Weisberg, *In an Uncertain World: Tough Choices from Wall Street to Washington* (Random House, 2003).

Page 221   Robert Kaplan and David Norton: Robert Kaplan and David Norton, "The Office of Strategy Management," *Harvard Business Review*, October 2005.

Page 221   Tekes has a $500 million: Robert D. Atkinson's *The Past and Future of America's Economy: Long Waves of Innovation that Power Cycles of Growth* (Edward Elgar, 2005) uses Finland's Tekes as a model for what Atkinson terms an "American ingenuity foundation." The Web site of Tekes, www.tekes.fi/eng, has numerous valuable case studies of government, private-sector, and academic collaboration with international partners.

Page 222   We must develop: *What Is a Critical Technology?* by Bruce A. Bimber and Stephen W. Popper (Rand, 1994) provides a useful structure for assessing technologies on a national basis. The biennial reports of the National Critical Technologies Panel during the Clinton administration are available online through the National Archives, but Google's search engine seems better at retrieving them than the archive's own search function, www.archive.gov.

Page 230   The availability of broadband: A number of different surveys of broadband penetration exist. I have chosen to use statistics from the Organization on Economic Cooperation and Development, www.oecd.org. The OECD's Directorate for Science, Technology and Industry maintains a useful time series of statistics on broadband penetration and use in all thirty OECD member countries.

Page 233   As detailed in Dava: Dava Sobel, *Longitude: The True Story of a Lone Genius Who Solved the Greatest Scientific Problem of His Time* (Penguin, 1996). Harvard economist Michael Kremer has been the pioneering advocate of prizes to stimulate innovation, with his work on incentives to create vaccines for malaria and other tropical diseases. See www.economics.harvard.edu/faculty/kremer/vaccine.html.

CHAPTER 10. WHAT'S GOOD FOR THE WORLD IS GOOD FOR AMERICA

Page 241   a leading world power: I am certainly aware of the controversies swirling around the idea of the United States' manifest destiny. My advocacy is not for a new imperialism. Anders Stephanson's *Manifest Destiny: American Expansion and the Empire of Right* (Hill & Wang, 1996) surveys the genesis of the concept and how it has been used to the present day.

Page 244   ranking the world's innovators: The Global Innovation Index is prepared by the magazine *World Businesses*, in association with the leading European business school INSEAD. It uses statistics grouped under eight headings—institutions and policies, human capacity, infrastructure, technological sophistication, business markets and capital, knowledge, competitiveness, and wealth—to create a ranking of 107 countries. In the 2007 index, the United States was judged a clear number one, with Germany second and the United Kingdom number three. Angola took the wooden spoon at 107th. Everyone, myself included, loves rankings, but these kinds of statistical snapshots should be used with a liberal pinch of salt as intriguing indicators, not as definitive judgments: worldbusinesslive.com/search/article/625441/the-worlds-top-innovators/.

Page 244   Investment bank Goldman Sachs: Jim O'Neill, global economist at Goldman Sachs, had the original idea of grouping Brazil, Russia, India, and China as key influences on the future of the world economy. His notion was expanded in a Goldman Sachs economic research report, "Dreaming with BRICs: The Path to 2050," by Dominic Wilson and Roopa Purushothaman (Goldman Sachs Global Economics Paper 99, October 2003). Numerous analyses have followed. An interesting video presentation on the BRICs can be found at www.gs.com/brics.

Page 244   "Golden Arches Theory": Thomas Friedman described his "Golden Arches Theory of Conflict Prevention" in *The Lexus and the Olive Tree* (Farrar, Straus & Giroux, 1999). He seems to have overlooked the fact that Belgrade had a number of McDonald's franchises at the time of the wars in former Yugoslavia.

Page 245   Saxenian calls "brain circulation.": AnnaLee Saxenian, *The New Argonauts: Regional Advantage in a Global Economy* (Harvard University Press, 2006), provides a structure for thinking about "brain circulation." Saxenian's argonauts are international entrepreneur/commuters, shifting easily between different countries and cultures, taking advantage of global networks of resources and knowledge.

Page 247   In a survey of 186: Booz Allen Hamilton and INSEAD, "Innovation: Is Global the Way Forward?" 2006. Available at www.strategy-business.com/media/file/global_innovation.pdf.

Page 250   *Global Competitiveness Report*: Michael Porter, Klaus Schwab, Augusto Lopez-Claro, and Xavier Sala-i-Martin, eds., *The Global Competitiveness Report 2006–2007* (Palgrave Macmillan, 2006). Some of the information in *The Global Competitiveness Report* can be accessed through www.weforum.org/gcr.

Page 256   Innovation expert and author Dorothy Leonard: My former teaching partner at Harvard Business School, Dorothy Leonard, and her partner Walter C. Swap added incisive insight in their study of knowledge cultivation entitled *Deep Smarts: How to Cultivate and Transfer Enduring Business Wisdom* (Harvard Business School Press, 2005).

Page 257   In the same spirit: Alec Wilkinson, "No Obstacles," *The New Yorker*, April 16, 2007, is a fascinating profile of David Bell and the new extreme sport of parkour.

Page 261   half of that funding: Current data on venture capital funding in the United States can be found at www.pwcmoneytree.com. The novel approach of Y Combinator is succinctly described on its Web site, www.ycombinator.com.

Page 263   "Each day we allowed Benjamin": The story of the then-young Benjamin Gardner is recounted in Howard Gardner's *The Disciplined Mind: What All Students Should Understand* (Simon & Schuster, 1999).

Page 267   "fireside chats": The Museum of Broadcast Communications, www.museum.tv, offers all of FDR's fireside chats through its online archive.

ACKNOWLEDGMENTS

The classic image of the lonely writer in his or her garret sweating over pages of foolscap is out of step with a digital era that embraces the power of Internet search, e-mail, group document editing, open innovation, and the jazz of great collaboration.

Many people helped shape this book. First, I want to thank my editor, Emily Loose, for the finest editorial experience imaginable—one made up of equal parts of empathy and support, professionalism, and unflagging smarts. Second, Lance Knobel, who works with me at Kao & Company, provided intellectual and research collaboration of the first water that at times resembled having Pete Sampras provide tennis drill. Donna Carpenter and Mo Coyle provided elegance, wit, and a foundation with their editorial contributions. My agent Helen Rees, with whom I have "jammed" for over a decade, handled the business arrangements with her usual flair. Marjorie McClain supported myriad administrative tasks associated with the book.

The scenarios contained in *Innovation Nation* were roughed out with the help of an exceptional group of San Francisco—based colleagues that included Peter Leyden, John Zysman, Michael Borrus, Niels Christian Nielsen, and Lance Knobel. A workshop hosted by the Center for American Progress brought together Neera Tanden, John Podesta, Ronnie Chatterji, Gene Sperling, Thomas Kalil, Josh Gottheimer, Ian Solomon, and Rob Atkinson.

Mary Walshok deserves special mention for adding to my understanding of the intricacies of regional innovation and for lending her San Diego zeal to several reviews of this book.

Many individuals took time from their busy lives to contribute interviews: Dean Kamen (DEKA), Vint Cerf (Google), Tony Tether (DARPA), Tan Chin Nam (Ministry of Information and the Arts, Government of Singapore), Philip Su (JTC Corporation, Government of Singapore), Nabil Ali Alyousuf (The Executive Office, Government of Dubai), Philip Yeo (Chairman of A*STAR, Singapore Biopolis), Chuan Poh Lim (Permanent Secretary, Ministry of Education, Government of Singapore), Sean Randolph (Director, Bay Area Science and Innovation Consortium), Craig Barrett (Chairman, Intel Corporation), Howard Gardner (Department of Education, Harvard University), Jay Cohen (U.S. Department of Homeland Security), Rob Atkinson (Information Technology and Innovation Forum), Erik Rassmussen (Innovation Council, Denmark), Linda Dozier (COO, In2Books), Stan Williams (Director, Quantum Science Research Group, HP), Steve Franklin (Gunderson Dettmer), Tom Melcher (Blue Bamboo Ventures), Uffe Elbaek (KaosPilots, OutGames), Brian Behlendorf (Collabnet), Miles Gilburne (ZGI), Bo Ekman (Tallberg Forum), and Reg Lewis (QB3).

Many colleagues added to my knowledge in specific areas. I would especially like to express my appreciation to Senator Hillary Clinton for taking an interest in this project. I would also like to acknowledge former Speaker of the House Newt Gingrich, and current Speaker of the House Nancy Pelosi for the opportunity to discuss the policy dimensions of *Innovation Nation* with them. Andy Krepinevich helped me find literature on the assassin's mace. Brian Persons, Ed Giambastiani, John Arquilla, and Andy Marshall have shaped my views on military matters. Robin Harper enabled me to understand the nuances of the Second Life community, while Peter Williams introduced me to the world of mountaineering and El Capitan. Matt

Gardner provided insights on the San Francisco biotech industry; Mark Bunger illuminated patterns of innovation in the nanotechnology industry, while KaosPilot team 12 supported some of the research; Mette Fresner's help was particularly valuable. And discussions with Richard Rhodes were an intellectual treat.

A number of friends and colleagues kindly read the manuscript and offered their suggestions: John Arquilla, Paul Saffo, Tom Singer, Mary Walshok, Gary Meller, Wayne Johnson, Ronnie Chatterji, Sean Randolph, Peter Leyden, Laurel Kao, and Mike Skurko.

Sometimes my behavior is a throwback to the sixties; one symptom is that I tend to write to music. Three recordings formed the hidden soundtrack of *Innovation Nation:* (1) Steve Reich, *Reich Remixed* (Nonesuch 79552-2, 1998) (played about two hundred times), (2) The Pat Metheny Group, *The Way Up* (Nonesuch 79876-2, 2005) (played about two hundred times), and (3) *Sunday in the Park with George*, London Cast Recording (P.S. Classics B000EZ9048, 2006) (played about fifty times).

Every book is the documentation of opportunity costs applied to one's personal life. My family has endured my absence during the gestation of this book, so it is more than fitting that it be dedicated to them.

Finally, I want to acknowledge my parents, both departed now, who came to the United States from China fifty-eight years ago in search of the American Dream. Their values, knowledge of the world, and love for this country continue to inspire me on a daily basis.

INDEX

ABOUT THE AUTHOR

John Kao, dubbed, "Mr. Creativity" and a "serial innovator" by *The Economist*, has had a many-faceted career: innovation thought leader, best-selling author, Tony-nominated film and theater producer, psychiatrist, Harvard Business School professor, sought-after advisor, and serial entrepreneur. He is the chairman of Kao & Company, an advisory and venture development firm that counts leading companies, government agencies, and political figures among its clients. He lives in San Francisco, California.

Innovationation.org is being launched as a portal enabling access to information on the many-faceted subject of national innovation strategy. It is intended to support interaction among a global community of policy-makers, domain experts, and concerned citizens.